D1591029

PUBLISHED WITH A

LITTLE SUBVENTION FROM

Figure Foundation

PUBLISHER FOR THE MASSES,

EMANUEL HALDEMAN-JULIUS

R. Alton Lee

UNIVERSITY OF NEBRASKA PRESS | LINCOLN AND LONDON

CONTENTS

List of Illustrations — *ix*

Preface — *xi*

Acknowledgments — *xiii*

Prologue: Odessa to Fin de Siècle Philadelphia — *1*

1. Forces That Shaped Him, 1889–1905 — *9*

2. The Beckoning World, 1905–1915 — *35*

3. Girard, Kansas, 1915–1918 — *57*

4. Little Blue Books, 1918–1923 — *93*

5. A Cornucopia of Books and Events, 1923–1928 — *127*

6. The Great Depression, 1928–1938 — *147*

7. Resurrection, 1938–1951 — *179*

Epilogue — *199*

Appendix — *205*

Notes — *221*

Bibliography — *237*

Index — *241*

ILLUSTRATIONS

Following page 126

1. Emanuel Haldeman-Julius at the typewriter, 1925
2 & 3. Emanuel and Marcet Haldeman-Julius
4. Emanuel and his Little Blue Books, 1947
5. Emanuel Haldeman-Julius
6. Emanuel and his sister Rose
7. Haldeman-Julius home in Girard, Kansas
8. Swimming pool where Emanuel was found dead
9. Former site of Haldeman-Julius's first publishing operation in downtown Girard

PREFACE

The tri-state region of southeastern Kansas held a well-kept secret: for the last three decades of the first half of the twentieth century, it was the literary and publishing Mecca of the United States, and thus the international center for Western civilization. The career of Emanuel Haldeman-Julius was the catalyst of this phenomenon.

His story is a remarkable one because it was a bootstrap operation of a boy in Philadelphia of a poor immigrant family of Russian Jews who came there at the turn of the century and rose to dominate the publishing world of his time. At the height of his success Haldeman-Julius knew every major author in the Western world of his time and most of the minor ones. He was a friend, or at least an acquaintance, of many other important people of early-twentieth-century America. Kings and presidents did not consult with him, but they read his Little Blue Books. How this man, Emanuel Haldeman-Julius, came to tiny Girard, Kansas, as a young man, established a successful publishing business, and remained there the rest of his life is another, less startling secret.

Few details are known about his childhood, but some give us clues to his highly complex personality. The nature of his boyhood life emphasizes this from the start. Don't bother me, don't touch me, don't involve me was his philosophy. His parents respected his isolation as long as he was not a nuisance about it. The family soon learned that he would indicate when he wanted company. He received his love for books from his father's work, his business skills from his mother, and garnered his love for appetizing

---

food from her skilled cooking. In addition, he loved music, possessed a pleasant singing voice, and could play the piano and violin. As an adult he developed a love of vibrant conversation and sensual sex. He also retained his need for isolation at various times, whether it was a ride in the country, the seclusion of his workplace, or a trip.

His desire to be alone led to an egotistical attitude at the pinnacle of his success. "Let the world come to Girard if they want to see me" expresses this phase of his personality. But most importantly, he was a Socialist at heart and had the good of mankind as his principal interest. He was consistently supportive of the downtrodden and the abused as well as a promoter of many social ideas and practices ahead of their times, such as civil rights and companionate marriage. His love of books endured his entire lifetime, and he was determined to educate the masses by providing inexpensive copies of books on a variety of topics from classics to self-improvement.

How did this young man who moved to New York City from Philadelphia come to leave his beloved "Big Apple" and resettle in a tiny town in Kansas become such a success in his chosen profession—publishing? This is the story of the man, his life, his business, his success, and his importance. Unfortunately, he suffered a premature and tragic death.

ACKNOWLEDGMENTS

Matthew Bokovoy of the University of Nebraska Press first called my attention to the need for a biography of Emanuel Haldeman-Julius because of his fabulous career in book publishing. He then lent his expertise in American Socialism through the various phases of publication. His knowledge of the secondary literature is truly impressive, and I appreciate his assistance during this difficult process. Any errors that remain are, of course, my own.

Emanuel Haldeman-Julius's papers were dispersed soon after his death. Alice Haldeman took her share, which was basically Marcet's papers, and deposited them in the Dailey Library of the University of Illinois, Chicago. Dean Harper and his staff at the Dailey Library were most helpful with these papers, which are called the Haldeman-Julius Family Papers. Henry Haldeman placed his share in the Lilley Library of Indiana University. The Haldeman-Julius Collection remained in Pittsburg, Kansas, in the Axe Library. Randy Roberts of the Axe Library is very knowledgeable about Haldeman-Julius sources and generously shared his familiarity with that collection. A special thanks to Steven Cox, who replaced Randy following the latter's promotion. In addition, former archivist Gene DeGruson of the Axe Library, who planned to write a biography of Emanuel with coauthor Sue Haldeman-Julius, photocopied many items from the collection at Lilley Library, and he added these items to the original Haldeman-Julius Collection in preparation for this undertaking. David

Vail of the Morse Department of Special Collections, Kansas State University, made the Sue Haldeman-Julius Collection available to me. I am grateful to all these archivists.

I also made extensive use of two of the three dissertations written on Emanuel Haldeman-Julius and his work. Andrew Cothran's "The Little Blue Book Man and the Big American Parade: A Biography of Emanuel Haldeman-Julius" (PhD diss., University of Maryland, 1966) and Dale Marvin Herder's "Education for the Masses: The Haldeman-Julius Little Blue Books as Popular Culture during the Nineteen-Twenties" (PhD diss., Michigan State University, 1975) are valuable because of their extensive research and because the authors were able to interview Emanuel Haldeman-Julius's siblings and children. The third, Melanie Ann Brown's "Five Cent Culture at the 'University in Print': Radical Ideology and the Marketplace in E. Haldeman-Julius's Little Blue Books, 1919–1929" (PhD diss., University of Minnesota, 2006), is difficult to cite because of its unusual system of pagination. Finally, I must thank my wife, Marilyn, for reading the entire manuscript and saving me from numerous errors.

PUBLISHER FOR THE MASSES,

EMANUEL HALDEMAN-JULIUS

PROLOGUE

Odessa to Fin de Siècle Philadelphia

This is the story of a second-generation immigrant who enjoyed a wildly successful career in the publishing world. He disliked his Jewish inheritance and sought, consistently and unsuccessfully, to escape it. He never completely shed the fact that his parents were poor Russian immigrants who were part of the great Jewish migration to the land of opportunity in the late nineteenth century. The story begins in Jewish Russia. The great Diaspora in the second century, whereby the Roman Empire dispersed the Jews from Jerusalem, resulted in a few Jews living in Russia and its environs, especially Ukraine and the Crimea area. The Russian Empire acquired great numbers of Jews with Catherine the Great's policy of expanding Russian territory. In 1772 she gathered in territory around Minsk and Kiev, containing a half-million Jews. She participated in the Third Partition of Poland in 1795, acquiring millions more to live in the Pale of Settlement, as the region was labeled. Official policy was to convert them to Christianity, but, invariably failing this, these people lived with the virulent anti-Semitism of their neighbors because they clung to their religion and because of their neighbors' envy of their successful acquisitive nature.

As Hans Rogger writes, Russian Jews "belonged to no Christian church, spoke a strange language (Yiddish) and wore strange Medieval dress." As a result, czarist Russia kept them in "the anomalous condition of citizens who were denied some basic attributes of citizenship, yet expected to fulfil all its obligations." The serfs were freed in 1861; the

Jews, therefore, looked forward to their turn at emancipation from their inferior governmental situation.[1]

A turning point came in czarist policy of second-class citizenship for them with the assassination of Czar Alexander II in 1881 from a terrorist bomb, but not in the direction they expected. His successor, Alexander III, proved to be decidedly anti-Semitic, and the miserable lot of Jews deteriorated even further with increasing persecution. The new czar insisted that his father's assassination was a Jewish plot and used this "as an excuse for anti-Jewish legislation."[2]

The anti-Semitic governor-general of Kiev, Alexander Drentein, for example, spread the word that the czar wanted retribution from Jews for the death of his father. *Pogrom*, a Russian word meaning "violence," was a process then considered to be extinct for "settling Judeo-Gentile controversies," but it was soon resurrected, especially in southern Russia. A typical one in Balta was described as follows:

> Among the arrested was a former Russian colonel. Authorities found on him a list of Jewish shops singled out for pillage. But soon the chief of police, the chief of the garrison and the district commissioner of police arrive, one after the other; at once the soldiers step aside, the freed crowd sacks the wine and spirit shops located in the neighborhood, gets drunk and proceeds to pillage and rob, with the assistance of the peasants from the city environs and the police. This is when the terrible and savage scenes of massacre, rape and pillage took place, about which the newspaper descriptions are fairly accurate. . . . The pogrom at Balta, terminated only today, was provoked by the active intervention of the local authorities, and not by their inertia. The result was 15,000 Jews reduced to poverty, forty killed or badly wounded, and twenty women raped.[3]

In Kiev alone, mob destruction cost Jews 2.5 million rubles (a ruble then was worth two-thirds to three-quarters of an American dollar). These pogroms prompted discussions in the British Parliament and the U.S. Congress, and protest meetings in London and New York City. President Benjamin Harrison, in a message to Congress, noted the "serious concern" of his administration over these pogroms and the resulting "harsh measures now being enforced against the Hebrews in Russia. . . . It is estimated that over 1,000,000 will be forced from Russia within a few years." He further noted that this issue was not "a local question." Other countries, besides the United States, would be affected by the migration. In fact, 2 million migrated, mostly to the United States, between 1882 and World War I.[4]

When Russian Jews refused to convert to Christianity, many died on the road to Siberia or later at a prison camp. For those who remained, the Provisional Rules of 1882 increased the existing restrictions that denied them the right to live or work where and how they wished. They were forced to live in the Pale of Permanent Settlement, consisting of fifteen western and southwestern provinces, and in the ten provinces of the Kingdom of Poland. The new rules denied them the right to own property in rural areas and set very limited quotas for medical and other types of professional education, as well as for serving as brokers or on juries. Families of men who ignored their military conscription were fined 300 rubles the following year. Jews were restricted in the choice of their domicile in villages, and contacts between peasants and Jews were inhibited. These developments resulted in Jews' increasing hostility toward the government and further retaliatory action against them in this endless cycle of violence. An ever-growing number of limits were placed on university and school admissions. Odessa, for example, had a population of 240,000, of which 106,000 were Jews. The quota for public schools was fifty-two Jewish students for the entire system. Under threat of exile to Siberia, lawyers were compelled to moderate their defenses of Jews in court. Jews were banned from Moscow on the eve of Passover, denying them access to the "newly constructed beautiful synagogue that was closed." The government shut down the silk industry, which gave vital employment to many Jews. Millions began fleeing to neighboring countries, many abandoning their meager possessions and eventually ending up poverty-stricken in Hamburg or Liverpool, port cities for emigrants to other cities in the world.[5]

In 1882, Alexander III put the finishing touches on these restrictions with "rigorous expulsion measures." "Tens of thousands of Jews" wandered across Russia, from east to west, seeking some kind of refuge.

"The pauperization of the Jewish masses became more acute," adding to the unexpected numbers emigrating elsewhere.[6]

Concurrently, there were several developments that facilitated this desire to seek a better life. Modern transportation was making migration easier. Steamship rates across the Atlantic became lower; at one point fares cost as little as $12. Accommodations were primitive as emigrants were herded down into the hold like cattle, but fortunately, the voyage was not lengthy, just highly unpleasant. There was also a growing emphasis on Russian nationalism, making Jews appear increasingly as unwanted outsiders and stimulating a growing internal anti-Semitism. This attitude was further encouraged by the periodic pogroms and other outbursts of popular wrath against Jews.

David Zolajefski and Elizabeth Zamustin were part of this mass exodus from the Odessa area, leaving a village some forty *versts* (a *verst* equals two-thirds of a mile) away. They were first cousins with rabbis on both sides of the family. A rabbi is not a priest or preacher but a lawyer who interprets Jewish law, in which religion plays a part. David's paternal grandfather was a cultured rabbi, a man of high standing and influence in the community, known and honored for miles around the village. David's father, Rabbi Nathan, made sure the boy received not only a Jewish education but also a secular one by attending the gymnasium, or Russian high school. He also, as was customary among Jews at the time, learned a trade; in his case he became a bookbinder (they were bound by hand at this time). After their marriage, David and Elizabeth took a grand trip to "Algiers, Turkey, and Arabia" for their honeymoon. David had lived through two pogroms as a youth, and he and Elizabeth, both twenty-five, decided to migrate to America, where their children would receive an education. Several of the relatives made the same decision. David's sister Rose and her family, as well as Elizabeth's brother Boris and his family, migrated to America.[7]

The Zolajefski family traveled to Baltimore, losing a daughter on the way who was buried at sea. A fourth child had died earlier and was buried in Russia, leaving Nathan, the oldest, and a daughter, Esther. Under the best conditions, the voyage took six days; bad weather or storms caused delays and made the trip more miserable. The men were separated from the women, and the women took care of the children.

One immigrant from the Pale described his experience. They were in steerage, and all the children slept with the mother, five persons in one bed. They had no bath during the seven-day voyage. The family had one cup of water per day for washing purposes. The mother had a loaf of black bread and some buttons of garlic for them to eat. The stench of the hold was the worst part of the voyage—they almost felt like they could touch it. It originated in vomit and was compounded by seasickness. One could only try to escape it by going to the deck and letting the fresh air revive them.

When a journalist who was traveling with the peasants overheard first-class passengers disparaging these unfortunates, he asked himself how the steerage travelers could remember they were human beings when they first must pick the worms out of their food. As they neared the end of their trip, they could then begin to fret over the inspections they would face on Ellis Island. Could they pass muster, or would they be turned back? If so, then what?

David found a job in Baltimore but soon discovered that bookbinders were more respected in Philadelphia and moved the family to that city in 1887. Emanuel arrived on 30 July 1889, their first child born in America.[8] David found permanent work in a moderate-paying job as a bookbinder for Eikhoff and Kraemer, and Elizabeth became a homemaker. "I cannot call you Zolajefski," his employer said, "because it is too long a name." It was too hard to pronounce, he continued, and besides, it was a Russian name. "You are an American now and need an American name. I will shorten it or, better yet how will Julius do?" This was agreeable, and when his first son was born in America the boy was registered as Emanuel Julius.

When Emanuel was born the family was living in a four-story brick tenement house at 237 Race Street on the north side of the city in a predominantly Irish neighborhood. The more affluent residents had moved out of the inner city, leaving these large houses for the huge number of immigrants flooding into the United States in the late-nineteenth-century City of Brotherly Love. Jewish women were modest and declined to have male doctors deliver their children, so Sophia Sachs, a female doctor, became the midwife for Elizabeth and signed Emanuel's birth certificate. The area bordered the Delaware River on the east and the Schuylkill on the west. Emanuel was frail as an infant, and Elizabeth often carried him to the Race Street wharf where he could inhale the fresh river breeze. As he was growing up, the family lived at 1326 Germantown Avenue in Kensington. It was here that Elizabeth purchased a small tobacco shop in one of the lower front rooms.

Children came rather frequently to this loving couple in America: Emanuel was followed by three girls: Rosalie (1892), Josephine (1894), and Lillian (1899). With six children to raise, Elizabeth was careful in buying food for her large brood. Fried chicken was a luxury; usually it was boiled—head, feet, and all—for its broth. Elizabeth often ate the head, saving the meatier pieces for the bread-winning members of the family. Emanuel watched "in repulsive horror" as his mother ate the head. Elizabeth, on the other hand, was a practical person and found humor in her son's reaction.[9]

Emanuel was fascinated with his father's profession, and this stimulated a love of books that would eventually become a passion. As he later observed, "seeing a book I could not afford to buy was worse than being hungry and looking at a bun in a bakery window."[10]

Sister Rosalie recalled Emanuel was "a very bright boy" but "misunderstood" as a child. His parents never did learn how to communicate with such a precocious boy, and as he grew older he became isolated and a loner. He suffered no remorse when he dropped out of school, took a job, and began to help temporarily in supporting the family. He would not return home until later in life.[11]

That Emanuel had a childhood he did not care to discuss is indicated by his first wife. Marcet recalled that she did not meet his family until they had been married four years and had three children. Almost all family correspondence was with Emanuel's older sister, Esther, and she expressed her own concepts, not those of the parents. From the time Emanuel left school at fifteen, Marcet noted, "his visits (home) were so infrequent as to be negligible." Manuel, as intimates called him, had a "casual attitude toward his family, indicating no strong familial memories, lasting fondness or normalities."[12]

William Penn built his City of Brotherly Love between the Schuylkill and Delaware Rivers. As the city grew, it expanded to the north and west. By the end of the nineteenth century and the depression of the 1890s, the worst the nation had yet seen, half of the population was composed of immigrants and their children. Electric streetcars, especially in the second half of the decade, made possible the mass urbanization of the native-born, middle-class masses. When they moved westward and northward, newly arrived immigrants filled their abandoned homes.

Philadelphia became known as the City of Houses, and its brick row homes achieved national fame. The older area between Vine and South Streets contained offices, retail stores, and entertainment. Small workshops, especially in printing and the garment trades, abounded. Most workers, rich and poor, walked to work. Blocks of row houses were scattered throughout. By this time South Fourth Street was one of the many shopping areas for recently arrived Russian Jews. The row houses were two-story, six-room brick structures large enough that enterprising housewives could use part of the house to set up some type of retail goods serving local customers. The Kensington area contained craft shops for bicycles, small metal shops, brushes, window shades, harness, and sundry other goods.[13] It was into this cosmopolitan city that Emanuel Julius was born and in which he grew through adolescence into young adulthood.

1

FORCES THAT SHAPED HIM, 1889–1905

What were the forces that shaped Emanuel's character? What childhood episodes made a lasting impression on his developing mind? We do not know, and it is impossible to discover, because neither he nor his parents left any written record of these early years. As an adult Emanuel wrote a great deal of autobiographical material—in fact, much of his writing is of this genre—but he did not see fit to write of the episodes of his childhood that influenced him prior to the age of ten.

What influence did his parents have on his early development? He admired his father and was especially impressed with his wit and ability to puncture superciliousness with ease. Emanuel greatly appreciated his mother's skill in debunking and in managing the family's budget. Usually, in a large family the oldest become leaders and the younger are coddled. As a middle child, did Emanuel feel neglected, unimportant? He certainly felt alone. Emanuel probably inherited more characteristics from his mother than from his father. His older sister, Esther, recalled that when she watched him and listened to him talk, it was as if she were watching her mother. His first wife, Marcet, would observe that "at his best he was much like his mother." A short woman inclined to stoutness, Elizabeth was well read and displayed good judgment in business matters. From her Emanuel inherited his business ability. He also recalled that his mother hated "persecution, prejudices, and oppression," no doubt stemming from her experience of living in czarist Russia. These characteristics, too, became an important part of him.[1]

Julius once referred to being "on the best of terms" with his father. "I liked to talk to him, for I was always amused by his dry, wry, sarcastic wit." David was often seen going to a steamship company with another Jew to buy a steamship ticket to bring over a relative living in Europe. Often there were other immigrants in their house. Once there was a peddler, two tailors, an old-clothesman, and a rabbi, all sleeping on the floor, dreaming of success in their new homeland.[2]

Emanuel often brought his father's lunch to work and frequently came early so he could observe the action in the bindery. He hated the smell of the glue but took an intense interest in the way his father went about the job of binding a book.

> He had a rack of the smoothest wood I ever felt, on which he sewed the signatures (sections) one at a time by hand. When the machines came in my father had to step aside, for he was too old to learn to handle thousands of books around noisy machines. His personal enemy—the machine—turned out jobs that aroused him to quiet, muttering scorn.

His mother took charge of the income of perhaps $1,000 annually (common laborers earned about $500 yearly). With this money she

> performed miracles daily that I, in my first decade of life, wondered at. So far as I know, she was never overcharged once in her entire life. She had an unerring impulse that led her to the places where she could get the best bargains in food, clothing and the rest of the supplies that must go into even a modest home. . . . She dealt with the practical things of life. (She was) given to bursting into a torrent of words—streams of hundreds of words—that would tear a fake or a piece of bunk to shreds. She, like her husband, was a great reader, especially of books which she approached in the spirit of pure skepticism. She was the kind of person who doubted every thing and everyone. . . . I look on her as the first debunker who ever came into my life.[3]

Marcet later wrote that Emanuel expressed the idea that he was "ill at ease in his home" when a child, noting that he had discussed this concept in a Little Blue Book titled *The Color of Life*. In one essay he has Fritz the bellboy lamenting "he had always been alone; had never known what it meant to have the love of a mother, the guidance of a father." In the same tome, Carlo de Mariano recalls that he was "a poor lad, whose family was living in abject poverty" and that "at times we were living in actual want for the things that keep us alive. It meant that I must go to work." The Julius family was never this destitute. Emanuel did not have to go to work when he did, but it did help the family live a more comfortable life. Finally, he has a young clerk soliloquize that "we come into the world alone, and stay all alone . . . and die alone. . . . [L]ife to me is a game of solitaire." Devastating words to loving parents.[4]

Religion played a small role in molding his thinking and attitudes. Although there were rabbis on both sides of the family, David did not attend synagogue, nor did he send his children. Emanuel did not write of this aspect of his childhood until he was an adult and had developed into an atheist and freethinker, so there is little reference to Jewry in his writing—no mention of synagogues, a good deal of discussion about his passion for good food, but no mention of kosher cooking in the home, no cantors, no Passover or Hanukkah, no bar mitzvahs. It was not until later in life that he discussed being a Jew. Did he blame his parents for the anti-Semitic taunts he endured during his childhood, "the fights and the disfiguring nose compliments of Irish Catholic boys"? We can never know.

> My home life was devoid of piety. Neither parent cared seriously about religion, and never thought I needed to absorb a mess of superstitious notions in order to earn a place in heaven. They were indifferent, for which I thank them. I'm not ready to say they were Freethinkers. They just didn't seem to care a damn.[5]

He did write candidly about Jewry long after he had matured as a reporter, writer, and publisher and had accumulated considerable work experience. Try as he might to deny or ignore his heritage, he could never escape it. Emanuel despised racial intolerance, a trait he found even among many liberals who surrounded him in his work. When a Jewish editor hired him, he complained, word went out among the staff that "Jews were ganging up to get rid of the Gentiles and take the bread out of their mouths." When he was the only Jew on a newspaper staff, he lamented, he was worked harder than anyone else but paid half the salary of the others. If he performed well, fellow staffers called him "a brilliant Jew"; if he wrote a clever story, he was "a witty Jew." He was never permitted to forget "his origins," and he consistently refused to accept this. He was certain the resentment could not stem from his religion, because as a boy he had rejected Judaism and become a freethinker. Is there such a thing as a Jewish race? he queried. Emanuel always thought of himself as "a member of the Caucasian race." Thus, he concluded, the only answer was "to smile and get to work." "It isn't comforting," he concluded, "but it works somehow." "Whatever you do," he warned fellow Jews, "don't look for pity and sympathy." This, of course, includes a good deal of self-pity that one is wont to express.[6]

Emanuel entered public school at age six and left when he finished seventh grade. It was not unusual at the time for male students not to attend high school. In fact, it was normal during this period. A contemporary, Dwight Eisenhower of Abilene, Kansas, born one year after Emanuel, was exceptional in completing high school by age eighteen. It is interesting, though, that Emanuel was the only child in the family who did not attend high school. Even Nathan and Esther finished high school, and Esther earned a college degree. This was not a planned development. It just evolved, in part because of Emanuel's indifference to school. The fact that not attending high school was contrary to family tradition meant little to him.

The Philadelphia school system used the children's reader written by Monroe, rather than the enduring popular one by McGuffey. Both authors, though, used the same approach: they borrowed selections from earlier texts and produced large doses of morality. Emphasis was placed on reading, writing, and arithmetic in the early years and on grammar and arithmetic in the upper grades. Geography and physiology were memory exercises, with the Latin name of bones being learned by rote. The adverse effects of alcohol and tobacco on the human body were emphasized, and the capitals of every state were memorized.[7]

Emanuel attended John Moffet Elementary School, where the principal,

David R. Baer, regaled students with his personal experiences in the Battle of Gettysburg. This public system of education was devoid of any theology. It was designed primarily to help the student cope with a world in terms of the three R's. The children were exposed to Bible passages each morning, "but we kids got so we didn't even listen" to them, he reported. Emanuel's education would not truly begin until he left school and was gainfully employed.

Emanuel later concluded that "all I got out of my years in the Philadelphia public school system was a smattering of U.S. history, a bit of geography, some grammar, arithmetic, and a few other basic subjects." He was "a fair student, well behaved, polite, and a little scared of everybody." He did not think anything there "harmed" him, not even the Bible passages every morning. He recalled that one day, upon returning to school after lunch, he was waiting for a freight train to pass and saw "a man jump under a car and put his head under a wheel." When he arrived at school and explained his tardiness to the teacher, she upbraided him as "an ornery cuss" and warned him "he should not look at sights like that!" Interesting advice to give to a child.[8]

Hugh F. Monroe was a close classmate at the Moffet school, a year and a half younger than "Mannie," as he was called by his chums. The two were not interested in grammar school but in enjoying life. They went rowing on the Delaware River and camping out overnight. Monroe recalled that a man named Benjamin Damrosh, who conducted a music school in Philadelphia, came to Moffet and offered to teach music lessons to anyone interested. "In just a short time," Mannie was "playing the violin perfectly" and demonstrating "a deep baritone voice." This was the beginning of Emanuel's lifelong love for good music.[9]

Emanuel had an outstanding history teacher who could become "exceedingly expressive during certain periods of American history." She was a short, brown-haired, gray-eyed, small-mouthed woman in her mid-thirties and was usually dressed in a tailored suit and white silk waistcoat. She came alive when she reached the Founding Fathers. Stalking up and down the aisle, she talked of their experience at Valley Forge, hunching her shoulders as if to keep out the cold and snow. The next morning they would take the streetcar down to the Liberty Bell, then walk a few blocks north to Ben Franklin's grave and Betsy Ross's house where the patriot made the first American flag. The teacher "was an actress who dramatized everything" in a wide-gestured manner. When Paul Revere rode, she strode up and down the classroom, re-creating his wild horseback ride. Every Redcoat was a villain, General Burgoyne was a vicious brute, as were Howe and Cornwallis. Dull decades followed until the Civil War period arrived. Soon "she was off on a white charger," glorifying Lincoln. Then came the Emancipation Proclamation—glorious document. "The Gettysburg Address was one of her greatest moments. . . . Then they turned dull again." She was unable to get excited over the Indian wars, but here the children had the Ned Bunting stories and the tales of Buffalo Bill to substitute for "Miss History."[10]

Later in his life, Emanuel wrote a series of vignettes about a preadolescent boy growing up in Philadelphia at the turn of the century, a delightful but challenging metropolitan area that shaped characters in different ways. The city had a great impact on his developing personality and taught him much about life that he could never learn in school. He quickly became streetwise.

To a small boy the world seemed to be a wondrous place where everything was a show. There was a public card-writer, a man in his thirties, with a flowing mustache and ink-stained fingers. He did fancy cards at a penny each. Emanuel had him write his name, which he did in a flowing Spencerian hand. He made ornate birth announcements with doves in the corner, a wedding card with an arrow shot through a heart, a death card lined in black with an hourglass showing the sand almost gone from the top half. His work was necessary at that time of prevalent illiteracy. Emanuel asked the tattoo artist to put an anchor on his arm and was told that, because he was only ten, he had to bring an approving note from his parents.[11]

For 5 cents one could aim a rifle five times at moving metal birds or, next door, "a Negro stuck his head through a hole in the back canvass" and you threw a baseball at his head. He was hit more often when more than one customer threw at the same time. When hit he would yell out loudly, "but he was a splendid, courageous sport and would cry defiantly for more throwers." People seemed eager to pay 10 cents, or even 25, for the chance to hit "a laughing, taunting Negro on the head with a baseball." Emanuel was told the man could not be hurt, because "he rubbed a certain oil on his head" that protected it.[12]

Public auctions were a free show where watches, silverware, albums, vanity sets, suitcases, pictures, statues, rugs, watch chains, and other sundry items were sold. The auctioneer was an impressive-looking fellow, "faultlessly dressed," with lots of wit and sarcasm. Emanuel had a good idea of what these things were worth and noticed that there were always two fellows in the crowd who were ready to increase the bid when audience interest dropped. Here he was introduced to the idea of a shill "and wondered why anyone" could do such things to honest, hardworking people. Once one of his sisters came with Emanuel and asked him to bid on a set of opera glasses worth $1.85. When they were knocked off to him for $3.45, he noticed that one of the shills had been bidding against him.[13]

Many goods were sold by street peddlers—an Italian balloon man who sold colored pinwheels that his wife and children made at home while he was on the streets; a black woman selling "Baltimore crabs," roasted chestnuts, and watermelon in the summer; a Jewish peddler with cucumbers, olives, and sliced pineapple; the peanut and popcorn man with his "whistling" contraption that roasted his wares (on the side he sold untaxed whisky at 5 cents a quart, of which Emanuel's father was a regular customer). Near the corner saloon an Irishman sold oysters in his place along the wall. The man was a Civil War veteran, and when he had a break in sales he would relate to the boys tales of the Battle of Gettysburg. You could buy almost anything on the street, if you had the price.[14]

The milkman who appeared every morning was a "tall, thin, brown moustached man in his 50s" who sat on a wagon with large cans of milk. He had two ladles, one for pints and one for quarts. His horse knew the route so well that he needed no guidance. He wore a straw hat with two holes for his ears, often with a wet sponge under it. Several sleigh bells hung on the back of the wagon to signal their approach to the neighborhood. Emanuel would hand the milkman a shiny pail and a dime, and he would ladle it full. It was an unsanitary procedure, according to modern standards, and the milk possibly was heavily watered, but the man, the horse, and the wagon all became an institution in the neighborhood.[15]

Butter was bought in bulk from a large tub from which the seller would scoop out an amount with a wide, wooden spoon. It was "a splash of pure, lovely, cool loveliness" that now comes in sealed cartons, no dirt, no contamination, no deterioration in flavor, no special appeal. The cracker barrel, close to the stove to keep its contents fresh, crisp, and dry, became a part of Americana with the "cracker barrel philosophers" and the "cracker barrel politicians."[16]

All this was replaced by the modern supermarket. The grand opening of Foodtown's market was advertised with a housewarming. The huge store was "as bright and shiny as a new Chevrolet, and the hundreds of items made one think that man had at last journeyed into the Garden of Eden, except that here one was expected to eat the apple (27 cents for a fair-sized bag) and piles of metal carts with goodies that even kings did not know about 300 years ago." The variety of goods was immense, and the frozen-food displays needed no covers to keep in the cold, a law of physics that mystified the average shopper. There was a corner for the bakery, where the finished products were tantalizingly fresh. A counter for ready-made goodies displayed potato salad selling for 29 cents per pound. A meat section turned out products made in a spotless kitchen by expert butchers and displayed pot roast, steak, tongue, brains, sausage, heart, hamburger, cut-up chickens, ducks, geese, turkeys, shrimp, fish, oysters. A shopper had to stop at the bakery, vegetable, butcher, delicatessen, and finally the grocery sections for staples. When one checked out with the cashier, the bill always seemed larger than it used to be. Emanuel recalled the dingy, small establishments where boys delivered purchases and many bought groceries on credit. Now all this was rolled into one giant market, with "Mom and Pop" stores in competition, trying to make a living on small sales as in the past with a nickel or dime profit on each item.[17] The way a man in the front window of Child's restaurant made flapjacks was "a form of art," and "the sight of those pancakes, covered with syrup, moved me to want a stack though too often did not have the dime. He worked, easily, quickly each cake, giving each a flip, and sending the finished order in to his customers. He was an artist."[18] Aker's fancy grocery store on Eighth Street had "really a great, talented gifted actor who pretended to be a mechanical man."

> His face was painted like the face of the groom on a wedding cake, but with more colors. He had sharp, red round splotches on his cheeks, his black moustache was painted on, his eyebrows were painted over so that they looked like patent leather, his wig was shiny black and parted in the middle, his hands were in white gloves, his movements were short and wavering, his hands moved in jerks, a few inches at a time, his eyes stared straight ahead as though made of glass, the insides of his nostrils were painted a fiery red, his clothes were the last word in formality—everything about him suggested an automatic man who had been wound up, the way toys could be wound up and sent crawling or walking. Everything was so precise about his [*sic*], so realistic, that one could take him for a robot, except for one thing that my sharp eye had detected. The skin of his neck acted the same way human skin wrinkles and moves. I knew he was a man, a great actor, an artist, even better than the flapjack performer down the street.[19]

Was Emanuel thinking of his mother when he wrote about Jewish cooks? He asserted:

> Old-fashioned Jewish women held on to their husbands when younger, beautiful women were stealing other husbands, through their "genius" as cooks. A twenty-seven year old curvaceous blonde could not compete with a fifty year old mama who turns out mitzoh balls with chicken soup, chopped chicken livers, apple strudel sponge cheese and almond cakes, cold gefelte fish with strong red horse radish stuffed kishke (goose neck), boiled beef, blintzes, homemade noodles in consomme, sliced smetena (sliced cucumber and small red radishes in a bowl of sour cream), borsht, and luscious potato latkes. Her challah is unlike any other bread ever made, shaped a little like a fish, with a braid on top, and varnished with an egg yolk that's applied with a goose

feather—the last loving touch of a sensitive craftsman. Her haman taschen are shiny buns stuffed with jelly.

He lamented the passing of "kosher" cooking. Where are the foods of yesterday, he wrote, when the matzo balls were really "made of eggs, matzoh meal, vegetable shortening, salt and pepper"? Is there any chicken fat in the modern chicken broth? He longed for a Jewish cookbook so that he might publish it and do his bit to preserve an art that was "threatened by our cafeteria hot-dog, hamburger and Coca-Cola, barbeque, quick lunch, and Ye Tea Shoppe styles that take good food and spoil it but that still satisfy the nerveless palates of lard-soaked chazirfresses." Good Jewish cooks, he noted, did not follow the book but operated by ear, by feeling, by impulse, by hunch. Critics warned that if you live on these dishes, you would surely die. "Isn't it a nice way to go?" he asked.[20]

The young boy took a boat to Red Bank, on the Jersey Shore, where he and friends would play all day. They worked up an appetite that Quakeress Elizabeth Monroe would satisfy with "a tin cup of strong, smelly, tasty vegetable soup with two large heavy crackers." One cup of that rich, nourishing soup was "a heavenly meal, especially after hours of hard playing," to which the boys were called at noon by a loud bell. She also furnished the two boats and operation of the park. There was a monument there to commemorate those who died in the Battle of Red Bank during the Revolutionary War. When the estate ran out of money, private philanthropy took over to continue its operation. It became known as "Soupy Island" after its delicious noon repast. Emanuel was small for his age and managed to be admitted long after he passed the age limit.[21]

Some of the older boys joined gangs and built shacks of wood and tin on city lots and lived in these huts. The boys lived by rolling fruit stands and stealing in other ways. They gambled with cards and dice. When the police knocked down their shacks, the officers would confiscate the gambling money. Emanuel recalled that W. C. Fields escaped this "shakedown" by building his tiny shack in a junkyard with the owner's permission.[22]

The boy remembered clearly the Peace Jubilee where "thousands of veterans" marched to the music of John Philip Sousa in celebration of victory over Spain in 1898. At an announced time the street was cleared and President William McKinley appeared in a carriage "drawn by high-stepping, racing horses." The president "kept his silk hat in the air while we cheered." It was "the most exciting show a 10-year-old had ever seen."[23]

Soldiers marched in parade to celebrate the victory. Emanuel marched alongside, keeping step, his head held back, "and the music seemed to keep my hair straight up. My flushed skin was alive with thrills." He loved it but discovered the marchers hated every step because they had already marched to the scene of the celebration, and were told there would be more exhausting marching later. Finding that the marchers were not enjoying their work was Emanuel's "first disillusionment as a patriot." Dogs ran up and down the street, barking. The children marched up to Delaware Street, where they viewed a wooden man-of-war that was more than one hundred years old. An armed American sailor stopped them with "you fellars Amer-r-r-rican citizens or Spanish spies?" and they assured him they were loyal citizens.[24]

When Emanuel was a boy, the "tall, shiny silk hat was the badge of respectability" and brought with it the timeworn jokes of boys throwing snowballs to knock the hats off. One of his schoolteachers was engaged to a handsome man who wore a silk hat when he picked her up at school. He wore a silk-labeled black Prince Albert, with striped trousers and patent leather shoes with black shiny buttons down the side. He was a bank teller who earned the magnificent sum of $25 weekly. When the snow fell, the city gentlemen came downtown in their horse-drawn sleighs, whip in right hand, reins in left hand, with the horses prancing, bells jingling. The boy loved to walk in the snow, hearing it crunch under his shoes, watching it swirl against a streetlight, to come home to his mother's cooking because the walk made him hungry.[25]

The snow also meant buying bundles of kindling and people carrying coal oil in a two-gallon can with a potato in its spout to keep it from jiggling out. He would bring coal oil home to his mother. Many of his friends had to cover themselves with additional clothes, newspapers, "and everything that might help keep out the cold." Then out came the sleighs again with their horses "sweating and blowing vapor." It was great to see the coal wagon arrive and the driver extending his chute to the cellar window and dumping the load in five minutes. Emanuel's father took "a great forward step" when he brought home one day "several delicate Welsback mantles." He lit a match "to send a flame throughout the cone-shaped thing." Then it was ready, and "the white light it produced was sensationally clear." But as these developments emerged, the horse-drawn sleighs disappeared, and motorcars appeared in their place.[26]

"It was painful to see the men huff and puff over the starter" of their automobile. If it was cold, it took many turns of the crank to start the engine. There would always be someone to yell, "Get a horse!" Then the motorcar would come down the street at thirteen miles an hour, frightening angry people. When the drivers began to have to buy annual licenses, they howled that their rights were being violated and that "they were being treated like criminals." Some refused to buy because they were conscientious objectors. But the state eventually won when they finally surrendered and purchased.[27]

In the spring, marble fever would sweep the city. The boys would chalk a line in the pavement and play until "their shooting thumb" became numb. They would count their wealth in "aggies," then suddenly give them up for spinning tops, followed by flying kites. Continually there was the craze of collecting the colored pictures of daring women scantily clad that came with packages of cigarettes. Suddenly a burlesque queen or a movie star would be worth ten marbles or two tops. This craze was followed by ball games in vacant lots. "Everything came in waves." The boys even played jacks occasionally, although this was considered a girl's game, followed by roller-skating in good weather.[28]

Once Emanuel's mother bought him a pair of roller skates for 10 cents. She received the quality she paid for. Emanuel had not gotten "around the corner" before one of the cast-iron pieces broke. He was unable to glue the pieces back together and returned them to the shopkeeper, who said he had warned his mother they did not come with a guarantee. When the snows came she bought him a 10-cent sled. Its runners were made of tin, not steel, and he received a split lip when he tried a belly flopper on it. The runners collapsed under the strain.[29]

Election nights were exciting. Men and boys started piling up wood during the day for an immense fire in the evening. Packing cases, crates, old furniture, anything that would burn was lit as soon as it got dark. The bonfire was set near the stockyards where Germantown Avenue in Kensington "spread out" near Third and Girard. A policeman was present, but his job was to make sure nearby houses were not endangered by the fire or the mob of people who would gather. There were fistfights, parades, wild speeches that promised anything and everything. No one ever heard of libel laws. Beer flowed freely. Patriotism was taken for granted by everyone.

The Fourth of July was also exciting, with the blown-out eyes and thumbs and fingers numbed, as well as the singed eyebrows. Once some coal miners visited Kensington with sticks of dynamite, "which they set up on a clothes line and set off one at a time." Emanuel "saw many an old enamel coffeepot practically disappear under a 10 cent Chinese firecracker that was every bit 12 inches high." A Happy Hooligan cost 10 cents and was heavy. Emanuel recalled a policeman picking up a juvenile arm that a Happy Hooligan blew off. Policemen at that time wore "ugly derbies and almost knee-length brass-buttoned coats and they always took their whisky straight, in sizeable glasses at a swallow followed by no water, by God!" Reading the Declaration of Independence took place in an open-air meeting a short walk from Ben Franklin's grave.[30]

The neighborhood the Juliuses lived in was often dominated by Irish Catholics and Germans. It was rough being a Jew there. The Irish called you Christ Killer and, if they caught you, would give you a good beating. In fact, Emanuel's crooked nose came from a street fight in which it was broken. At night gangs of teenagers and older boys roamed the streets "looking for bearded Jews and when they found one they would beat him up."

There were Italian boys "walking the streets, carrying buckets" in which they collected dog manure. Emanuel could recall years later his "horror" at the "whitish, dry, powdery manure" they sought. He had no idea how much they received when they sold it and thought perhaps it was used to fertilize "flowers and all kinds of exotic plants." It was a practice that probably "commanded a high market price" but a repulsive one that held no interest for him.[31]

For a time large numbers of Hungarians began crowding out the Irish and Germans from their traditional neighborhoods. They were fleeing their native land from high taxes and military conscription. Once a father took a couple of boys and one of his own into a saloon, Emanuel recalled, where "he quaffed a large nickel beer and the boys had soft drinks." The Hungarians were "young, swarthy, husky fellows with bristling black moustaches, good teeth, clear blue or gray eyes . . . light colored vests, white shirts with scrolly red trim and long sleeves that ballooned from elbow to wrist, a big porcelain pipe, and at least ten pounds of paprika."

Four to six men lived in a room that cost each about $1 per week. Someone always brought a ham for Sunday meals, along with beer. They also liked raw hamburger with chopped onions, vinegar, garlic, "and the inevitable paprika." Emanuel soon learned to eat the raw meat, which shocked his mother for "she had strong scruples against such practices." Emanuel taught the Hungarians English, and they reciprocated by teaching him the Yiddish language.

When Emanuel was about sixteen, a young Hungarian boy suffered from an unknown disease. He worked at the slaughterhouse at Third and Girard until one day he was taken to the local hospital, where he soon died. One of the men gathered the boy's belongings and sold them. He came to Emanuel's mother and gave her three dimes and five pennies for the debt the boy owed her. A dozen men and "half that many women" attended the funeral, where the men drank beer and men and women ate ham and hamburger and sang songs, mournfully at first, then gaily. Despite their loss, "life was being lived again."[32]

The Hungarian men came to America first, made some money, then sent for the women. Emanuel found the women to be "beautiful and fragrant." They laughed or flirted with their husbands or sweethearts. They were usually small women "with black hair, oval tanned faces, flashing eyes, red lips . . . round breasts, and strong bodies. They made life soft, beautiful, warm, and cozy." These women contrasted with the former inhabitants, who "wore ugly clothes, fought in their homes and in the streets, got drunk, and went hunting for Jews to beat up, were priest-ridden, ignorant, crude, and given to sudden bursts of violence."[33]

Emanuel remembered the cobblestones on Cadwallader Street where, as a boy, he watched Italian and Irish laborers lay the stones. They tamped them in with heavy wooden thumpers "in a delicately-timed routine," much like two section hands driving a spike rhythmically into a railroad tie. One could see that the men loved "those happy, lilting, staccato cadenzas." The workers transformed "a noisy activity into an arpeggio," he recalled later, "that enthralled me."[34]

All saloons had watering troughs outside where the horses could get drinks of water while the teamsters enjoyed their beer inside. On hot days a teamster would dump a pail of cool water on the horse's head, and in response, "the horse would rear up, shake its head, and then, after the first shock, act as though it would like some more." After ten minutes of this, a tired horse would leave the trough thoroughly refreshed.[35]

Flea shows were presented in "freakish theaters." Emanuel recalled one named the Dime Museum on Arch Street. Human freaks were displayed on the third floor, as well as a mechanical chess player with an expert chess player hidden inside, human embryos encased in alcohol, women who showed everything "up to their garters," midgets, giants, hermaphrodites, a bearded lady, a man with a rubber skin, a contortionist, a fire-eater, a sword swallower, tumblers, acrobats, a unicyclist, a tramp comedian who brought lit cigar butts out of his pants, a juggler, a marksman who could knock a cigarette out of a woman's mouth by aiming his rifle behind his head with the aid of a little mirror, a knife thrower.[36]

Emanuel saw a show named "Hanlon's Superba" as a boy and recalled it vividly years later. The stage was a huge frame before which one of the Hanlon brothers pretended to do calisthenics before a mirror. There was no "mirror," but another brother behind the frame "acts in close coordination with the performer out in front." This act ran for years. He received a pass for letting the company put up two posters about the show in the window of his mother's shop on Germantown Avenue.[37]

"Roughnecks" were attracted to the Kensington theater with admission of 10 cents for the gallery. It was an atmosphere of "noise, smoke, yells, whistles, hisses, guffaws, stamping, and over everything else the stench of urine, for there was no toilet and all peed against the rear wall." The atmosphere was Elizabethan London, "except that we had no orange girls." Later, Emanuel learned that the girls who sold oranges to men in the curtained stalls "also sold them something else."[38]

"Anything that carried the hint of a show would find" Emanuel in attendance, even the Chamber of Horrors, known as the European museum. This exhibit was "intended to bring patients to the clap doctor upstairs." The wax figures included Louis Napoleon "with most of his middle section exposed for he was being treated by a urologist for some disorder of his plumbing system." His eyes would open and shut and he would inhale and exhale. "The figures of syphilitic men were ghastly," and many men "fainted while looking at the living examples of their miseries." A barker would approach men and ask if anyone needed a doctor. A special section of the show included the torture chambers of the Spanish Inquisition, and nearby were the war paintings of the great Russian artist Vereshchagin.[39]

Emanuel occasionally attended the Jewish theater on Arch Street, in the area of homes of the Drews and Barrymores. The audience was the best show there. They came prepared with "huge packages of food—salami, hard-boiled eggs, pickled green tomatoes and cucumbers, legs of chicken, goober nuts, oranges, apples, bananas, bagels, rye bread, hard candies, and sunflower seeds." Boys went around with huge pretzels on a stick, a penny each. The audience yelled and screamed, occasionally at each other, and wept when an innocent character was wronged. When the villain falsely accused the hero of stealing, the adult next to Emanuel yelled, "You're a goddam liar." Emanuel loved the Jewish comedians more than the serious actors. One of them pretended to get $5,000 from a father for marrying his daughter. After the ceremony, the $5,000 was not forthcoming. Finally, after the guests had left, the groom approached his father-in-law and pointed to his fly with his left hand, shook his right fist, and cried, "Unless I get the $5,000 now not one button will I unbutton!" Emanuel attended these shows free, again compliments of posters displayed in his mother's shop.[40]

For the older young set, there was always the lure of New York City—car parties were the big-city version of a country hayride. Twenty-five or thirty would hire a streetcar, cover it with bunting, and pound on small drums or tin pails, shake cow bells or rattles, and sing or josh each other.

The fellows wisecracked "fit to make the girls die laughing." The more aristocratic would build the trip around taking in a show, or the more affluent would extend the trip to a dinner and then a Broadway show starring a Barrymore.[41]

Emmanuel's "round little mother's inconspicuous tobacco and candy store at 1326 Germantown Avenue" sported a cigar-store Indian. This was a "frightening" Indian chief with a tomahawk in his right hand and "a huge bunch of [tobacco] leaves" in his left. It was carved by a man who formerly shaped ship figureheads. The chief seemed like "a person rather than dummy" with his bold colors of red, green, yellow, ochre, and brown. His headdress and feathers seemed to flutter in the wind, as did his cloak. Hands and legs were carved separately, then attached with screws. His mother could have purchased a metal Indian, but Emanuel passionately pleaded with her to buy one carved from an old ship spar of white pine. The Indian's paint was freshened once a year when a traveling painter appeared while making the rounds of four states, brightening up cigar-store Indians "for a few dollars." They brought the Indian inside every night to protect it from the elements and from theft. After these Indians had been "junked up by the tens of thousands," collectors bought them for $500 if they were in good condition. These Indians were not standardized, as the carvers were true individualistic artists. When Emanuel's mother sold the shop for $300, a 900 percent profit over what she bought it for, she had no idea that someday the chief alone would be worth more than that.[42]

The organ grinder happened to be in front of the store once when it was raining. He put Peter, his monkey, under his coat so he would not catch cold. Even in the store, the monkey shivered with the damp cold. Emanuel could see him shaking and gave him a piece of banana. The Italian let Emanuel hold the little fellow, and he could feel him tremble, looking out from his jacket with wide, wondering, frightened eyes.[43]

Once when he was eleven Emanuel felt an uncontrollable urge to get out into the country, as the city was becoming uncomfortable for reasons unknown even to himself. He walked to Girard and Fifth and caught a streetcar for Fox Chase, at the edge of Philadelphia. He was prepared with a paper bag containing hard-boiled eggs, slices of jellied bread, an apple, an orange, and a banana. When he got off, he walked north until he was "really in the country." The grass and weeds were up to his waist. The sun was out, and he realized for the first time he could see the blue sky with "lacy white clouds floating softly, seemingly just beyond the tops of the trees."

He tried to pass everything through his fingers—the weeds, the grass, the hundreds of bugs, smelling "a dozen new aromas." He ate slowly, lying in the grass with bugs everywhere. "Each bite tasted good." He rested on his back, smelling the good earth. He rose rested, and continued to walk north until he could hear rumbles of an approaching storm. First the rain came gently, then harder, and he foolishly ran under a tree with the lightning crashing around, but "it felt good, and safe, and beautiful." The tree would protect him, he thought. He was "getting soaked to the skin," his hair was flat against his scalp and down on his forehead. The storm died down. He walked back to the streetcar line, then rode back to the city with its offensive smells and distracting noises, refreshed.[44]

Emanuel enjoyed attending Italian funerals—"always the best show in town." There were black coffins for old men, violet ones for old women, gray for the middle aged, and white for the young. Some of the musicians were from Luigi Creatore's band, which played in the park and which Emanuel enjoyed listening to because Creatore was "an explosive, temperamental, fiery, tempestuous, raging rip-roaring conductor" when he directed the men in a fast score. His contortions of "weaving, jumping, ducking, and head-shaking" always left the boys waiting to see how much his "long, black hair got mussed up."[45]

Once Emanuel had the entire day off from school and spent the time with free tickets to the zoo. He had seen elephants and giraffes at the Barnum and Bailey circus, but here he could "nestle right up to the bars or windows of cages that held long, terrifying pythons, and other reptiles, frightening alligators, beautiful lions and tigers, amusing , devilish, and impish monkeys." The children watched zookeepers at feeding time, throwing buckets of meat to lions. Many thought the wild boars were ugly, but Emanuel saw "beauty" there. They "were picturesque, fascinating, dangerous, admirable." It was "wonderful to hear the lions roar as their meal approached, the birds with their gorgeous feathers, their lovely forms." The "red and blue assed baboons," the zebras' stripes, the enormous elephants, the little foxes—all were beautiful sights to the young city dweller.[46]

At roughly the age of fourteen he heard William Jennings Bryan deliver his famous "Prince of Peace" sermon to "a huge Academy of Music audience." Emanuel found the "Great Commoner" to be an "ignorant, stupid, narrow minded, malicious man with a magnificent voice that invariably impressed his audience of 'yokels, and Bible-thumpers.'" As Bryan expressed it, he was "more interested in the Rock of Ages than he was in the age of rocks." This was a kind of rubbish that delighted Bryan's hearers and brought him the support of the parsons.[47]

The local cathouses intrigued the boy. Emanuel first heard of them from "people who whispered about them" in his mother's shop. There were two of them in the Kensington district, a $1 one and a $2 one. Most of Philadelphia's prostitution took place downtown in the Tenderloin district, but Mrs. Murphy set up her two shops on Germantown Avenue. Mrs. Murphy was "hugely fat," a big-boned woman with "beautiful and kind young eyes, the strength of a workingman." She had had experience in this business before opening her own houses. She proved to be a "first class depositor" at the bank on Girard Avenue.

Mrs. Murphy ran a tight ship. She met the "trade" at the door and rejected the unwanted (of which there were many, such as drunks and the rough fellows who scared her girls), and knew exactly how much time a girl should allow each customer. Occasionally she would have to dart out of the front room, knock loudly on a door, and yell "Time's up!" Although there was a bouncer present, Mrs. Murphy often "bounced the drunks and trouble-makers" personally. Customers had to be careful with their language around her. On busy paydays, impatient young men would call out, "Jeez-Chrise, can't you hurry that guy up, I'm boinin'?" she would respond, "No use Jesus Christ here. I don't like it." The seventeen-year-old Western Union boy, who was always in uniform and carried a loaded gun, delivered messages to girls and told the younger boys of the $1 house activities. Mrs. Murphy would not admit Emanuel and his twelve-year-old friends until "they had hair down there," the Western Union boy informed them, so there was "nothing to do but wait." But Emanuel discovered he could gain admission and observe the activities by running errands for Mrs. Murphy, such as mailing letters for her. Sometimes he had to wait five minutes while she finished her letter, and this gave him some time to observe activities. The Western Union boy told them that some of the girls were married and got "put in by their husbands," and there was "a coming and going of girls all the time." Sometimes a pimp brought in a girl and Mrs. Murphy paid him $20, but she would not allow him to remain, as that was bad for business. The girls, Emanuel recalled, were always kind and generous.

There were usually eight girls in the $1 house and six in the $2 house. Cops were on the "free list." On the boys' way home from school, the girls would knock on their windows to signal to them that they had a letter for them to mail. The young boys would run other errands—to the candy shop, the drugstore, the laundry—for which they received never less than a dime, and sometimes a quarter. Emanuel recalled that the girls were "all beautiful creatures, young, smelly with perfume, and far more courteous than the people we had dealings with closer to home, and often right at home." Mrs. Murphy had a son who was a doctor, so she knew which doctor to call if a customer complained of a dose of the clap or a girl needed an abortion. She paid off the police and made sure no one got rolled in her houses. She wore black widow's clothing and was always jolly—well, most of the time. She believed her function in life was noble and necessary, and she protected herself, her girls, and her patrons. Most of her girls were Irish, with a few Italians, blonde Germans, and an occasional light black. No business was conducted on Sundays or holidays. When Mrs. Murphy died, "thousands mourned" and half of her estate went to the church. The local police precinct sent a wreath. Her business establishment meant that there was no streetwalking in the neighborhood, although violence, cruelty, and drunkenness abounded.[48]

The summer when he was fifteen, after attending a Salvation Army meeting, Emanuel decided on impulse to visit their new hotel in Boston.

The ten-story hotel was up to date with hot and cold showers on each floor, and it was "fresh and clean." He looked for a job and found one in a cheap restaurant. He was assigned to work the lunch shift from 11:00 to 1:00, for which he could eat his fill and be paid 50 cents. He figured he could get by on the 50 cents until he found more lucrative employment. After one hour, though, the boss gave him 50 cents and told him to enjoy his meal; his services were no longer needed. While eating a bowl of beef stew, he asked the employer why he was being fired. The boss replied that it was because he lacked experience. Perhaps he broke too many dishes. In any case, the boss had closely watched him carrying dishes and perceptively concluded Emanuel was not "a professional dish carrier." He found other employment.[49]

He enjoyed his visit, except for the noisy Elevated, but it stopped at midnight so he could count on six hours of rest each night. He lunched at Pie Alley nearby for his main meal of the day. Again his ingenuity came to the rescue of his meager resources. He bought coffee and a blueberry pie for 5 cents and purchased a 35-cent banquet ticket. He kept the 35-cent ticket, got in line, picked up a huge meal, and paid with the 5-cent ticket. For some reason, perhaps because he saw so much cheating on the streets, this did not prick his conscience. He toured Boston, heard speakers at the Commons, Sunday-night lectures, and debates at the socialist hall. Socialism was receiving much national attention at the time, and he spent a good deal of time that summer in the socialist reading room. He wore a blue hat with shiny black visor, much like sailors wore, and "this increased solicitation" from street walkers. He found occasional work and hit up his older sister for a few more dollars to continue his vacation.

He made the acquaintance of a man in the socialist reading room who invited him to participate in his scheme. Emanuel and others would act as serious customers in a clothing store, and the man would steal suits when the attention of the clerk was distracted. It was an easy dollar a day for him, and one could live nicely in Boston on that sum. He spent his summer as happy as could be, but autumn and school eventually arrived. As Emanuel expressed it, he was free, happy, and had youth, but all good things have to end. He was ready to return to Philadelphia. He completed his vacation with a slice of cold watermelon for a penny, a slice of pine-apple for a penny, and a one-cent bagel when he arrived in Philadelphia. He told his family of his summer adventures while "eating heartily of his mother's cooking" and slept seventeen hours before waking. He neglected to describe his petty larceny of cheating the eatery, and his dollar-a-day job as an accomplice in theft. This streak of larceny would return to haunt him later with his income-tax problems.[50]

Meanwhile, on the excursion to Boston, Emanuel was absorbing the theories of Marxism, which had begun in Europe as a response to Victorian capitalism and to the Industrial Revolution that was abolishing the preferred position of the skilled craftsman. Then, as Marxism migrated across the Atlantic, it began to mutate. New York City appeared to socialist immigrants, with its small industries and dense, stable neighborhoods, like the Old World they had left. Led by Morris Hillquit, they provided the core of socialist thought at the turn of the twentieth century. But the further west they migrated, the greater changes appeared to be, with Chicago and Milwaukee and their urbanization and large industries. Led nominally by Victor Berger, these socialists were a contentious lot, and factions frequently splintered off, sometimes permanently, sometimes over trivial issues. As they struggled to adapt Marxist ideals to the different conditions they found in their new surroundings, they faced a test in the railroad strike of 1877, which morphed into a great national uprising against grinding poverty and class privilege. Some accepted a strictly secular view of their political and economic condition, while others believed the Sermon on the Mount was their ultimate goal and that they were their brothers' keeper.[51]

Socialism took a more radical turn in California. In the Land of Hollywood, Jack London spoke to, and for, the movement through his numerous articles. He was succeeded by Upton Sinclair, who supported American involvement in World War I through the Social Democratic League. When the New Deal proceeded to build socialism "bit by bit" through President Franklin Roosevelt's New Deal programs, Sinclair believed his Utopia was approaching.[52]

During his California trip and later, Emanuel also absorbed the theories of socialism by periodically visiting the local headquarters at 1305 Arch Street, where he listened to speakers such as James B. Connelly, Joseph E. Cohen, Fred Long, and Eugene V. Debs. There were many kinds of socialism being hawked at this time in nineteenth-century America. The more radical ones preached violence and a type close to communism, while the brand espoused by Debs, which attracted Emanuel, was basically designed to implement the Golden Rule. Fundamentally, it proposed government ownership and control of the means of production and distribution of all goods, governed by an impartial body of equals. This would include, on the national level, transportation, mail service, maintenance of military force, public safety, education, health, utilities, recreation—basic functions of any government. These moderates rejected violence, preaching peaceful means of acquiring power through the ballot box, by majority rule.[53]

While in his teens, Emanuel was particularly taken with Ella Reeve. When she visited Philadelphia he liked to take charge of the literature that was always present at a socialist gathering, take up collections, and make "little speeches." Emanuel helped the "little Socialist firebrand" arrange a speech at the Baldwin Locomotive Works. He especially enjoyed assisting George Kirkpatrick, whom he thought was "the genius of the Socialist lecture platform." Kirkpatrick's speeches consisted of "two hours of oratory, appeals to reason, wit, sarcasm, irony, poetry, verbal thunder and lightning, sound knowledge, the latest in science." But his most profound memory was the visit of Eugene Debs when Emanuel was "about seventeen." Debs was "the most impressive man" he had ever known. His speech was "magnificent," Emanuel thought. "He spoke rapidly, now at the top of his rather shrill voice, now at a soft baritone; now he scolded the workers for enduring the evils of capitalism. He ridiculed the aristocracy and I remember the scorn he aimed at the rich American girls who were marrying poverty-stricken European counts. He called them counts and other no-accounts, which brought a short laugh. . . . He thundered against war, using a full sentence that I heard him repeat many times over a period of 25 years."[54]

It was the socialist literature that attracted Emanuel most. Lacking

the money to purchase, he would read a pamphlet at the party headquarters, replace it on the rack, and select another—pamphlet after
pamphlet. He would thumb through the books, decide which he wanted
to read, and stop at the Free Library on Chestnut Street to check them
out. He was twelve or thirteen when he discovered Robert Ingersoll's
pamphlets. When he finished reading one, he went for a walk. At that
time he held no belief in God and challenged God "to do his stuff. . . .
He could strike me dead before I reached the next corner." When he
was not struck dead, he decided that if there was a God, "he didn't
give a damn about what I thought or did." But Emanuel had no time
for doubts. Then, he noted, he began "reading in earnest," abandoning
the Horatio Alger and Frank Merriwell stories and "soaking up the
classics." These great speeches and the travelers who gave them whet-
ted his appetite to see and learn more of the outside world awaiting his
conquest. He was especially impressed with the socialist emphasis on
literature and on educating the masses.[55]

This was the great age for oratory in American history when many
people found their finest entertainment in attending a Chautauqua or
listening to a good orator. Ingersoll, a well-known agnostic, was one of
those speakers who cast a spell over Emanuel as well as other listeners.
He was able to combine both tears and peals of laughter with his calm
delivery. It was said that Eugene Debs, after hearing Ingersoll speak, took
him to the Terre Haute depot for his trip home and decided to travel with
him to Cincinnati to explore Ingersoll's concepts further.[56]

Emanuel seldom wrote of his siblings, so it is unknown what he thought
of his three younger sisters. He liked and respected his older sister, Esther,
because she was a teacher, and with some income she could loan him small
sums occasionally. When his older brother, Nathan, died, his wife asked
Emanuel why he was apathetic and did not grieve for him. He replied, "I
never liked him anyway. He used to torture me."[57]

Emanuel's father was a practical man, but he understood his son rather
imperfectly. Emanuel could never be a bookkeeper like Nathan, nor a
teacher like Esther, he concluded. This left the boy with the choice of a
trade, like his father, with a preliminary training period or apprenticeship.

At the end of the school term, when Emanuel was thirteen and would be fourteen in July, David told his son that when boys in Odessa were that age they began to think of a career, of striking out on their own as adults. He suggested to Emanuel that it would be folly to waste the whole summer, as he had been doing in exploring Philadelphia the past summers. Emanuel agreed. He was anxious to get a real job and make some money, even if he had to contribute some of it to help support the large family.[58]

He found employment in a sweatshop factory hiring hundreds of boys his age to make guns, ships, and other wooden toys. It was run by a rich German family in Kensington. Child labor was used exclusively, except for the supervisors. The children were paid $3 weekly, with payday every other week, minus 5 cents for ice water. By modern standards the hours were long. On weekdays they worked from 7 a.m. to 6 p.m. with an hour for lunch. On Saturdays it was from 6:35 a.m. to 1:00 p.m. He was put to work painting wooden parts—and loved it—for a while. After several weeks the novelty wore off and he missed wandering the streets of Philadelphia. In addition, his fellow workers were foul-mouthed brutes, and he longed for school to start again.

Then his father told Emanuel how important his small contribution was to the family budget. He was bright, and he could attend night school and continue his job. Emanuel felt he had no choice but to yield silently, and he enrolled in Brown's preparatory school for night classes. He had to give up his piano practice time, but someone left David a cheap violin in payment for a debt. Esther arranged to give piano lessons to the sister of a violinist, and in exchange the violinist would instruct Emanuel in violin. Emanuel loved the violin much more than piano, and his love for music prompted him to save his money to attend the opera one night and hear Caruso sing *Aida*.

Emanuel was determined to get away from the dreadful toy factory, though, and one evening at the dinner table he announced his job had been terminated. David rightfully suspected he had quit, but Emanuel convinced him he would get another job. Trouble with algebra and Latin forced him out of Brown's, and he transferred to a local high school to take night classes of his choosing. In his late teens he got a job of his liking, learning a trade with the *Philadelphia Press and Record*.[59]

Emanuel was soon prepared to crisscross the country in a quest to find himself and seek a proper occupation by obtaining experience in different jobs that would help him hone his skills as a writer and editor.

2

THE BECKONING WORLD, 1905–1915

Socialism became one of the great centers for intellectual stimulus in Emanuel's life. "I have never heard better talk before or since," he asserted. "I listened to the conversation of those I thought superior in information and mental ability." It made him "a full-fledged left-winger at sixteen." The socialist organization in Philadelphia had an excellent library and also a steady, impressive offering of outstanding speakers. Left-wing politics was in its heyday following the victory of the conservative Republican forces under William McKinley in the presidential election of 1896. The leaders of the Socialist Party—Eugene V. Debs, Ella Reeve Bloor, George Kirkpatrick—were emerging as proponents of the great cause, a movement that became very attractive to aspiring young radicals. Socialists preached revolt, and this had an appeal to certain discontented youth. The party also seemed to discern what was wrong with society and had the answers to solve the problems.

> For those who came to maturity during the last decade of the nineteenth century, the emerging world of American Socialism dominated their intellectual life. Those were the days in which youthful illusions still shone bright. No war had come to blight youth's generous impulses with the hard practicality of greybeard's designs. Europe was then a goal, not a chaos. Above all, to the dissatisfied youngsters of the epoch . . . Socialism was bathed in a literary atmosphere.

As uninviting as the average "headquarters of a local might be, there was usually a bookcase filled with pamphlets and more substantial volumes bearing titles that suggested flight from harsh reality. And not flight alone. Revolt. It was a logical haven for youthful discontent."[1] Emanuel was impressed that the headquarters always had pamphlets available from which he could learn something.

> Robert Ingersoll had the most lasting impact on Emanuel's thinking on religiosity and freedom. He was especially impressed with the philosopher's thoughts on this topic as expressed immediately after the Civil War. I see no reason why the white and black man cannot live together in the same land and under the same flag. The beauty of liberty is, you cannot have it unless you give it away, and the more you give away the more you have. I know that my liberty is secure solely because others are free.[2]

Emanuel dropped out of the Philadelphia school system without formally attending high school. After leaving the toy factory, he enrolled in some night classes and took a job as an usher in Keith's theater. This was not the end of his education, but rather the beginning. He started by reading Old King Brady and the Frank Merriwell stories, which were available to him free in his mother's shop. Then he turned to the Horatio Alger books he could check out at the Children's Branch of the Free Library.

David Julius was determined that his bright young son be exposed to the classics and introduced him to the writings of Tom Paine, thus beginning his lifelong quest for further knowledge through self-education. The writings of Paine and some of the pamphlets of Robert Ingersoll—both of whom were debunkers—impressed Emanuel, making him a lifelong freethinker, as they did thousands of other readers. The difference was those thousands of other readers soon returned to their original faith. Emanuel did not, as he had no original faith to which to return. He became a committed admirer of these two writers, even as he absorbed Balzac, Maupassant, Tolstoy, and Gorky, to whom his father also introduced him. He read Herbert Spencer, Longfellow, Poe, Shakespeare, Dickens, Dumas, Hugo, Carlyle, H. G. Wells—a fine list for an eager young mind.

At this time, while he was reading these classics, Emanuel was learning his trade as a copy holder for the *Philadelphia Press and Record*. He rounded out his education in Philadelphia by further reading in the classics on socialism. He often visited the local headquarters on Arch Street, discussing these principles with local members, reading the *Communist Manifesto*, and attending the occasional lectures of Eugene Debs. "Ed" Moore, a millworker, was a fanatic on socialism, and James B. Conant, a devout Catholic, gave public speeches that impressed the young lad. Conant called George R. Kirkpatrick the "genius of the socialist platform," and Emanuel listened enraptured to his speeches on "The Hypnotism of the Working Class" more than fifty times until he could repeat it by heart. He heard Joseph Cohen and Fred Long expound on Marx's *Capital*, which he found difficult reading. During this period of his life he also secured the rudiments of writing through "haunting" the shelves of economics and sociology at the Free Library. By the time he left for New York City, he was ready to begin writing for newspapers. As Harry Golden observes, when he reached adulthood Emanuel was "probably the best read man on the continent."[3]

A turning point in his life came when he accepted employment as a bellboy at $16 monthly with Miss Mason's School for Girls at Tarrytown-on-the-Hudson, where some four hundred "pretty and rich virgins" learned how to be proper wives for wealthy husbands. Through close supervision, the girls were well protected from possible scandal.[4] There was little for him to do on the job, so the school's library became the focus of his life. The librarian was "old, tiny, wrinkled, gray, bent and cranky," but the two got along famously because Emanuel wanted to learn and she was intrigued with the idea of tutoring a young mind. She became engrossed in developing his mind, and he became "the only person in the world who could talk to her at any time and get courteous treatment and intelligent concern over the state of my intellect." She fed him every word written by Emerson, who impressed him with his "realistic, hard-boiled mind unclouded by superstition and mysticism." On the other hand, he considered some of Emerson's essays to be weak because "the author rejected his own better work and let himself express ideas that were dim-shadowed, vague, remote from reality, and devoid of his usual vigor, health, and naturalism." She had him read Carlyle's *Sartor Resartus*, which he found "delightful." Then came Mark Twain, to whose home she took him one evening. When Emanuel began writing short essays for the *New York Call*, she would neglect fifty girls to read and criticize his pieces and tell him what she liked and what could be improved.[5]

She introduced him to Washington Irving, whom he read for entertainment and his graceful prose style. She took him to Irving's home and grave, then pointed up the Hudson to places that Irving wrote about and what had happened there. She drove him to Twain's home, where "they met again." The librarian told Twain of Emanuel's ambition to become a writer, and "he nodded slowly." He was in his seventies, and "release was soon to come."[6]

When the librarian gave him a book of essays by Hamilton Wright Maybrie, he informed her that the author might be famous but he thought his writing was "rubbish, trash. She smiled approvingly." One evening Maybrie came to the school to lecture. Emanuel could not sit with the young female audience, but he was permitted a chair in the hall where he could listen. Miss Mason introduced Maybrie as "one of America's great writers and most important literary critic." Then the lecturer presented his "inspirational rot and conventional ideas, clichés, and dull verbiage," as Emanuel described it. When he finished the librarian escorted him out and paused to introduce him to Emanuel, saying he was probably the only one who heard him tonight who had read his works. Maybrie "beamed and smiled slightly." Emanuel said, "Yes, I have read your books, but I can't say they were any better than your lecture and that was my idea of an inferior performance." He expected Miss Mason to fire him, but she did not, perhaps because of the librarian.[7]

Emanuel decided to go to the Labor Church to hear a lecture by "the country's most vindictive and savage bigot," Anthony Comstock, author of New York State's infamous law setting standards on pornography. Comstock bragged about the "carloads of literature he had confiscated, of the thousands of pictures, devices, periodicals, pamphlets, and other forms of expression" he had destroyed. He discussed the "many people he had sent to prison, how many had committed suicide." Emanuel was surprised at how many young people were in attendance, and how none of them were challenging Comstock's views. Then, "a short, stout woman" stood up and called out, "How many people have you murdered, Anthony Comstock?" Comstock thundered back, "I am being interrupted by one of my old enemies, Emma Goldman." She was accompanied by Alexander Berkman and Ben L. Reitman. The accusations "came thick and fast," but the crowd was with Comstock. Goldman charged him with "destroying works of literature by Rabelais, Boccaccio, and other classics." "I don't believe in protecting the classics when they are filthy and immoral," Comstock yelled. "Think of all the adolescent boys who have been driven to masturbation by these writers of classical obscenity, and how many of them have been made insane by their masturbation, all being brought on by reading the classics." And so it went, with Goldman and her friends challenging Comstock with obscenities in the Bible. To this Comstock responded that the Bible was not a classic but "the word of Gawd!" Emanuel thought Comstock was "a nasty neurotic, smut-obsessed fanatic."

Goldman and Berkman were well-known anarchists who declined to join the Socialist Party but were known and liked by party members. When she first met Eugene Debs, Goldman found the party leader to be "genial and charming as a human being" and thought his views to be "very much like her own." In fact, she called him an anarchist and he did not refute her. Goldman and Berkman were living together in a nearby apartment, and Emanuel, who was impressed by their ideas, "made several visits there" and "got to know them quite well."[8]

The Rand School of Social Science stood about a half-dozen blocks from the Goldman apartment. It was a three-story building with a restaurant in the basement operated by the socialist Piet Vlag. A library, bookstore, office, and classrooms were located on the first floor. There were additional classrooms on the second floor, and rooms on the third floor were rented to socialist writers and speakers, some of whom lived there permanently. Emanuel spent much of his time there, reading socialist newspapers and periodicals. "The place was quiet and inviting," he said. "I felt my mind expanding several notches."[9]

At that time Goldman was editing her pocket-size magazine, *Mother Earth*. Emanuel "admired and enjoyed" Berkman's *Prison Memoirs of an Anarchist*, a story of his attempt on Henry Clay Frick's life and the twenty-eight years he spent in the Pennsylvania penitentiary in punishment for that deed. Emanuel told him how much he enjoyed his story, and "from then on he was my friend." Whenever Berkman got into trouble with the police and had to hide out for a while, it was a "cinch" for Emanuel to find his hideout and "delight" his editor with stories he would submit on Berkman. Usually the anarchist had not committed any crime, but when there was any outbreak of violence the police would automatically begin their investigation by questioning him. Berkman was the "student" type of radical, whereas Goldman was "the fiery agitator and mass orator."[10]

The librarian let him read her copy of *Smart Set*, and he became acquainted for the first time with George Jean Nathan and Henry L. Mencken. He disagreed with Mencken's political and economic views but liked his philosophy of life. Twain was never a socialist, but Emanuel believed "he had radical ideas about economics, hated imperialism, and was more of a critic than a supporter of capitalism." Soon after Twain died, in 1910, Emanuel put some of his ideas into an article titled "Mark Twain: Radical," for which the *International Socialist Review* paid him the handsome sum of $10. Emanuel was especially pleased when he discovered that the issue also carried essays by William "Big Bill" Haywood and Debs. During this period he wrote short essays for the *New York Call*, a socialist daily. The librarian helped him with these articles and taught him "a little about the use of words, punctuation, spelling, construction and the like." A short time after he went to New York City to work for the *Call*, he was saddened to read the librarian's obituary.

Emanuel's essays caught the attention of the editor of the *Call*, Louis Kopelin, and he was hired at $15 weekly. He packed his bag, kissed his mother, said good-bye to his father, and left. No scene, no crisis, observed his sister Rosalie. "He just left. He wanted to get out into the world and Momma and Daddy didn't mind. They knew he would be alright. Daddy said 'when he's ready to come back, he'll come back.'" He never looked back or returned, bound for the Big Apple with less than $2 in his pockets.[11]

Writers for the *Call* at the time included such luminaries as George R. Kirkpatrick, Allan Benson, John Spargo, Charles Edward Russell, Morris Hillquit, Joseph E. Cohen, John M. Work, and John Wanhope. All were leading figures in the eastern wing of the Socialist Party. Against this pantheon of writers, Emanuel had to wait some time to see his name in print. It was not until June 1911 that he published his first story for the *Call*. Titled "Business," it told the story of the infamous Triangle Shirtwaist Company fire. In his account, a middle-class Jew named Jouralovitch, unconnected to the factory, made immediate arrangements for the production of black armbands with the words "We Mourn Our Loss" printed on them and exploited the disaster by selling ten thousand of the armbands.[12]

He wrote Sunday features on George Bernard Shaw and art, and wrote sketches on everyday people, stories he later gathered together for his Little Blue Book *The Color of Life*. Collectively, the stories attempt to create a philosophy for dealing with the everyday issues of life, optimism versus pessimism, of true love requited. Many of them dealt with Emanuel's having to cope with pessimistic editors who failed to understand the significance of his stories, who procrastinated on stories until it was too late for resolution. He wrote "like a demon" on labor problems and socialist news. He had a whimsical streak and often used the pen name Patsy O'Bang for this type of writing.[13]

Emanuel found himself to be the subject of an essay appearing in the *Call*. The article reported the organizing of the Socialist Literary Syndicate, and he was its manager, hard at work, contacting the country's leading socialist writers to persuade them to join the syndicate's activities. Louis Kopelin, now in Washington DC, as national correspondent for the National Socialist Press, endorsed the syndicate, advising socialist editors across the nation to check into its possibilities for stories for their newspapers.[14]

Given the competition he faced from the other *Call* writers, Emanuel had to look for a position elsewhere if he wished to advance himself. Kopelin interviewed Victor L. Berger, the first socialist elected to the U.S. House of Representatives, who was planning on establishing a new newspaper, the *Milwaukee Leader*. Emanuel loved the Big Apple but wanted more than anything else to write and thus was willing to move to a job that offered the best prospects for his talent.

He moved to Milwaukee with a $3 raise to report for Berger's *Leader*, a week before the first edition was printed. Berger, who enjoyed low-life jokes, always referred to Emanuel as "My Lettle Shew." He covered city hall, the jail, the sheriff's office, the morgue, and the police and fire departments. He "held down three men's jobs," beginning every morning at 7:30 and going to 5:00 p.m. and writing five to seven columns daily, all for $18 a week. In addition, Emanuel often received night assignments because the city editor, Chester M. Wright, "believed in the gospel of toil."[15]

One item he covered involved a woman murdered by "her frustrated lover." Emanuel brought in his story and a picture of the woman. When killed, she weighed "at least 222 pounds." Wright did not want to waste space on "a homely woman" and instructed Emanuel to return to the murder scene and get a better picture, "even if it was ten years old, so long as she was pretty." He returned to the house where the family was in mourning, and there, on top of the coffin in the parlor, sat a picture of the woman when she was young and pretty. He had no time to ask permission but "barged in" and grabbed the picture. In the process the sawhorses tumbled and the coffin fell on him. To the horror of the family, he darted for the door with the picture, yelling at the family not to worry, that if any damage occurred the *Leader* would cover it. Stunts like this endeared him to the editor, but Emanuel's ribs "hurt for weeks."[16]

Carl Sandburg, then in his thirties and unknown, occupied a desk next to Emanuel's on the third floor. He was assigned labor issues. Sandburg was a "plodder," Emanuel recalled, who turned out "dull pieces that no one read except the labor leaders he mentioned." He never discussed himself with his colleagues but was always ready to listen to others. "Everyone knew he was secretly addicted to poetry," Emanuel reported. Sandburg was, in truth, a plodder for the Socialist Party, or as his biographer described him, a "foot soldier." It was after he moved to Chicago that he became known as the poet of the Windy City.[17]

A reporter named Manley worked for the *Milwaukee Journal* and became Emanuel's "pet rival," whose main goal in life was to beat him on "exclusives." Emanuel teamed up with the police reporter of the *Wisconsin News* to meet every morning to swap stories. This fellow was not a stickler for the facts—"little white fakes weren't unethical," he insisted—so the reporter gave Emanuel his fakes and the latter added a few refinements to them. Emanuel's city editor was aware of what the pair were doing and acquiesced in their farce. Thus the city's *Journal* editor "would raise hell with Manley every time he came on one of our police yarns that poor, helpless Manley" had missed because "they never happened." Manley had "to spend several hours each day running down my tiny touches of fiction."[18]

One of these stories involved a mother working in her kitchen who saw her two-year-old girl fall out the third-floor window of their flat, hit a clothesline, and fall safely into a basket of clothes. "Do it again, Mama," begged the child. The mother rushed the child to the hospital, which was part of Emanuel's police beat, and had her checked out. Emanuel reported this story, but he and his *News* cohort always used addresses in the middle of a vacant lot or beyond the end of a street, "so we had the poor bastard running all over town" to check out their fictitious stories.[19]

Emanuel and Manley fought over one story for weeks without any faking. A Greek candy store operator would give candy to "good looking young virgins" to entice them into his fancy apartment, which had a "magnificent bedroom covered with mirrors." One time the fellow seduced a young maiden who was eight weeks shy of the age of consent and was arrested for "contributing to the delinquency of a minor." The district attorney was a socialist, and to him Manley was "a reactionary reporter for a capitalist newspaper," so Emanuel had "the inside track on information" on the case "from the beginning." The district attorney presented the court with "lurid pictures" of the den of iniquity, but they became court property and could be used only with court permission. He "whispered" to Emanuel that the pictures were in a certain drawer and that the judge would never know if they disappeared "for a few hours." When Emanuel had the pictures reproduced and returned to the drawer, Manley could not yell "fake." Manley appealed to the judge, who then accosted the district attorney, who responded that the photos were where they were supposed to be.[20]

Another incident involved Emanuel writing a story laced with quotations from Shelly, Byron, and Keats, a magnificent feat that appeared on page 1 of the *Leader*. Wright, who loved to razz Emanuel, had some of his henchmen greet Emanuel every morning with lavish praise about his article and how great a writer he was. When they went to a restaurant, "a waiter, properly instructed," would ask for his autograph, or a bartender would throw his arms around Emanuel and exclaim how he was inspired by the essay. Even the mayor called and congratulated him as a credit to the *Leader*, and said that Milwaukee should be proud of its great writer. Victor Berger, in on the scheme, promised to write an article on the essay and have it translated for his German-language weekly. Even the public librarian asked for the original manuscript for preservation. The praise was so heady that it took the young writer several days to realize he was being "spoofed."[21]

Wright piled more and more work on Emanuel and "showed him gratitude by some dirty trick." He taught him the "valuable lesson" of ignoring inspiration and getting "down to work." At first Emanuel would "groan and suffer over an article by writing it out in long-hand, correcting it, retyping, and then go" over the thing again. Wright taught him "how to lay out my notes, pull up to a machine and let loose," how to write "what I had to say and then merely read it over for spelling and punctuation, with only an occasional word changed." When Wright moved to a new job as editor of the *Chicago World*, he asked Emanuel to go with him. This socialist newspaper's circulation had sky-rocketed when the city's major newspapers went on strike. The budding young reporter received the immense sum of $30 a week.[22]

It was in Chicago that Emanuel began to realize he was sadly lacking in social graces. To remedy this defect he watched how celebrities acted. He began restraining the impulse to crack his knuckles in public and making sure that the spoon was not left in his coffee cup. He had learned from John Spargo, the English socialist who was on the *Call* staff, to break off a small piece of bread and butter it rather than butter the entire slice.

He noticed that people did not like to see one remove "nose crusts" or eat with one's hat on. With practice he could soon "eat in such a way as not to destroy the appetite of anyone within range." He had his hair cut once a month and made sure to "scoop out the real estate under his finger nails." He was attempting to make his manners presentable to "intelligent people, not to shine among social parasites."[23]

Emanuel never liked Chicago, which he found "too big, too cumbersome, too clumsy, and too ugly." While there he was able to do some writing for the socialist paper *Coming Nation*, which merged with *Appeal to Reason* in 1904. Compared to his beloved New York City, his stay in Chicago "wasn't any too happy." When Wright was named editor of the *Los Angeles Citizen*, he invited Emanuel to accompany him. The latter agreed, because he knew Wright would put him on "the pie wagon" and believed he still had much to learn from Wright about editing. Compared to working on the *Chicago World*, the new job was like "having five days off each week." He had to accept a pay cut of $5 a week, though, rather than the usual pay raise when moving. In short order the two took over operation of another weekly, the *Social Democrat*, for which Emanuel was paid nothing because Chester told him he "wasn't really needed" at the *Citizen* and could not be paid for both jobs.[24]

Stanley B. Wilson, owner of the *Citizen*, decided he wanted to publish "a good looking monthly magazine," the *Western Comrade*, to take care of the aesthetic and literary needs of the growing socialist movement in the West. When Wright was offered the job of editing the *New York Call* in 1914, Emanuel had to leave the *Citizen* because Wilson considered him to be "Chester's problem." So Emanuel was on his own when he accepted the editorship of the *Social Democrat*.[25]

The *Western Comrade* was failing, with its circulation at only 850, so Wilson gave it to Emanuel for "nothing." Emanuel "did everything except print the thing" and soon had its circulation up to 1,500, with him clearing $100 a month and "making him a rich man." He wanted desperately to write, and now he was the owner and manager of a magazine! Editing the *Social Democrat* and the *Western Comrade* still gave him plenty of free time to read and write and to meet people. He spent the next eighteen

months in the Los Angeles area enjoying the beauty of the countryside—
"the mountains, the ocean, the magnificent homes . . . the marvelous
women." "Hollywood was just becoming glamorous" at that time with
its silent movie industry.[26]

On one occasion Emanuel had the opportunity to meet Jack London at
a movie studio where London was negotiating to sell movie rights to one
of his novels. Emanuel found the famous left-wing novelist was "rather
tall, well-built, trim, neat," informally dressed and wearing a huge Texas-
sized hat. When he wrote about the encounter in the *Western Comrade*,
Emanuel called London's hat a sombrero. London subsequently invited
him to his ranch in Sonoma County, and during their conversation he
scolded Emanuel for misnaming his hat. In what Emanuel called a "non-
sequitur," London questioned if he could not be "straight" about what
was *on* his head, then how could he hope for Emanuel to be correct about
what was *in* his head? In a subsequent letter, London responded sharply.
"Dear Comrade," he wrote,

> just a word of advice from an old man to a young man. Get over, as
> quickly as you can, being provincial and insular. In the first place, a
> sombrero is not an abominable head-gear . . . except to a provincial,
> insular ghetto Easterner such as you are. Second, I do not wear a som-
> brero. The hat you saw me wearing in Los Angeles was not a sombrero.
> Don't you see how utterly you lost out on all your counts? And why in
> hell did you want to bring in sombreros anyway. What had that to do
> with me? What does the public care about how to estimate a sombrero?
> Don't you see my boy, hell and the newspaper offices are full of men
> who do careless work as you did, and who are as insular and provincial
> as you are. Of course, the connotation of provincialism and insularity
> is egotism. My boy, I am giving you a lesson that should be worth
> everything to you if you can take it to head and heart.

A month later London wrote to Emanuel again.

> I may conclude you are dreadfully careless. Of course you never saw
> me in a sombrero. You know you did not see me in a sombrero, and

you know I know you never saw me in a sombrero and on that basic lie you built your New York ghetto prejudice against the sombrero, and put that over on your readers as well. There is no excuse for this intellectual (yes, and ethical) harlotry of yours. You lie when you put such things across upon your readers and on me, and when I drive back at you, squarely between the eyes, you bewail your sad state and squeal your antecedent slavery.

Enough already—Emanuel got his point about the sombrero.[27]

Emanuel quoted London as saying that he was more interested in his ranch and its stallions than he was in writing on socialism. London agreed that he wrote for the money, and Emanuel thus portrayed him as "a mercenary . . . acquisitive penman." This made London "look like hell" when the story appeared in print, and the noted author again took umbrage, calling Emanuel "a lot of bad names." London then again invited him to his ranch, but Emanuel had to decline because it was "such a long trip . . . up near San Francisco." Besides, he had had enough exposure to the famous author's ego.

At this point in their exchanges, Emanuel regretted not telling his readers of London's racism in his reference to Jews as "sewer rats, the novelist hated Negroes, and despised the Japanese." London was "a Nordic blonde, a superman, a member of the elite," who believed "inferior races" should be "exterminated." He left all this out of his story because he thought, by doing so, he was serving socialism by "suppressing an unpleasant fact" about one of its luminaries. He later concluded he would have given better service to socialism if he "had told the whole story." London, he concluded, "was a worshipper of brute strength and violence." To him, Darwinism "meant the rule of the powerful, who, with clubs and cannon were to let loose an orgy of blood and wipe out the world's inferior people." In the 1930s, when Emanuel read of what Hitler, Goebbels, and "the rest of the Nazi gangsters" were doing in Europe, he concluded that London "was America's first and most talented Nazi."[28]

Emanuel analyzed London's fellow sociologist Upton Sinclair, noting he had "hurt himself" by his "gullibility," or what he called "spookology."

Sinclair objected to this use of the term "spookology" and insisted that his research and theories were based on science. Although Emanuel considered them "low and reprehensible," he liked Sinclair, admired him "in many ways," and hoped to see him abandon mysticism and "turn to sane, realistic thinking."[29]

When Emanuel arrived on the West Coast with Wright, Los Angeles was still hearing reverberations from the McNamara case. General Harrison Gray Otis, owner and publisher of the *Los Angeles Times*, was a labor-baiting reactionary who used his newspaper to further anti-union causes. Debs described him as "the most venomous foe of organized labor in the United States." When his *Times* building was dynamited in 1910, some labor leaders suspected Otis himself of the deed, but most observers concluded that it was the work of radicals. The McNamara brothers, John and James, along with Ortie McManigal, were arrested and charged with the crime. Public opinion immediately concluded that these radicals were guilty, and subsequent court procedures were followed closely.[30]

The prosecution brought in William J. Burns and his detective agency to gather information about the defendants' activities in Los Angeles, and Clarence Darrow of Chicago was recruited to defend the brothers. Darrow was accused of trying to bribe a juror and soon was on trial himself. Emanuel noted that although the State of California failed to convict Darrow, the famous lawyer "had to go through many months of effort, worry, and expense." Emanuel considered Darrow "the wittiest, most humorous man I have ever known." Darrow was a popular speaker while he was in Los Angeles, telling listeners "what he thought was the matter with the damned human race." These speeches were Darrow's "indirect way of meeting the torrents of abuse from the *Times*, which thirsted for his blood."[31]

Emanuel described Darrow's legal approach as "fight, fight, fight—a constant, endless, tireless pounding away at the facts." The lawyer was an extrovert who loved people and crowds. Though not a socialist, he "felt sympathy for all leftists, including the Anarchists." Darrow, Emanuel knew, rejected both socialism and communism and was "an FDR type of New Dealer." He was a freethinker and presented his thoughts with "wisecracks, gags, epigrams, jokes, irony, and satire."[32]

Darrow, in many respects, was similar to the editor and novelist E. W. Howe. Both were freethinkers and atheists; Howe was a reactionary individualist, while Darrow leaned to liberalism. Once the two were asked to address a large gathering. The governor, in introducing Darrow, referred to the audience of ten thousand as "intelligent people." When Darrow began to speak, he adjusted his glasses, looked over the crowd, and said to the governor, "Hell, man, there ain't that many intelligent people in the whole world."[33]

An essay Emanuel wrote for the *Western Comrade* presaged an issue he would return to in his Little Blue Books. Titled "The Conquest of Prudery," it presented a "naturalistic view of sex" along with a diatribe against Victorian prudery. He had always tried, Emanuel asserted, "to speak with equal frankness to both sides concerning sexual matters." He admitted this had caused him problems in the past, but "prudery and sex ignorance were being attacked from many sides" and he "predicted that sexual prudery would follow cannibalism, witchcraft, and slavery" into oblivion. He certainly was accurate in this prediction, at least for the coming decade, the Roaring Twenties.[34]

Editing the *Social Democrat* and the *Western Comrade* also brought Emanuel into contact with Job Harriman, the man who ran for vice-president with Eugene Debs. Harriman also conducted a good race for mayor of Los Angeles, but when the McNamaras confessed to the *Times* bombing he was "left out on a limb," as one of the defense attorneys expressed it just days before the city election. Harriman suffered from advanced tuberculosis and drove himself "to overexertion and to an early death." Debs once referred to him as "the Uriah Heep of the Socialist movement." About the time he met Harriman, Emanuel received word from Wright inviting him to join him at the *New York Call*, an offer that he accepted with alacrity because it meant a return to his beloved Big Apple.[35]

Emanuel needed to make arrangements to leave the West Coast, and he resigned as editor of the *Social Democrat*. Harriman was working on a colonizing scheme "many miles north of Los Angeles [and] needed an organ to promote" it, and he sought to acquire Emanuel's magazine. He offered Emanuel $1,000 in stock in the *Western Comrade* for the journal, which Emanuel accepted and then sold for gold pieces. Meanwhile, he had saved $1,500, and with the gold to help pay his way to New York City, he "felt prosperous."[36]

Emanuel believed his time in California had been productive. He now felt confident in himself "as a writer and manager" and believed he could perform well on "any newspaper or magazine that struck my fancy." More importantly, he loved his work and always felt like he "was being paid for playing." Though he was glad to leave California, he believed his experience there had "rounded him out" and prepared him "for any situation in the field"—a cocky attitude, perhaps, but Emanuel was never lacking in self-confidence.[37]

Emanuel considered his time in Los Angeles to have been well spent. There had been numerous women—Eugenie, Myrtle, Maud, Clara, Ruth, Constance, Becky, "and some others I can't recall." He enjoyed his profession so much that he would be "willing to pay for the privilege of doing the work." He recalled that Milwaukee was "an attractive town and full of changing, friendly, delightful people," while Chicago was "only big and ugly." He was glad to leave Los Angeles:

> It was garden of roses without aroma, winters without snow, manners without culture, beautiful places, buildings, homes and scenes that made me think of the sets erected in the movie studios, a population eager to be duped by mountebanks, evangelicals, and con-men; a heaven for circuses; a headquarters for fanaticism, snooping into people's private lives and beliefs.[38]

He entrained for the East Coast on his twenty-fifth birthday, 30 July 1914, eager to return to "the great, beautiful, majestic, magnificent, exciting, thrilling, exotic, dramatic, charming" New York City. When he arrived at Needles, California, it was "perhaps 120 degrees, hot as the hinges of hell," but for some reason he kept his jacket on. The popular topic of conversation on the train was the war in Europe between the Central Powers (Germany, Austria-Hungary, and Italy) and the Allies

(Great Britain, France, and Russia), along with "the avowed hostility to war by Socialist leaders in important positions." The war "did not seem real to us in America," he wrote, but Europe was engaged in a conflict that the pacifist socialists had been unable to prevent. Most Americans seemed to view the war as "a vast sporting event" while they were "cozy and out of harm's reach."[39]

His traveling companions were more interested in what to eat at the next stop. Three times a day the train paused at a Harvey House where they "enjoyed the best of food" for 75 cents, served by "pretty waitresses in attractive uniforms." The waitresses were so well organized and efficient that, with advanced notice of a train's arrival, they could feed seventy passengers in twenty minutes. The trip consumed eight days, and Emanuel "realized anew the vastness of our country," pleased with the idea that if his parents had not migrated to "the land of the free" he might "at that moment be carrying a gun and looking for someone to shoot." Instead, he could looked forward to a "lifetime spent in writing." He was on his way to become Sunday editor, literary critic, and reviewer of music and plays. New York City was "calling" for him to return, and he was "glad."[40]

His pay at the *Call* was a meager $25 a week. He rented a large room on the east side of Washington Square at Benedicts for $4 a week, including maid service. He "always stood well" with the apartment employees, because he "always had a pocketful of theater tickets." He received more services than "the other residents did with their cash tips." A married Columbia University professor lived next door with "a Negro woman." Down the hall lived a homosexual surgeon who would entertain his "favorite boys most of whom were musicians and actors." On the floor below there was "a beautiful and charming girl" named Anna Marcet Haldeman, who was a "successful" Broadway actress. He never spoke to her during the months they lived there, because he "had plenty of time to comb the town for interesting and stimulating company."[41]

Having worked for Wright for several years on various newspapers, Emanuel knew his boss quite well. "He knew every phase of editing, and I had sense enough to appreciate his usefulness, though I never had respect for his nature or intelligence," Emanuel mused. He "disliked the man's pettiness, his quickness to take offense, his butler-like kowtowing to men of importance or power, his subservience to respectable authority, his contempt for intellectual and artistic ideas, his silly pride, his fits of smothered rage, and his brown-nosing of those who might do him a [good] turn." On the other hand, Wright "could show up with nothing on his desk worth putting into type. Five hours later he'd produce a paper." Despite his experience with the *Western Comrade*, Emanuel still had much to learn about editing.[42]

When Emanuel arrived in New York City in early August 1914, Europeans were already ferociously killing each other. Most people on the street and the English-language newspapers opposed Germany, but "there were many who supported the Hun." The editor and the editorial writer for the *Call* were worried over the behavior of the leftists in Europe who ignored the socialist opposition to war and "came to the support of their rulers," especially in Austro-Hungary, France, and Germany. "Nothing to do but wait," Emanuel noted, so he settled into his job of editing the Sunday Magazine on music, art, and an occasional news assignment.[43]

Joshua Wanhope occupied the desk next to Emanuel's. He was from the British Isles, in his late forties, handsome with a luxurious mustache, a strong body, and a beautiful burr. He had been a sailor before becoming a socialist writer and speaker. Like so many self-educated intellectuals, he possessed "candor, directness, honesty, freedom from prejudice and bigotry." Wanhope insisted that "the war was of no concern to Americans" and believed that both the Allies and Central Powers should be opposed for "indulging in imperialistic warfare."[44]

Alexander Woollcott was a writer who failed to gain Emanuel's respect. He liked money but refused "to sell himself to anyone with jammed moneybags." When he received a tempting offer from Hollywood, he responded that "when I take up street-walking, the street will be Broadway, not Hollywood Boulevard." He once interviewed Emanuel and profiled him for the *New Yorker*, and "it was an awful piece," Emanuel argued, for which he was paid $75. Emanuel did not realize that Woollcott was "supposed to be a boor with a passion for insulting people." He never called Emanuel "a single bad name" and perhaps was showing him "the courtesy due one who was the subject of his professional interest for a few hours."[45]

Diamond Jim Brady, Emanuel discovered, was not "an artist," but a hog. He would begin a meal with five dozen raw oysters, go through "several dishes of chicken, beef, venison, fish, frogs, lobsters, numerous desserts, and end up with champagne." When he died, a doctor told the press that Brady's stomach was "about eight times the size of an ordinary man's digestive organ."[46]

A waiter informed Emanuel about his contacts with Robert G. Ingersoll, who was popular even among members of the Union League Club. The famous freethinker loved "the best liquor and enjoyed the finest cigars," was a lover of life and "a great mixer." A priest approached Ingersoll's table one evening and asked, "How can you dare disagree with Sir Isaac Newton? He believed in God." Ingersoll responded, "How can you dare to disagree with Newton? He was a Protestant."[47]

Charlie Seal was a self-taught machinist who lectured in the evenings. His "Merrie England" was an outstanding piece of socialist propaganda, and "God and My Neighbor" was an exposition of freethinking— both "minor classics," Emanuel said. Another proletarian intellectual fellow worker labored in a textile mill approximately fifty-four hours weekly for about $13. He told Ed Moore, a "vinegary" millworker whom he disagreed with on socialism, that "I know I am here on my own volition." "Well," responded Moore, "by God, I know I'm not here on my own volition." There were numerous "proletarian intellectuals," self-taught, who could declaim with the best of them on obscure Marxian philosophy.[48]

Living in Greenwich Village with the Brevoort restaurant nearby meant seeing many celebrities. In 1914, Emanuel claimed, one could not "throw a hard roll 10 feet" without hitting one. Good meals cost $2, and a tip of 15 or 50 cents insulted no one. At breakfast one day he saw Theodore Dreiser, Upton Sinclair, Max Eastman, Floyd Dell, Clara Tice, Eugene O'Neill, Frank Harris, James Hunecher, Clement Wood, James Oppenheim, Guido Bruno, and Alfred Kreymborg. A short time later he encountered Edgar Salters, George Jean Nathan,

Don Harold, L. Lewelyn and John Cowper Powys, Charles Edward Russell, Robert Carlton Brown, William Marion Reedy, Thomas Seltzer, Hendrik William Van Loon, Eugene Wood, Horatio Winslow, Andre Tridon, Maurice Becker, Art Young, Anton Otto Fisher, Horace Traubel, Stuart Davis, Robert Henri, George Bellows, Jo Davidson, and Glenn Coleman. On his way back to his quarters, Emanuel passed Bob Minor, Max Endicoff, Berkeley Tobey, Harry Kem, Courtenay Lemon, Herman Sampson, B. Russell Hertz, Witter Bynner, "and a few members of the Strunsky tribe." At this time "the blight of bally-hoo and crass commercialism" was still in the future, as well as "high rents, expensive studios, night clubs, and phony cafe bohemianism." It was still "a cheap, handy convenient neighborhood for poor artists and struggling writers and poets."[49]

One day Harold Stearns appeared at his door, seeking breakfast. The young man explained that if people filled him with intoxicating drink they should assume "a moral obligation" to provide him with bed and breakfast. His clothing looked slept-in, and when Emanuel recommended he turn his collar inside out, he responded that "I've already done that." When he complained of Emanuel's neat, prosperous-looking condition, he was told to look for one of the many plentiful jobs then available. Harold explained that he could write, and liked to, but he insisted on writing "when, how, and what I please." "We gifted ones," he insisted, "can't meet deadlines" and we "refuse to be hacks," so he would have to continue "to live as I'm doing now." When Prohibition arrived, Harold and his friends headed for Paris.[50]

In October 1915, Louis Kopelin offered Emanuel a 40 percent raise to become his editorial assistant for the *Appeal to Reason*, a newspaper that enjoyed a circulation of over 750,000, which made it the leading socialist newspaper in the world. Leaving New York City and moving to tiny Girard, Kansas, would be an enormous change, but Emanuel decided to take the risk, viewing this as an important opportunity to advance in his career.

The *Call* had kept him busy, but it had also provided him with column after column with which to write and experiment. "He wrote regularly and often and . . . some of what he wrote was good; some quite bad; most of it obviously rushed, hurriedly conceived, written rapidly under the threat of impending deadlines." Now he was headed toward a completely new life in rustic Girard. Little did he know that the town would bring major changes in his life and provide the setting for his transformative career in book publishing.

3

GIRARD, KANSAS, 1915–1918

After living in the Big Apple, what a shock for Emanuel to arrive in tiny, bucolic Girard in late 1915. Fortunately, it was at night and good comrades were there to meet him at the Frisco railroad depot. This seat of Crawford County had a population of roughly two thousand and was just a few miles from the heart of the tri-state mining region of Kansas, Missouri, and Oklahoma. Girard is about a hundred miles south of Kansas City. Its residents were moderately well-to-do citizens who were practicing Presbyterians and Republicans, but Crawford County also contained large numbers of recent immigrants from southern and eastern Europe who came to work the nearby coalfields. These people made the area a stronghold of socialism. Girard was also home to the world's largest socialist newspaper.

Julius Augustus Wayland had begun publishing his socialist newspaper *Appeal to Reason* in Kansas City in 1895. The paper had difficulty making financial ends meet, and Wayland decided to find a less expensive home for it. A Kansas native and well acquainted with small towns, he searched the state and discovered Girard, which he described as "the prettiest little town I found in three months hunting for a place to make my home." He chose it for his new residence in 1904 because of the various European ethnic groups in the nearby coalfields and the anticipation that he could reduce his overhead in a small town, and thus rescue the *Appeal* from extinction.[1]

A capitalist at heart, Wayland thoroughly enjoyed making money from his two main pursuits—publishing his newspaper and dabbling in real estate. When questioned about this apparent conflict with the ideals of socialism, he and his supporters pointed out that Frederick Engels was a British capitalist and Morris Hillquit a well-known New York corporate lawyer. Later, Emanuel ignored the issue, claiming that Wayland was first and foremost a businessman.

Wayland quickly discovered how unpopular socialists were in this arch-Republican community with an occasional brick thrown through a window of his printing plant. But he was an optimist and always carried his socialist literature with him as he toured the countryside during weekends, passing out his message and explaining the true principles of his political beliefs. Although remaining hostile to the term *socialist*, the citizens of Crawford County could not help but like the odd fellow and listened to his explanations without agreeing with anything he said. Besides, he provided employment for many locals in his printing shop.

Wayland made the *Appeal to Reason* the most successful socialist newspaper in the country through his Appeal Army. This was simply his Honor Roll, as he called it, or hustlers of new readers. These promoters would enjoy a large discount if they could collect a group of subscribers receiving copies at the identical address. Some activists were able to make a living through the differential of the 50-cents-per-issue subscription rate and Wayland's group rate. Later, his new editor, Fred Warren, put Grace Brewer in charge of a weekly column titled "The Appeal Army," in which she would reward them with a few lines of type if they did anything significant, such as adding new readers. Wayland also sold advertisements—again, contrary to socialist principles—and by using these techniques he was able to build its circulation through sending coupons to teachers, union members, legislators of all types, and newspaper editors throughout the nation. Socialist speakers often went on tour with the price of admission being an annual subscription to the *Appeal to Reason*.[2]

Many *Appeal* stories dealt with "poverty, crime, child labor, prostitution, suicide, unhealthy working conditions, alcohol," all the world's problems that were the result of capitalism, socialists argued. These were topics Emanuel had been writing about for years for other socialist newspapers, which was the main reason Kopelin had recruited him.

Eugene V. Debs and other leading socialist writers covered the nation's major labor issues for the *Appeal*.[3]

On 30 December 1905, former Idaho governor Frank Steunenberg was killed outside his home by a bomb. Pinkerton detective James McParland obtained a confession of the crime from Harry Orchard, member of the radical Western Federation of Miners, claiming that "Big Bill" Haywood (president of the Western Federation of Miners), Charles Moyer, and George Pettibone, all of Denver, hired him to do the job. A secret complaint was filed in Canyon County, Idaho, against them. The governor of Colorado signed extradition papers on a Saturday night when they could not get a stay of execution. The trio were put on a special train as the only passengers to Idaho and were indicted for murder on 6 March 1906. Organized labor was incensed over this kidnapping, and Eugene Debs wrote his famous editorial "Arouse, Ye Slaves!" for the *Appeal to Reason*. Distraught over the death of his parents at the same time, Debs traveled to Girard, and the *Appeal* hired him to write for the newspaper at $100 weekly.[4]

By 1910, Fred Warren was running the *Appeal*, leaving Wayland time to pursue his other obsession, real estate. But Wayland soon became involved in the "Fred Warren issue." Warren was outraged over the kidnapping of the labor leaders, and after the U.S. Supreme Court judged the kidnapping to be legal he offered an award for the kidnapping of former governor William Taylor of Kentucky, who had murdered his successor, then fled to Pennsylvania, and thence to Indiana, where governors of these states refused to extradite Taylor.[5]

Neither President Theodore Roosevelt nor Harrison Gray Otis of the *Los Angeles Times* was amused by Warren's ploy. Otis labeled the *Appeal to Reason* an "anarchist" newspaper and dispatched reporters to join the federal agents haunting Girard, searching for negative stories. Tales were fabricated that Wayland, who had lost his wife in an automobile accident the previous year, had seduced a fourteen-year-old orphan girl, Minnie Austin, and took her to Missouri, where she died during an abortion. The Roosevelt government charged him with violating the Mann Act, and the mass-media attacks proved to be too much for the melancholy Wayland, who committed suicide. Warren was forced from the editorship of the *Appeal* soon after, and Wayland's sons, Walter and Jon, who had inherited the newspaper, hired Louis Kopelin as managing editor.[6]

Four years later, in 1914, Europe was plunged into World War I, a conflict socialists opposed because of the party's stand against the use of violence. Socialists opposed the war because workers were allied across national boundaries and they believed workers were being exploited by the warring capitalists. Unofficial American support for the Allies meant a decline in the popularity of the *Appeal to Reason*, and it was soon skidding into insolvency. It was at this time that Kopelin decided the newspaper needed fresh blood on its staff and offered Emanuel a job.

Meanwhile, events were transpiring outside Emanuel's little world that were affecting the course of history of the United States. The Triangle Shirtwaist Factory fire occurred in 1911 and greatly altered the course of industry and the quest of reformers to achieve industrial improvements. Emanuel covered this story for his newspaper. The Triangle company employed hundreds of young girls at low wages, for long hours and under dreadful working conditions. After the fire it was discovered that the doors were locked to prevent the girls from leaving early. The desperate girls were unable to escape, and 146 perished. This tragedy prompted Senator Robert Wagner of New York to investigate and to commence a lengthy program of reform in factories, child labor, and conditions of labor in general, culminating in the Wagner Act of 1935.[7]

The turn of the century also saw the rise of American "captains of industry." Henry Clay Frick of U.S. Steel, John D. Rockefeller of Standard Oil, Andrew Carnegie of Carnegie Steel, and the Big Four of the Central Pacific Railroad were being investigated by journalists called "muckrakers" and having their practices exposed to the public. Periodicals such as *McClure's* and *Cosmopolitan* lent their pages to these reformers, and the "savants of capitalism" rapidly became the abomination of society. The public eagerly absorbed the stories, as Americans were longing "to understand the mental and sociopolitical mechanisms at work behind the facades of power." Jack London and other writers used their novels to expose the activities of these "Nietzschean supermen" as antipathetic to the needs of society. To London, such activities meant that "feudalism still held the modern world in a hammerlock."[8]

Meanwhile, Prohibition was making steady progress as state after state prohibited the production or sale of alcoholic beverages. In a short time these reformers used the patriotic issue of conserving grain for the prosecution of the war effort and achieved a national reform that during the following decade proved to be a miserable failure, except for the abolition of the decadent corner saloon.[9]

Finally, President Theodore Roosevelt became the champion of American farmers when he established a Country Life Commission in 1908 to study means to improve rural life. He recruited Liberty Hyde Bailey, director of the College of Agriculture at Cornell University, to direct the investigation. Bailey examined farm towns and their services. Although the commission contained some notable personnel, such as Henry Wallace, of *Wallace's Farmer* fame, and Kenyon L. Butterfield of the Massachusetts Agricultural College, "it never really got off the ground." American society was deeply interested in the development of the automobile and city life and industry, and the country "hicks" had to wait for their "day in court."[10]

When Emanuel stepped off the train in Girard he was met by Kopelin and John Gunn, a valued assistant in making the *Appeal to Reason* project function. Gunn, twenty-two, and Emanuel, twenty-six, would became close friends. Gunn later described the latter as "a short, slender fellow, with wirily-knit bones and sparkling eyes, who was bubbling over with vitality, curiosity, and conversation at that late hour and after a long trip." After stopping to look at the *Appeal* plant, the trio talked for an hour or two in Kopelin's apartment. Then John escorted Emanuel to a corner of the courthouse square where they had rented an apartment for him. Often, in the months and years that followed, Emanuel and John would spend their evenings walking the streets of Girard, "talking about books, ideas, life, ourselves." Emanuel was "eager for all that life had to offer and what it did not obviously offer, he would seek out with a mind that was bold and restless and insatiable."[11]

Emanuel also began to develop a sense of what living in a small town would be like. He had passed through small villages on his transcontinental train trips but had never experienced them in action: their generosity in time of need or crisis; their clannishness in time of danger; their fear of the unknown; their pettiness; their ignorance and pride in such; their courage; their unshakable prejudices; their obstinate opposition to change; their unquestioned acceptance of brother's keeper; their unreasoning hatred of socialism when surrounded by its positive features of their public schools, their highways, their post office, their city water system, their national, state, and local parks, their radios. Emanuel would feel the full brunt of their animosity toward big-city ways, Jews, liberals, left-wing writers, outsiders. Later, living on his farm, he argued that he was just like them, but he was not. His current secretary, a native of Girard, noted the difference, not in the farms, but in the occupants. He was "odd" because he was smarter than the average farmer, a screwball, a national celebrity. So the natives were friendly to him because of his printing business, but aloof in camaraderie, based on their fear of his "differences."[12]

A few weeks after Emanuel arrived, Mrs. Warren Wayland introduced him to the town's prize female banker and heiress to a modest fortune, Marcet Haldeman. Emanuel and Marcet had been aware of each other's existence when they lived at the same rooming house in New York City, but they had never been formally introduced. A few days later Marcet, wrote her aunt Jane Addams that she was "enjoying a thrilling ["thrilling" was crossed out and "interesting" added] and absorbing friendship with Emanuel Julius, a brilliant Russian Jew (just my age) [he was twenty-six, she was twenty-eight]. . . . I thank heaven he is here, for we have the most marvelous times."[13]

The Haldemans were an important family in their native Cedarville, Illinois. John Haldeman married Anna Hostetter, and they had two sons, Henry and George. Sarah Weber married John Huy Addams, a miller, and they had two daughters, Sarah Alice Addams and Jane Addams (later of Hull House fame in Chicago). Henry Haldeman married Sarah Alice Addams, and they had one child, Anna Marcet Haldeman, who was born in 1887. Henry was trained in medicine at Leipzig, but after he married Sarah Alice the couple pioneered in Girard, where they quickly assumed leadership roles in the small community, principally because they owned the bank. When Henry died, in 1905, Sarah Alice operated the bank until her death, in 1915. Marcet felt compelled to return to Girard to take over operation of the bank, because of her love for her mother and her devotion to the family heritage.

The rumor arose, and persists today, that Sarah Alice's will stipulated that Marcet must return to live in Girard for one year to receive the inheritance. This requirement is not in the will, so the question becomes, where did the idea originate? It is not unreasonable to think that Marcet initiated it to save face with the hometown folk by offering a reasonable explanation for why she would abandon her beloved East to return to dreary Girard. It was for a significant monetary bequest.[14]

Marcet was a very bright young woman, and she headed east to boarding school when she was fifteen. She attended Bryn Mawr, as did her aunt Jane, and completed her studies at the American Academy of Dramatic Arts in New York City in 1910. From 1910 to 1913, working under the name Jean Marcet, she toured in Cecil B. DeMille's stock company, which appeared in New York City, Philadelphia, Baltimore, Montreal, Newark, Cincinnati, St. Louis, and smaller cities.[15] She adapted well to her new eastern culture in the big cities, learning to smoke cigarettes and picking up other such habits as a "cultured flapper" of the Roaring Twenties would acquire. Then the death of her mother produced a major personal crisis, and she concluded she must return to tiny Girard and assume her familial responsibilities. This transition back to home was not easy for her, especially when she decided to sell her parents' house and live in an apartment. She shipped the furniture to Cedarville, where she placed what items she wanted to use in the old Victorian house and stored the remainder in the barn. This action suggested that she might not plan to spend the rest of her life in Girard, and this is how the residents of Girard interpreted her action.

While in college, Marcet had written to her mother expressing her amazement that she had lived in Girard for "so long" and yet retained "so much charm and bigness and breadth of mind." She was "glad" she had spent her childhood there and appreciated "all that I have learned there," because that background made her ready for "just so much more all that has come since." Marcet said that she could never live in Girard again and expressed the hope that "it will not be long" until her mother came east "and we will live here." She was then living on West Fifty-Second Street, in the Big Apple. Then Marcet found employment in a traveling show, and that was the end of those plans.[16]

In addition to pursuing an acting career, Marcet also was trying to develop her writing skills. She possessed a good deal of talent along these lines and had a book manuscript ready to seek a publisher. Knowledgeable friends suggested Doran and Company. She had a friend who knew Sinclair Lewis "quite well," and at that time he was connected with the company as a manuscript reader, so they invited the famous author for lunch. Marcet made a point of not mentioning to Lewis her manuscript, titled "Marcet's Fairyland," but sought only to be a good hostess. She and her friend concluded that he had "a splendid time . . . a royal good time!" and they felt like "scheming wretches and awful hypocrites." Marcet built up her courage and sent him the manuscript the next week, with a cover letter of "eight or nine lines" that she had taken an hour to compose.[17]

She received a quick response. Lewis replied that he had found the manuscript not "available for our use." It was "charmingly written," but "in general structure and idea" it was "too much like a tremendous number of children's books" he had evaluated "in the last few years." The meeting of "children with the fairy folk is a very common idea," he kindly observed. He expressed the hope that she would develop her talent "to move out of the ordinary line." He asked to see "anything else by you. . . . [T]his is not mere politeness, I mean it quite definitely." He also was "glad to see Mrs. [Grace] Michelson's illustrations" for the book.[18]

Sarah Alice Haldeman died on 19 March 1915 in a hospital in Chicago where she was receiving radium treatments for cancer, and Marcet and Aunt Jane were at her bedside. Alice had been devoted to philanthropy and "uplift work." Like her sister, Alice was interested in "promoting the welfare of humanity in general." She spent years working with orphans and other needy children in securing educational training. Nothing gave her "more pleasure than to be surrounded in her home with young people . . . to use her unusually large and carefully selected library." The local newspaper's tribute noted that she had "a wonderful mind" and was capable of reading "a work and then repeating it nearly word for word." Her work as a writer "showed literary genius." Alice had traveled extensively and had "many friends and acquaintances in European countries and carried on a large correspondence." She was a key figure in organizing and launching the state's circulating library system.[19]

When Marcet returned to Girard in 1915 she found she had grown away from her friends intellectually during her time in the East, as often happens when one leaves a small hometown. She "shocked" the ladies of Girard with her language, smoking, and radical ideas. For instance, she suggested they take the money they gave to foreign missions of their churches and that given for the home missions and use it to "fix up the disreputable dance hall" the boys and girls of the county used, "and the women could take turns chaperoning there." Her older acquaintance responded to this suggestion that when the young people had money, "they spend it for drink." "Of course they do," Marcet replied, "they have no other pleasures available but that and sex." The lady blushed and said, "It would break your mother's heart to hear you talk like that." Marcet answered, "To hear me speak the truth? It breaks my heart that one truth is so sordid, and it breaks my heart that we sit by and do nothing." She added, "This older generation is too set in its ways." When they refused to take her suggestions seriously, she organized the "Jolly Club" of boys and girls of the nearby poor mining towns and rented and renovated a hall for holding dances and recreation. She also purchased seven acres of land for $600 and built "a baseball diamond, tennis courts, and recreation grounds for the younger children." She planned on hiring the older boys to do the maintenance work on the baseball diamond and the track, because "children always like a thing better if they make it themselves, and besides it keeps them out of mischief if they have to work in the earth."[20]

Marcet described to "Auntie" Jane the first dance she sponsored. After a "hard day at the bank" she "pulled herself together" and went to the hall, finding some two hundred people gathered for the "lunch" and dance that evening. Some five families with babies in their buggies also came to watch the festivities. Things were going "merry as a wedding bell" when some of the men "began to show the effects of their frequent visits to the Blind Tiger next door." One of the girls, "in a throaty, excited voice," informed her that Tony Rider was "killing a man outside." Marcet knew Tony "from way back" and realized that although there was not "a finer miner in the County" when sober, he had already "been up" for assault when drunk. She went outside to see what was happening and found the miners standing by and doing nothing to stop the brawl. She spoke sharply to them and they then broke up the fight. "At that inopportune moment the music stopped," and as word of the fight spread inside, the crowd insisted on seeing what was happening. Marcet stood in the doorway, telling them it was a fight and they could not come outside until after the next dance. "We want to see," they insisted, and she responded, "You can't," and stood her ground, blocking the doorway. "The crowd sullenly turned back." Then it was time to close for the night, and Tony appeared, refusing to leave. "Come, Mr. Rider," she said calmly, "I want to close up." He refused to budge until she reminded him they were old friends, and then "he got up and shambled out." The last thing she saw when she left was Tony "clinched against his enemy." But most people said "it was the nicest dance they ever had" and were eager for another one next payday.[21]

Marcet went to the county jail every Sunday afternoon to give a talk to the inmates. The jail was built "years ago" and had "no heat but an old stove." There were currently thirty prisoners in a jail that was built to accommodate eight. The Saturday after they received their sentences she read them "The Man without a Country," and she reported "you could hear a pin drop." She sat against the bars so that those in "the inner sanctum" of murderers and those who committed mayhem could hear. The men up close "leaned their foreheads against the bars and pushed their fingers through other bars and closed them." Whenever she looked up to make a point, she saw only "intense eyes" and fingers. She continued with *Tom Sawyer* and appreciated the "chuckles and laughs" from the prisoners "as much as any that ever came to me across the footlights."[22]

She was elected a delegate to the Republican county convention in the spring of 1915 and had to deliver a speech. It pleased her to stand before the Girard people in the crowd, "lots of whom have been ripping

me up and down behind my back, and I told them a few plain truths."
The Christian minister had "preached about me and against me. His
remarks were the *one* topic of conversation here for over a week." He
thundered that she was "tearing down the Church of Christ" with her
negative influence. Her friends were "furious," and her boys at the camp
promised to "lay for him and learn him a lesson" if she gave the word,
"but I didn't care much." When the county caucus ended, she drove to
the camp and "danced until twelve."[23]

Later that year, Marcet chose the coal-mining town of Ridley, near
Pittsburg, to learn firsthand how the local people lived. Everyone warned
her that she did not realize "what she was getting into and that it wasn't
'safe.'" But she soon found out that although the natives were "a rough
lot they are a warm-hearted, eager-minded folk and that—chiefly through
ignorance, I think,—the people in Girard and Pittsburg grossly misrepresented them."[24]

She "greatly feared" tunnels and underground places so much that
it amounted to a phobia, but she felt compelled to see where the people
worked. She "*had*" to understand them because "they come to me with
all their problems," so she went down into a mine with them. She found
the situation one of "the blind leading the blind."

She learned much working with her "girls" in sewing curtains and
other renovations for the hall she had planned for community activities.
Mary, a twenty-two-year-old who had been married and divorced from
"a perfect brute," told her about Jo's background. Marcet remembered
the "vivid, wistful Italian" quite well and was told he had killed a girl. He
was currently on "payroll," she was told, "from Leavenworth prison."
He had received a ninety-nine-year sentence for the murder and served
four years before his friends won a parole for him. Marcet recalled that
Jo was "one of the best club members I have and whenever I dance with
him and realize how full of vibrant, joyous youth and strength he is," she
reflected that many states would have given him the death penalty. "Her
very soul cried out against capital punishment" as a result. In addition,
the director of the state girls reform school told Marcet that one-third of
her inmates "come from our district and of that percent the big majority

come from our county." Marcet faced a monumental task of bringing healthy entertainment to these young people, especially against the strong opposition of the "establishment" of Girard.[25]

Many years later, Marcet's daughter Alice wrote this description of her mother:

> It is not difficult to describe my mother's physical appearance, for she was a petite brunette, barely five feet tall. Her eyes were her most notable feature, as they were dark, velvety brown, intensely expressive and beautiful. She had an excellent profile—perfect nose, even white teeth and, above unplucked wide eyebrows, a truly noble brow. Her feet were small and dainty, her hands blessed with evenly and aesthetically pleasing tapered fingers which graced her conversations and lent an air of composure to all her photographs. Given these details of appearance, one can say that her essential aura was one of fineness. . . . Little Bo-Peep (for this is what everyone affectionately called her, from the mayor of the town to the filling station attendant) . . . was much loved by the citizens of Girard.[26]

In all her roles Marcet eagerly sought the advice of her "Dearest Auntie" Jane Addams. Marcet was willing, even eager at times, to lay bare her soul and confess her innermost thoughts and desires to her aunt. Marcet and her mother almost always included a visit to Chicago and Hull House during their summer travels. At Alice's insistence, Marcet learned to spin and weave at Hull House's labor museum, and became acquainted with her first African American, a cultured fellow who associated with whites on a basis of equality, an unusual occurrence at that time. She met Julia Lathrop (later head of the Children's Bureau of the Department of Labor), Florence Kelly, and other well-known social workers. W. E. B. Du Bois and Dr. Alice Hamilton, the first woman to hold a chair at Harvard University's School of Medicine, also appeared, as did a famous Russian woman who had assassinated a Russian general and escaped from a Siberian prison to migrate to America.

With the death of her parents, Marcet also took over management of the Haldeman family's financial assets in Cedarville. Mary Fry lived there

and took care of Marcet's paternal grandmother, Anna Haldeman Addams, who had had "a mellowing influence on Jane Addams." It was Aunt
Jane who encouraged Marcet in her theatrical career, which she pursued
despite the opposition of her mother. It was Jane and Marcet who were
at Sarah Alice's bedside when she died.[27]

In April 1915, shortly after her mother died, Marcet decided to draft
a will and name Jane as her beneficiary. She wrote her aunt that she was
"trying to do everything pretty much in the same order that mother did
after father's death." Her mother had filed a will, so Marcet would do
likewise. If she married, Marcet wrote, she would have to change the
document, but at that moment it seemed to be "the best thing for everybody . . . to leave [her possessions] to you." She was sending Jane a copy
of the will "in case the original is lost as father's was thanks to slip shod
management at the courthouse."[28]

In the fall of 1915 Marcet reported to her aunt that her bank was
"doing splendidly better than ever before in its history." Another bank
was opening that week, and to meet this competition, Marcet was working
with an architect to change her bank's front to stone and "make some
changes inside." "I want the place where I work and spend my life," she
said, "to be beautiful—with a simple dignified beauty." She added that
she belonged to the Girard Commercial Club and was getting used to
being "the only woman among 125 men." She also noted that "it has been
good fun to watch" the Girard female friends evolve from a small-town
view of her "to a more simple natural one."[29]

Marcet and Emanuel had both come from the East to bucolic Girard
at about the same time. It was a cultural shock to both, although more
so to Emanuel, as Marcet was familiar to small-town mores. Living in
the same small town and finding someone of the opposite sex with similar problems and interests seemed marvelous. They had many common
interests—in life, in thoughts, in amusements, in books—that no one
else in town had, thus drawing them together. They began dating, and
had become more serious between October and December 1915. By January 1916 they were discussing their love for each other, and by March
they were thinking of marriage—a real whirlwind courtship. First, they

needed to resolve problems—the extensive property she had inherited, her grandmother in Cedarville, his obligations to his job—clearly this would be a modern marriage.[30]

When contemplating marriage to Emanuel, Marcet naturally sought her aunt's advice. Although the lovers had many surface differences, they had many mutual interests in their thoughts, in their writings, in their zest for writing. She and Julius were separated that Christmas, Marcet joining the family in Cedarville for the holidays and Emanuel traveling to Oklahoma City to cover the state socialist convention. She wrote him that he "didn't know the difference your being in Girard means to me." Their love continued to blossom, and by March 1916 she was asking him to seek Aunt Jane's advice about their future. She wrote him:

> I do love you—so much that is bubbling full of joy whenever I think of it. My soul fills with peace when I realize that the years ahead of me will be spent with you—warmed by your tenderness and made beautiful by your comradeship. My mind cannot fathom the miracle of happiness that has come into my life. But with my mind heart and soul I thank whatever Gods might be—and vow by them—to try always to be worthy of it.

But Aunt Jane was taking a cautious approach to the romance, and Marcet asked Emanuel to write to Jane to reassure the doubting aunt. He agreed and wrote Jane:

> Well, things have become serious—terribly so. I don't entertain the slightest doubt that I love Marcet. . . . Please don't think she has a sudden emotion. . . . I think that Marcet and I should marry. I know I'll be happy with her. I'll try to make her happy. She is willing to take a chance. . . . Let her. We disagree about a number of things, but temperamentally we are compatible and that means everything worthwhile. . . . Marcet has her work and I have mine. We go to different worlds but we return to a new sphere of our own creation that gives each of us a feeling of bliss. . . . Marcet understands me, but she doesn't know me, which isn't

bad. . . . The fact remains that I have developed efficiency to where I am (for more than five years) completely independent.

A short time later, Marcet wrote Jane that "Julius wants me to marry him and, unless you find some sound and strong reason against my doing so, I shall." Three days later she poured out her heart and soul to "Auntie" in a long (thirty-three-page) handwritten letter. She wrote:

> When Julius [a strange reference to her beloved] first told me how much he cared, three weeks ago tomorrow, I answered that I did love him deeply but that I was not *in* love with him. And that is exactly how I felt. . . . He said that this was his first great love and that worried me. I told him why—because he had no way of correlating this experience and so giving it its real relative value whereas I could "place" my love for him almost exactly.
>
> He is one of the best comrades I have ever had. Father, Tom and Euterpe [close college friend] are the only other people with whom I have ever had anything like so comfortable a sense of natural harmony and have enjoyed such splendid adventures of the mind. And although he is quite as self-centered as I am [she was not], he is extraordinarily fair-minded and has my own notions of "self" liberty. I like to be with him. I invariably give him my best self and seem to draw out all that is best in him.
>
> But, of course I know that while this was all very lovely, it was hardly fair to Julius who was having his song of songs. But through it all I felt such a yearning for Tom I thought I should die.[31]

Mary Fry wrote Marcet about the "unhappy affair" with Tom. She did not identify him, except that he was a married man. She believed that the only cure Marcet had for recovering from this affair would be to "give your love to one like Julius—to one who loves you above all others, and to whom you are his very life. His letters are so sincere, so frank, and so satisfying. He must be a poet and artist."[32]

In March 1916, Marcet was very busy working on the address she would deliver the following month as secretary of the Kansas Bankers

Association at the state convention. The governor would speak, and she would follow the next day. At the same time she was getting her campaign for a new county jail under way, and preparing for another public dance, while simultaneously she was trying "to visualize what kind of life Julius and I would have together."

The next Sunday the two had "supper" together and talked "at length." She made Emanuel "understand exactly how I felt." She wrote Aunt Jane that she told him, "I do love you. I have a profound tenderness toward you. I feel a beautiful sense of being at home with you. I trust you and it gives me happiness to be with you. I have been in love and I know the difference. I have a feeling that I may fall in love with you and then I may not. I honestly can't tell." She continued:

> I asked if he had ever been ill from any sex experiences and he said no. I believed him absolutely, for he is temperamentally truthful, but I have lived too long in this world to have my belief in anyone and I explained this to him and said if I should decide to marry him I would have to have a doctor's certificate corroborating his statement. . . . Julius knew that I had had an unhappy love mix up last winter—and I said whether we stay friends or whether we marry, Tom will never come into your life through me—except that I shall always love him. I could no longer stop loving him than I could stop loving Euterpe. But you must promise me never to ask who he is. Aunt Jane if Julius hadn't agreed to that—I would have skipped everything right there. But he did and I felt he did so sincerely.[33]

Marcet attended the Republican convention the next Tuesday and told Jane that she might have a potential career in politics. She heard a speaker who was using a copy of *Appeal to Reason* to denounce socialism. "How the conservative element in this county does *hate* socialists," she noted. "I could scarcely make you realize how bitter and intense the feeling is." If she did not marry Emanuel, she "could become a big woman politically in this state." But here she was, planning to marry "a Socialist!!! and a Jew!!!" She concluded, though, that she did not "care *what* they said." She admitted that her habit of smoking cigarettes would be a political liability, but she refused to "give them up."[34]

She was so "heart-sick and tired" after the convention that she went home and got "drunk, dead drunk." When Emanuel called and talked to her while she was inebriated, she told him she would marry him. She later concluded that she had not been in "that condition for seven years" and admitted to him that she had been "pickled" when she made the promise, but she still meant it. She was now able to confide that "if Tom should become free, I shall still stay with you." Emanuel understood all this, and they agreed they should continue their careers and "be completely independent of each other." Emanuel had "become dear to me beyond words . . . and we need each other."[35]

Marcet described her fiancé at this point as slightly over five and a half feet tall, with a stocky build, though not heavy, clear, gray eyes, black hair that was sometimes parted on one side, or sometimes combed straight back, with long, thick eyelashes, a high broad forehead, a well-shaped, generous mouth, and a square, firm chin. Women, she observed, "are invariably drawn to him and their interest—at first at least—is as invariably reciprocated." He seldom drank, except an occasional glass of wine, or a brandy, but enjoyed his tobacco, especially a pipe and cigars. Marcet called attention to his self-centeredness but noted that his many positive characteristics overshadowed this weakness.[36]

Jane Addams announced the couple's engagement on 6 May 1916, and Marcet's paternal grandmother, Anna H. Haldeman, announced their marriage on 1 June. Marcet and Emanuel signed the marriage license that same day in Cedarville, erroneously listing his mother's maiden name as Zamost.

Before they married, Marcet and Emanuel signed an unusual "limited liability contract." It included the following elements: Marcet would not ask for alimony in case of divorce; both agreed to a "sharp distinction" between sexual loyalty and love; both should be free "to have full social freedom" with the opposite sex; both should have "freedom for passing affairs without cause for recrimination or reproaches on the part of the other"; both agreed "to eliminate adultery in itself as a just cause for

divorce"; "because marriage without love is prostitution," if love should
die, it would be "reason without recrimination or reproach for divorce";
and in such case, there would be no alimony; if there were children, both
would provide for them. This type of relationship would later become
known as a "companionate marriage."[37]

Marriage and ordinary family life had become the norm for Americans
at the end of the frontier. Marriage had been a sacred and divine institution as accepted by both Protestants and Catholics, and divorce had been
limited to childless couples. By World War I, "novels, plays, and works of
social criticism" derided marriage as an outmoded institution, and there
was a corresponding decline in divorce. Judge Ben Lindsay of Denver
offered an alternative with his widely cited "companionate marriage"
to cut down on the frequency of divorce. In this approach, two young
people would live together until they were certain of each other's love
and then arrange for a wedding ceremony. Afterward, the young couple
could proceed with having children. This would curtail the divorce rate
and also make a better life for children.[38]

One of the bridesmaids described the wedding in Cedarville, which
took place on 1 July 1916 at the Haldeman home:

> The whole outdoors was so lush and green and the inside of the house
> was just beautiful. . . . Just at noon [Marcet] in her pretty dress of
> white taffeta and georgette and Emanuel in a light gray suit took their
> position in the doorway that led into the dining room. . . . The guests as
> I remember were Grandmother Carrie Smith, Dorothy North, Grace
> and Peter Michaelson . . . Aunt Flora Giteau, Aunt Laurie Addams,
> [Marcet's] grandmother in her wheeled chair. . . . As I delve back into
> my memory it seems that [Marcet] told me that [her parents] stood
> in exactly the same place when they were married. . . . After the wed-
> ding there was a . . . big wedding cake . . . and yellow roses. Then the
> telephone began to ring and telegrams and messages came in all day
> long. It was very exciting. Presbyterian pastor Alfred H. Morrison of
> Newton performed the ceremony.[39]

Telegrams arrived from Emanuel's father, mother, sisters, and brother, all reporting sadly that they could not attend owing to the distance. Most disheartening was one from Jane Addams telling of a health complication that kept her in Chicago—she was "Terribly disappointed." "Dearest Auntie" invited the newlyweds to Chicago and a lunch. "Please ask Julius what Socialist friends he would also like to invite to the lunch."[40]

Two weeks after the wedding the newlyweds were back in Girard. Emanuel had a letter waiting for him from Eugene Debs. "My Dear Comrade Julius," Debs wrote:

> The cards announcing your marriage to Miss Anna Marcet Haldeman on June 1st came in my absence and I avail myself of the earliest moment to tender to you and your bride my most hearty congratulations upon the happy event. . . . Knowing what fine souls you are and how supremely worthy of all that makes life rich and full and complete. I hope most earnestly that all good influences may combine to realize all your beautiful dreams and noble aspirations.[41]

Emanuel had previously interviewed Debs concerning his race for the U.S. House of Representatives from the Fifth District in Indiana. Debs did not run for president in this cycle, and Allan Benson ran in his stead on the Socialist Party ticket. When Emanuel returned to his desk he wrote a series of essays on the 1916 presidential campaign.

Shortly before the wedding, Jane Addams had made a significant proposal to the couple. She suggested that "because Julius does not seem particularly attached to his own name," they might take the name Haldeman for their married name, or Julius Haldeman. It was not "a legal matter" for the woman to take the husband's surname, but "one of custom." This change might be done before it was necessary to sign legal documents such as deeds. Jane talked this over with a friend the day after speaking with Marcet and Emanuel, and her friend was "shocked" by the idea, so Jane withdrew her suggestion. But in July Jane brought up the issue again, and again a few months later. Emanuel was attracted to the idea, having long sought to avoid any Jewishness, and early in December he appeared before A. J. Curran, a Kansas district judge in Crawford County, and announced he wished to change his name legally to Haldeman-Julius.

The reason, he stated in his petition, was "to perpetuate the family name of his wife, whose maiden name was Anna Marcet Haldeman and that the name of Haldeman will continue to be used in connection with the various businesses and institutions in which it has so long been used."[42]

Soon after the wedding, Emanuel heard from an old acquaintance, much like one would after winning a lottery. Chester Wright heard of his marriage to a wealthy heiress and asked for a loan of $1,000. Emanuel feigned shock at the suggestion: "Surely you don't think that because I married a woman of means that I am therefore able to draw on her." What was Marcet's belonged to her, and what he had was his. He had only $2,000 in certificates drawing interest, and "that money is tied up, and I want it to remain so." He further noted that his income came from wages the *Appeal* paid him and that from that income he had to pay half of their household expenses. A socialist colony in Missouri also appealed for money, but this too he had to refuse. "I think I shall get up a printed form," he concluded, to announce that he was not available as a financial contributor.[43]

The newlyweds were in a whirl of activity in their own spheres. Emanuel was busy writing and receiving regular pay for it. The couple early decided to share their common expenses of the apartment, utilities, and groceries, and each kept his or her own earnings. Marcet was kept busy with bank business, fending off the competition of a new rival bank and with her duties as a state banking association officer. They were expecting their first child in May 1917.

At the same time Emanuel, was facing a crisis with the *Appeal to Reason*'s declining subscriptions that dropped drastically after the United States was drawn inexorably into the European conflict. The *Appeal* had opposed the United States' entry in the war, and its popularity had declined correspondingly, especially after the socialists lost the presidential election of 1916 by such a large margin. Something dramatic had to be done. Among other actions, they changed the name from *Appeal to Reason* to *New Appeal*. "We are about to receive our death blow," Emanuel wrote Jane Addams.[44]

A majority of European socialists supported their governments' prowar status, but in the United States the vast majority opposed U.S. involvement before and after entry on the Allied side. Meeting in national convention in St. Louis in April 1917, American socialists voted overwhelmingly for peace. The minority who supported President Wilson's position were among the better-known American socialists, such as John Spargo, Upton Sinclair, Allan Benson, A. M. Simons, and William English Walling.[45]

The American declaration of war on 6 April 1917 and the meeting of the socialists that month split the party. Emanuel's old friend from the *Call*, John Spargo, called on members to "make whatever sacrifices may be needed to enable our nation and its allies to end the war as speedily as possible." The minority, including Emanuel, resigned from the Socialist Party and formed the Social Democratic League, which supported Wilson, who insisted that "the war was necessary to save liberal democracy." Kopelin also joined the league, with Emanuel as its acting assistant secretary. On the front page of the *New Appeal*, Emanuel spread the news that Girard was now the headquarters of the new pro-government movement in American socialism. This branch of socialism supported the war effort when Congress declared war. Emanuel's byline disappeared from the *Appeal to Reason* until January 1918, when the *New Appeal* was launched as a replacement.[46]

When Kopelin was in New York City in 1917, prior to his embarking for Europe, he met with Allan Benson and suggested he write Emanuel about joining the *Appeal* staff as a writer at $100 weekly. Benson was asking the high salary because he knew that the *Appeal* needed him to survive. Emanuel gave Benson a position but only paid him $50 for two weekly articles. He explained to William English Walling that both he and Kopelin were drawing only $50 weekly. A short time later, Emanuel complained to Walling that the Loyal Socialist Mission was failing to send information about events in Europe that he could use in the *New Appeal*, forcing him to rely on other sources. (With the Armistice, of course, the Social Democratic League became a footnote in history.) He also shared his idea of publishing Benson's account of why he joined the league as a thirty-two-page booklet. This is Emanuel's first mention of the format that he would later expand to sixty-four pages for Little Blue Books.[47]

"Sacrifices may be necessary to enable our nation and its allies to win the war as speedily as possible," Emanuel wrote in the *Appeal* on 21 April 1917. The United States declared war on the Central Powers, thus resolving the issue through making it a question of patriotism. After this Emanuel's byline disappeared from the *Appeal* until January 1918, when the *New Appeal* was launched as its replacement.[48]

Emma Goldman wrote that Emanuel was "quite right that it does not worry me that the Socialist vote has gone down" in the election of 1916. She knew this was inevitable, because there was no reason the "average worker" would vote "for those who at best must waste their time in endless resolutions and certainly can do nothing for the workers within the capitalistic regime." She disagreed with Emanuel that this would "hurt other things besides the political element," confident that "those who think at all are outgrowing the voting mania altogether." As to his reference to the "new crop of crazy laws" Kansas was enacting, such as the recent criminal syndicalism law, "the revolutionary wave is spreading all over the country" and she held "the political element responsible." She believed America was "in for a period of espionage which will excel anything that exists in Russia." This was a perceptive prediction of the Red Scare that was to engulf the United States following the war.[49]

After extended negotiations, Emanuel and Kopelin bought two-thirds of the *New Appeal* from Walter and Jon Wayland for $50,000. Marcet's bank provided Emanuel's share of $25,000. Marcet thought this a bargain price considering the newspaper's assets of "its paper, its book department, and other sources of income." This arrangement was quite satisfactory for the Waylands, as Walter settled their third with his brother, who never had an interest in editing and needed the money for his mining ventures. Walter became a one-third-interest partner and was named president of the corporation, while Kopelin became vice-president, Emanuel secretary-treasurer, and Marcet a director. Emanuel received a weekly salary of $50 along with his share of the annual profits. Marcet and bank officer Oscar Shaeffer were "amazed" when they examined the *Appeal's* books and discovered what a money-maker the corporation was.[50]

Marcet found herself in "a very perplexing situation." Here she was, "a good Republican, planning and working for the success of the largest and most powerful Socialist paper . . . in the world." She found herself seeing "things altogether different as Manuel's wife. One thing is sure," she wrote Aunt Jane, "Manuel is very, very happy and heart and soul in his paper and that makes *me* very, very happy, I can tell you."[51]

The newspaper crisis had an important effect on Emanuel, and his articles and interests took a significant literary turn. He collected fifty sketches he had written for the *Comrade*, the *Call*, and the *Appeal to Reason* and arranged for the *Appeal* to publish them in paperback as *The Color of Life*. Marcet began writing a four-page sheet titled "The Booster" that surveyed the current economic situation in Crawford County and Girard and the advantages of investing in her bank stock. The *Appeal* printed it, and after its first issue appeared, in February 1917, Governor Arthur Capper wrote to congratulate her. Emanuel believed Capper's letter "should be exploited" for advertising, but nothing came of this.[52]

Late that summer, Aunt Jane arrived for the christening of their baby, Alice. Emanuel had questions: What was the actual service composed of? Marcet read from the Book of Common Prayer: "Dearly beloved, for as much as all men are conceived and born in sin—" Emanuel interrupted, "She wasn't. They'll have to cut that out." Marcet continued: "None can enter the Kingdom of God except that he be regenerated." Emanuel interrupted again: "Regenerate! The idea! Our beautiful little angel!" And so it went. "But mother's granddaughter must be christened so we will have to get through with it," Marcet declared. They finally decided on the Presbyterian service because it was simpler than the Episcopalian one.[53]

In early September, Marcet wrote Jane that Emanuel was "white-washing the barns and attending to all sorts of needed little details. He takes Alice with him quite often." When Alice was put in the car, "she promptly goes to sleep, perfectly serene, even when we speed up to 45 miles an hour." Marcet and Emanuel were beginning "to wonder how we shall ever hope to interest her. But perhaps she may be able to derive a slight thrill from her first air-ship ride or better still from learning to fly one." Alice was three months old, and Marcet worried over her developing "too rapidly.

I can't abide precocious children. But I think, as a matter of fact, she is just an unusually healthy and thoroughly normal youngster."[54]

In late October, Emanuel wrote to his brother Nathan about taking care of their father, who was quite ill. Nathan thought the oldster might be of some help on the farm. Emanuel responded quite pessimistically:

> Frankly, I don't see how I can arrange to take care of Dad. . . . I cannot interfere as to who shall do the work. . . . [I] keep my hands off as to who Fry shall employ. I know that father would prove of considerable value, but that is beside the question. . . . Putting excuses aside, I feel I can't be fair to Marcet and obtrude my family affairs. After all, Marcet does not know our people and it isn't fair for me to expect her to open to them. She is loyal to me, but I don't think that I should expect that loyalty to go to the extent that you expect and suggest. Marcet has a kindly feeling toward the folks, but after all, they are my folks and not hers. Not that we would not be proud of father, for he is a splendid father and an exceptional one in many ways. In addition to my love for father, there is a great deal of admiration. He has been a sturdy spirit fighting severe odds, it almost breaks my heart to think that as he is getting old he must begin to feel a certain helplessness. I have done all I could so (and I honestly believe that I have been rather liberal) and I certainly intend to do more from time to time. I would rather that we were as loyal as Esther, who has been the pillar for so many years.[55]

That same day, Marcet wrote Jane that they had decided to "keep the beautiful old place" (the farm at Cedarville) so that "perhaps when our children are growing up we can go there every summer regularly (as the family had been doing for years)." Meanwhile, if the current situation were to continue they would need to have a thorough discussion and reach a definite agreement on their arrangement for Mary Fry to continue to care for Grandmother Addams, as some troubling financial details had recently come to light.[56]

Marcet and Emanuel had a long discussion with Mary about financial decisions she had made in Grandmother's name, and on 31 August, Marcet wrote Aunt Jane a detailed (thirty-three typed pages!) account of the "peaceful" confrontation so there would be a family record of it. Mary was paid $500 annually to handle Grandmother's financial affairs, and Marcet asked her for an accounting. Mary turned over her bank book and vouchers—an area that Marcet thoroughly understood, of course. Marcet found "several things": a large proportion of the checks were made out to "loan" or "cash," Mary had not always deposited the full amount Marcet sent to cover Grandmother's expenses, and there were several entries regarding checks made out to Mary's husband, Homer Fry, long after he had stopped working on the farm. Emanuel then confronted Mary for a definition of "loan" in his "nice quiet way." Mary responded that "I have put that much from my own personal account to your grandmother's." Marcet asked her why she had deposited only $250 of the $350 she had sent Mary for July. Mary responded that she had to pay some bills with the $100. After extended conversations, Marcet and Emanuel decided that, in an innocent way, Mary was honest but had "unconsciously developed into a little machine that worked perfectly grinding away to the advantage of Mary's family and to the expense of grandmother and myself." They decided that "the whole state of mind is wrong here" and that changes must be made.

"From now on," Marcet informed Mary, "she would run Grandmother's household and her own household as *one*." Her new rules for Mary included the following:

1. Mary has no right to give away anything that is not her own personal property.
2. Grandmother will receive the usual $4,000 annually. Mary will draw $25 monthly of that sum for herself.
3. Should a nurse become necessary for Grandmother, Mary's $25 monthly will stop until the house is back to normal.
4. No more checks would be made out for "cash" without an "exact statement" of how each penny was spent.

Marcet had "faith" that Mary would "stick" to these arrangements.[57]

Marcet wrote Homer that she thought it a good idea if the two would draw up a contract for him to manage the farm, and she enclosed $30 to pay his expenses to come to Girard for this purpose. She stipulated a five-year contract in which she would provide the farm and its buildings and he would provide his machinery and labor; they would share the annual profits equally. A certain amount of manure would be spread each year, and the crops would be rotated. She would "put the fences in good shape for you and then shall expect you to keep them in good repair." Emanuel was going to help Marcet with "her end of running the farm."[58] Marcet had a power of attorney drawn up for Emanuel to help her carry out "a certain contract between" her and Homer for farming four hundred acres of land in Stephenson County, Illinois.[59]

This increased interest in the Illinois farm resulted from more than just financial concern. After the United States declared war on the Central Powers, in early April 1917, Congress enacted a Selective Service System that went into effect the following month. This included registering all men between twenty and thirty years of age. This draft would be administered by local boards of civilians. These draft boards proved to be "sensitive to local conditions" but also "susceptible to local political pressures." The law exempted men with dependents, and many local boards exempted all married men, but other boards applied a more narrow definition of "dependency." The draft board of Crawford County proved to be susceptible to local political pressure to take a narrow interpretation of dependency, especially for its relatively numerous young men of socialist tendencies.

Because of these developments, Emanuel, who was twenty-seven when the United States entered the war, began to cultivate a great interest in agriculture, as draft boards tended to exempt farmers from the draft so that they could continue production of foodstuffs for the war effort. Louis Kopelin was the first local socialist to go, drafted into the army in June 1918. Then President Woodrow Wilson changed his plans and furloughed Kopelin to join a special commission that would go to Europe and talk with socialists and politically liberal laborers there. Other commission members included A. M. Simons, Charles Edward Russell, George D. Herron of the Republic of Switzerland, John Spargo, Frank Bohn, and Alexander Howat, all prominent socialists, with Howat then serving as president of the Kansas unit of the United Mine Workers of America.[60]

The commission was charged with traveling to England, France, and Italy to work among socialists and "the working class in opposition to the German propaganda which wrecked the Russian Empire and made it subservient to the desires and wishes of Germany." Kopelin was named secretary of the group, because his years of experience in editing socialist newspapers gave him "a wide acquaintance among the socialists not only of America but of all foreign countries as well." His role was "to give publicity to its work, so that the socialists of America may, through the columns of the *New Appeal*, learn what the working class of Europe is doing to sustain the war, and he is to give through the Socialist newspapers of Europe the working class news from America." This left Emanuel to edit the *New Appeal* by himself, or Marcet would assume this role if he were also drafted to help carry on the work of the commission.[61]

But Emanuel was also an obvious target for Crawford County's foes of liberal political thinking, and he and Marcet had to fight to keep him from being drafted. Marcet testified, as part of the registration process that Emanuel went through to gain exemption, that she was dependent on him. She had to care for their baby, and thus it was incumbent on Emanuel to take care of her business interests. She was also responsible for overseeing her grandmother's financial interests, which accounted for her husband's statement that the couple's obligations in this category were agricultural in nature, including their own farmlands and those of her grandmother.[62]

Marcet also testified that two of the draft board members were currently political candidates for the Republican ticket and were trying to "make a hit with the Republicans by hitting the *Appeal* a blow." B. S. Gaitskill was the Democratic candidate for nomination for state attorney general and was "piqued because Louis [Kopelin] went and has been hard [heard] to say openly that he would see to it that Manuel went." Emanuel argued that he was placed in the category of unmarried and childless men because he was a socialist.

The *Kansas City Times* carried a story that Emanuel's local draft board had changed his status from 2-A (second round of draft) to 1-A (first round), and that after Emanuel appealed to the president the board returned him to 2-A upon the recommendation of Provost Marshal General (Enoch H.) Crowder. The *Times* article was quite misleading, as it portrayed Marcet as being very dependent on him for support. J. I. Sheppard, a Fort Scott attorney, was the Haldeman-Juliuses' legal representative, and he wrote the editor of the *Pittsburg Daily Sun* to ask the news media to correct the *Times*' numerous misrepresentations. It was "well understood by all that know them that she is a woman of independent means," Sheppard wrote, and the couple had never suggested otherwise. On the contrary, Emanuel had responded "no" to the question of his wife's dependence on him. In the Industrial form Emanuel completed, which the draft board rejected, he based his claim on his operation of the farm in Illinois. Emanuel was "instrumental," they emphasized, "in causing the *New Appeal* to declare openly its support of our Government in the war against Germany."[63]

Marcet suffered a serious health crisis in 1918, becoming a victim of the influenza pandemic in 1918–19. She almost let Jane walk into "the dragon's jaws," not realizing how contagious this deadly virus was. Jane had planned on visiting the family in Cedarville, but a speaking engagement took her to Minnesota. Marcet had "disinfectants burning," and the family recovered, but Jane's visit had to be canceled. Marcet telegraphed Emanuel the news, and he wrote that the situation sounded "terrible." He believed he would "simply die if Alice doesn't get well soon." He rushed to Cedarville to find that Alice had not contracted the flu; he and Alice were able to avoid the plague, but the house became "a land of shush and no-no." Father and daughter slept in a room "furnished PDQ" by Marcet while "she was pleasantly drunk with fever."[64]

In discussing the preparations to testify, Marcet told Emanuel she believed it "would be sheer madness to swear to anything but the truth." She calculated that the two owned almost $100,000 in property, but Emanuel wanted her to swear to $25,000. "Impossible. . . . Impossible! And sheer madness!!" After further thought, she decided that the $18,000 they owned in mortgages was "recorded in Grandmother's name" and the two small farms "were the only properties in *my name*." She emphasized to him that "we must be able to absolutely *prove every statement we make*." She also listed Emanuel's bank stock of $5,000 because she saw there was no way "you can avoid listing it." She strongly urged him "to be sure to go over the questionnaire with him [Oscar Shaeffer of her bank] carefully a final time before you turn it in."[65]

On 19 August 1918, Emanuel and Marcet appeared before B. S. Gaitskill, the draft board appeal agent for Crawford County, to testify as to their "financial standing." Gaitskill refused to allow them to make complete answers, and when they tried to correct their answers on the printed report, "he refused to allow us to make the corrections."[66]

Emanuel was asked his wife's "worth," although the questioner failed to connect these questions with Emanuel's status of managing the affairs of Marcet's grandmother's farm. Gaitskill's quizzing sounded more like an inquisitive neighbor engaged in a fishing expedition than a government official carrying out his duty to determine the financial worth of the town's richest banker. He asked Emanuel, "What is your wife's worth?" His response, "At the present time approximately $100,000." What is her approximate annual income? About $3,000. "Does your child have any income?" No. What is your annual income and earning? "I would say about $3,000." Is either your wife or your child dependent upon your labor, either mental or manual, for support? No. The inquisitor asked Marcet how much stock she owned in the State Bank of Girard, and she responded, $18,250. She stated she owned $12,500 in the *New Appeal* corporation, two unimproved farms in Kansas, and "a piece of unbroken ground in Iowa," worth $4,000, that had been in her family for years. The Haldeman family owned $75,000 in first mortgages, the income from which went to her grandmother. Marcet was really trying to be helpful and honest. She even stated, when asked, that she owned $1,500 in Liberty bonds and $1,000 in War Savings Stamps.[67]

The couple was "shocked" when they received a letter from Secretary of War Newton D. Baker. Emanuel had Sheppard write the War Department to appeal his classification. It was obvious Baker had access to these official records, since the letter that Emanuel's wife and child "were independent" and that Emanuel, while taking an interest in his daughter's future farm, was not indispensable to its successful operation. Therefore, his reclassification to 1-A was "entirely appropriate."[68]

Marcet wrote her close friend Euterpe about their ordeal. Because Kopelin was drafted and Emanuel was overworked at the newspaper, Marcet was doing the work of the associate editor so as to be thoroughly trained by the time Emanuel "himself, has to go to war." The county draft board members "wanted to play up the fact that they had not been afraid to make a man of Emanuel's caliber and my husband go just like the rest." They were angry over Crowder's telling them that Emanuel belonged in class 2-A, and refused to "send him any classification card at all."[69]

Marcet wrote Aunt Jane of her fear that Emanuel would be drafted and she would have to take over the operation of the *New Appeal*. Emanuel argued convincingly that she could run the operation. "You know the policy as well as I do," he reassured her. "You know our style, you know the mechanical make-up of the paper, you can write, you can edit and if you keep your wits about you can pull off the circulation stunts." She confessed to "Auntie" that "there is just so much of the actress in me that I *can* simply quit being myself and be Manuel while he is gone." But she was fearful of failure. "You don't know how deeply I love him and you don't know how disappointed he will be if I fail him. . . . I would rather die—I mean literally—than fail Manuel."

Emanuel was formally appealing his classification that day, and Marcet was certain it would be rejected, because Gaitskill had been overheard to say "it was all very well for Jake Sheppard to get Louis Kopelin furloughed after he was sent to war. It was a slick trick," Gaitskill said, "but he would have Kopelin in the trenches inside of sixty days" and "would see to it that Haldeman-Julius went too, that those *Appeal* people were pretty slick and he would see to it that they didn't get out of their duty."

Marcet was also having trouble at her bank. Gaitskill wrote the state banking commission to complain about Oscar Shaeffer and told the city commissioners that they could not put city funds in her bank, as they had just voted to do, as long as Oscar was bank president. Marcet told Jane that she had "a talk with Mr. Gaitskill that that worthy won't forget and a successful correspondence with the Bank Commission . . . and a heart to heart talk with each of the city commissioners. Everything was adjusted and peace reigns once more." Oscar did not resign, and Marcet noted that

"I won't be dictated about my bank by a lot of bullies." She did think, though, that Emanuel should resign as a bank director, "as this *Appeal* matter ought to be kept entirely separate from the bank." Officials of the competing bank "went to some of our best customers and misrepresented the facts about Oscar and things he said" and informed them that "if our customers continued to do business with our bank they would have them boycotted. So I got those men of the new bank together and told them that if they did not leave our customers alone I would have to take action. That our Government had declared itself in its attitude to men and corporations who tried to use the war for their personal purposes."

Marcet reported to Jane that Emanuel had met one of the draft board members on the street and carefully inquired about his case. Emanuel was the only one whom the board had put in class 1-A who had a baby, and he asked the man if it would make a difference in his case if Marcet was pregnant. The board member said "it would make a great deal of difference and Manuel told him I was." The member suggested he appeal his classification and present an affidavit that she was pregnant. Marcet was not absolutely certain, however, and "just suppose I should be mistaken. That would be a pretty kettle of fish. We are having this baby because Alice need[s] a little sister or brother and with no thought of this [draft issue] in mind." The Armistice, signed 18 November 1918, ended this uncertainty over Emanuel's draft status.[70]

In May 1920, Emanuel traveled to California, where, among other things, he had the opportunity to visit several conscientious objectors who had avoided conscription. He talked to Roger Baldwin, "a fine young fellow . . . who served a year in prison" for refusing to submit to the draft and would become head of the National Civil Liberties Union (later the American Civil Liberties Union). He also spoke with Albert Seiler, whom he knew when he lived in California before the war and who had just served time in Leavenworth federal prison. "Thank God I didn't have to go," Emanuel wrote Marcet. He was astonished at how many of his friends were being arrested for violating the numerous criminal syndicalism laws that states enacted during the Red Scare following the Armistice. "Nothing is to be gained by fighting the state," he noted. "If going to prison would help, I would go to prison. But it doesn't."[71]

In a letter to Euterpe describing their conscription problems, Marcet expressed her motherly pride in baby Alice, now nearly two years of age:

> Incidentally, you know, I have a very charming little daughter. She is really a little lamb. Lovely golden-brown curly hair, eyes that are some-times lilac-grey and sometimes as blue as violets. I carried her a full ten months instead of nine and she has always seemed to be a month ahead of the average baby of her age. At age eleven months she walked with the assurance and balance of a youngster of a year and a half and at twelve months danced to the Victrola with such an abandon that was really quite startling. I regret to state that she is very self-willed and at nine months actually stamped her foot at me. . . . She is a happy buoyant little soul and by handling her by my method of treating her as a little chum, she is developing into a winsome, alert personality. We want to have another child. She must have a little sister or brother, or, in spite of fate, she will get spoiled for she is one of those youngsters who attract unusual attention. Alice was also the "apple of her father's eye" and "a daddy's little girl."[72]

Aunt Jane wrote Marcet about her problem with carrying her baby to term. She was thankful that "both you and the new baby are in the world and I don't like to remember how near you both were to the confines." She recommended a "baby nurse" until Alice was "strong and normal." Jane also suggested Marcet engage "a nurse girl for Alice, to keep her out of doors as much as possible both for her good and your quiet."[73]

Marcet had contracted a serious disease late in her pregnancy. This was an albuminous condition, the presence of a protein in the urine symp-tomatic of kidney disease. Albumen is manufactured by the liver, and its levels help doctors diagnosed liver and kidney diseases. Low levels of albumen cause fluids to leak from the blood into the body's tissues, causing swelling, especially in the legs. Dr. O. M. Owensby in Pittsburg, Marcet's physician, detected this problem and put her on a strict diet of milk and water and "absolute rest." He warned her that if the condition continued he would have to take her to Kansas City and induce labor. She told Jane that she felt "perfectly safe in his kind and capable hands." She continued that she could not imagine "what a lively and vigorous little creature it is in its present habitat." She added in a postscript that Emanuel had just returned from Pittsburg with the report that her "specimen showed a marked improvement." Dr. Owensby had added milk toast and malted milk to her diet.[74]

If this medical problem was not enough distraction, Frank O'Hare arrived in October 1919 as a "house guest" for two weeks. Much of Marcet's health problem stemmed from working too much and going up and down stairs nineteen times a day. She raised the salary of Florence, their maid and cook, from $5 to $8 weekly, but this did not help her feelings sufficiently to overcome the hardship of serving twelve meals daily, so she neglected the other housework. Marcet had to help her so that everything was "smooth and quiet and I was neat and clean" for Emanuel when he returned home from work every day.[75]

Mr. O'Hare, "while quite a dear," proved to be a considerable burden. His wife, Kate Richards O'Hare, had just been sentenced to federal prison in West Virginia, then transferred to Missouri, for an antiwar speech that authorities insisted violated the Espionage Act of 1918. As a result, Frank was broken physically, unable to eat or sleep, and needed much rest. Marcet had him help her clean the chicken house, and this induced him to remodel it. When he arrived in Girard he was "a nervous wreck," but this diversion helped him "sleep like a top" until 10:00 a.m. or later. But this meant that either Florence or Marcet had to fix his breakfast. In addition, Marcet reminded Jane, "you know what it is to have anyone in that condition of nerves for two weeks."[76]

Marcet updated Jane on the children. Josephine, the child they had adopted earlier, had skipped third grade and was "making good" in fourth. Alice, age three, was "the most inventive little soul." She was currently playing with a deck of cards, making houses out of dominoes for the kings and queens. Then suddenly, she makes a long "too-too" out of the cards. One day at Sunday school she was in an exercise for Rally Day and she and her friend Mel Jenkins "led the procession on to the platform and

behaved with much poise, Alice singing with gusto and her little voice
ringing out above the others. When she saw us her face broke into smiles,
she arose and waved to us and told Mel quite audibly that there were
'Daddy and Muddie.' She quite won the audience by her naturalness."
Marcet was beginning Alice in the Montessori method, with herself as the
instructor. Montessori was developed by Italian physician and educator
Maria Montessori based on her research on "special needs" children. It
is characterized by emphasis on independence or "freedom within limits"
and respect for a child's natural dependence. This concept spread to the
United States in 1911. By the time Marcet discovered the theory and
practice it was in decline in this country. She told Jane that she should
see how Alice "obeys her father. Yet he is always gentle with her. But, like
Joey [Josephine], she stands in wholesome awe of him."[77]

Henry Haldeman-Julius was born in Pittsburg, Kansas, on 1 November
1919, increasing their number of children to three. The second had arrived
in August 1918, when Alice, Marcet, and Marcet's friend Ruthie Bob were
in front of the Crawford County courthouse, and Alice heard a cry from the
basement. Upon investigation, Marcet found a group of children brought
in from the mining community of Ringo whose parents could not care for
them. Until a definite decision was made about them, they were placed
in the women's division of the county jail. One of the children, Josephine
Wettstein, approached Marcet and took her hand. Marcet decided instantly
she would take the nine-year-old girl home, if that were possible. She wrote
Euterpe that she was unable to resist "the wan, frightened, bewildered
little creature" and was indignant that the county "should treat a mere
child in any such fashion." Marcet and Emanuel soon adopted Josephine
and raised her as their own child, This sudden expansion of their family
forced a decision, and the couple traded a farm in Kansas that Marcet
had inherited for a 160-acre farm at the eastern edge of Girard with the
usual farm cottage. After Marcet's modifications and extensive expansion,
the cottage took on the aspects of a large house with lots of room for the
children to play in and acquire numerous kinds of animals.[78]

In January 1920 Marcet wrote to Emanuel's mother that she wanted
to make the trip east for a visit but did not want to leave the *Appeal* for

such a long trip. It was not until that September that she was able to get away with her girls to visit the Julius family in Philadelphia. Esther afterward wrote Emanuel that they were there from Saturday afternoon until Monday morning and that the family enjoyed them "immensely." She thought Marcet was "the most charming woman in the world . . . and Alice promises to be just as charming and beautiful and graceful as the mother." Josephine was also "a most lovely child." Nathan took them to Atlantic City to visit his family and for a swim in the Atlantic. Esther expressed the hope that "in the near future" Emanuel could bring Henry and his entire family for a visit.[79]

4

LITTLE BLUE BOOKS, 1918–1923

Following the Armistice, Emanuel tried to prepare for his uncertain professional future. As subscriptions for the *New Appeal* declined after the war, he explored other avenues for a vocation. Soon after the Armistice was signed, the president of the W. T. Raleigh Company wrote that he had Emanuel's letter of 17 November 1918 expressing an interest in moving to Stephenson County, Illinois, and joining this health product firm. He asked Emanuel to send examples of literature he had written for selling commodities through the mail. Fortunately, Emanuel did not pursue this avenue of occupation for very long, as the decade ahead was one of upheaval, of rejecting old values, concepts, and habits. Instead, in February 1919, Emanuel published his first two numbers of the *New Appeal*'s "Pocket Series."[1]

Geoffrey Perrett asserts that the Roaring Twenties "reaped the first fruits of universal secondary education" because "for the first time nearly the entire adult population could read, and did." The age saw flappers dancing the Charleston, rouging their knees, listening to jazz, patronizing speakeasies and other sources of illegal alcohol, making bathtub gin, smoking cigarettes, flagpole-sitting, playing mah-jongg. The motto, if an age can have one, was "Live fast, die young, and leave a good-looking corpse."[2]

The decade also "marked a revolutionary advance in literary taste." The best-selling books of Zane Grey, Harold Bell Wright, and Booth Tarkington yielded to Sinclair Lewis, Eugene O'Neill, and Ernest Hemingway. More importantly, it resulted in a revolutionary expansion of reading, led by the Little Blue Books of E. Haldeman-Julius. The average American broke the monotony of a long commute to and from work by whipping out his latest Little Blue Book from a shirt pocket and reading Shakespeare, as did his more affluent, sophisticated, scholarly neighbor. Emanuel also quickly discovered that Americans of that age were vitally interested in sex education but unable to find it in their library, and he gave it to them in large doses.

When Emanuel was about fifteen, he had an experience that greatly influenced him when he was an adult. He stopped in Nick Brown's used bookstore at Pine and Fifth and bought a 10-cent copy of Oscar Wilde's long poem *The Ballad of Reading Gaol*. He crossed the street to a small city park, found a bench, and proceeded to read. It was winter, but he was so engrossed he did not notice until later that his "hands were blue," his "wet nose" was numb, and his ears "felt as hard as glass. Never, until then, or since, did any piece of printed matter move me more deeply," he reported later. Forever after that incident he thought "how nice it would be if such pamphlets could be picked up easily and inexpensively whenever one wanted to buy them." Then, in early 1919, once he was a part-owner of the *Appeal*, he took this pamphlet and *The Rubaiyat of Omar Khayyam*, marked them for printing, and handed them to his typesetter. They were printed on newspaper bulk paper, measured 3½ x 5 inches, and sold for 25 cents. He prepared a broadside to advertise them and sent it to the 175,000 names on the mailing list of the *New Appeal*.[3]

Before this endeavor could go any further, Kopelin returned to Girard. He, too, had been giving much thought to their future. While he believed Emanuel had done a good job ensuring the survival of the *New Appeal*, he had an important investment in the newspaper and saw "a bright future for it." William Wayland would approve any decision the two editors made, and they decided to concentrate the *New Appeal*'s energies on obtaining amnesty for the nation's political prisoners.

In the 16 November 1918 issue of the *New Appeal*, Emanuel declared for the new cause that the experience of World War I had on socialist thought and, of course, its political personification, Eugene V. Debs.[4] Debs had given a speech in Canton, Ohio, in June 1918 that a jury decided violated the wartime Espionage Act, and he was sentenced to ten years in prison. Emanuel then wrote to the Department of Justice to make a special appeal for Debs, referring to him as a "political prisoner." An assistant in the department responded that "political prisoner" was an "inaccurate term," as the Espionage Act was directed at "intentional obstruction of the prosecution of the war." The *New Appeal* then "took up in a big way the amnesty issue in general and the Debs issue in particular." Emanuel talked to Debs in Atlanta prison and then stopped in Terre Haute to interview Eugene's brother, Theodore. Emanuel wrote a special "Amnesty Edition" and a call for the "Appeal Army" to get this edition into the hands of "millions of people." In the 1 March 1919 issue the newspaper temporarily returned to its familiar name, the *Appeal to Reason*.[5]

In May 1919 Emanuel traveled to the nation's capital to interview Attorney General A. Mitchell Palmer to discuss Debs. Palmer's house had been bombed, further increasing his antipathy to radicals, and he asked Emanuel if he could review his story before it was published. The journalist agreed, but when the attorney general had not returned it within a fortnight, Emanuel informed him it would appear on the front page of a special Fourth of July edition. It depicted Palmer as a vindictive enemy because, he claimed, Debs had not said he was sorry for his war speeches and that he would not request clemency; until he did, though, his release "would not be considered." After Debs was transferred from Moundsville prison in West Virginia to the federal prison in Atlanta, Emanuel came home.[6]

Meanwhile, on the inside pages of the *Appeal to Reason*, Emanuel was waging another kind of campaign: an effort to sell the cheap books he had just published. The book division of the *Appeal* had occasionally published a book in the past. For example, it produced Upton Sinclair's *The Jungle* in serial form in 1906. This was not an entirely happy venture for Fred Warren, because he and Sinclair fought over the publishing rights when Sinclair signed a contract with Doubleday for the book version, which seemed to conflict with Warren's serial rights. Emanuel now began to envision a larger role for the book department.[7]

On page 2 of the 22 February 1919 issue of the *New Appeal*, an advertisement read: "Greatest Prison Poem Ever Written." Wilde's book, *The Ballad of Reading Gaol*, was offered to readers for 25 cents. It was the first volume in the Appeal Pocket Series. By 5 April the book department was ready for a "price-smashing" sale. For thirty days readers could purchase the *Ballad* for 15 cents per copy or ten for $1, and copies of the *Rubaiyat of Omar Khayyam* could be purchased for the same price. By late May the book department had twelve titles in the Pocket Series and was proclaiming that the experiment was working. The other ten titles were *The Original Documents of the German Revolution; The Soviet Constitution; Russia: A Challenge*, by Upton Sinclair; *The Piece of String*, by Guy de Maupassant; *This Misery of Boots*, by H. G. Wells; *A Trip to Utopia*, by E. Haldeman-Julius; *The Coltar's Saturday Night*, by Robert Burns; *Elegy in a Country Churchyard*, by Thomas Gray; *The Deserted Village*, by Oliver Goldsmith; and *The Fall of the House of Usher*, by Edgar Allen Poe.

He later explained what he was trying to do through this experiment: "I thought it might be possible to put books in the reach of everyone rich or poor, though mostly poor—books that they would want, and which they could chose for the sake of the books alone. By that I mean that I dreamed of publishing in such quantities that I could sell them at a price which would put all books on the same cost level."[8]

Emanuel explained the popularity of the Pocket Series: "The success of the Little Blue Books in the Pocket Series has proven the aptitude of the workers for the classics. The reason is apparent. Here are books that are so cheap that the poorest worker can buy them; they are short so that they can easily spare the time to read them; they are convenient in size, so he can carry them in his pocket to be read on the way to work, during the lunch hour, at any time that he has a few minutes unoccupied."[9]

He also explained his choice of titles he was publishing as being what was good for poor people, not what he wanted them to read. He was an atheist but published books on religion; he was a socialist but published titles promoting other political ideologies. He published books he liked, confident that his readers also wanted to read them.[10]

Emanuel considered ignorance the root of all evil; therefore education was the source of good things. Man was basically ignorant, influenced by medieval superstitions, and until this was cured by education, man would be unhappy. Emanuel's Little Blue Books were a large part of his campaign for the common man to educate himself. Education in its broadest sense was the only means by which man could become civilized, and Emanuel believed the printing press was man's salvation. He would use his presses to spread culture and understanding among the masses through his books, and the masses would gain salvation through self-improvement.[11]

This proved to be a daring venture into a new type of book publishing. Publishers usually faced the dilemma of wanting to print "worthwhile books" but needing to profit from that endeavor. The trend in the twentieth century had been toward making money, not printing "worthwhile books." Emanuel devised a scheme that allowed him to achieve both goals. He was determined to produce only "the best literature," but through experimentation he discovered that he could turn a profit by publishing in volume. His margin of profit was occasionally measured in fractions of pennies, but his huge volume of cheap paperbacks, various sales pitches, massive advertising, the modern technique of transfer, and his business acumen permitted him to revolutionize the industry.[12]

The paperback was not a new concept, but between the Roaring Twenties and the Cold War, publishers produced paperbacks in order "to reach a larger audience through serious work." Emanuel saw his mission as educating the masses through cheap classics—a use of the transfer concept of emulating the upper, or educated, classes through reading the "best works" and at the same time satisfying their basic instincts of seeking further knowledge of sex and "how-to's" of various kinds. The contemporary paperback publisher Penguin Books pursued V. K. Krishna Menon's vision of "an inexpensive library of engaged non-fiction."[13]

The Charles H. Kerr Company provides an outstanding example of publishing to educate the masses. By 1913 the company was publishing 40 percent of the hardbound copies listed in the socialist catalog. Its efforts to involve the mass of party workers made them "the unsung heroes of American socialism." The company drew its strength from its base. When it needed operating funds, Kerr appealed to the rank and file to purchase a share of stock in the company. This produced the necessary funding but also permitted Kerr to retain control of the company by limiting the purchase to one share.[14]

It was not long before Haldeman-Julius received an important recommendation from an unexpected source. In 1914 the socialists had established a special college in Fort Scott, Kansas. Following the socialists' relative success in the presidential election in 1912, Walter Mills agreed to move his School of Social Economy from Chicago to Fort Scott in order to merge with the drive for the new college, financed in part by the *Appeal to Reason.* Founded by Jake Sheppard and joined by C. B. Hoffman of Enterprise, Arthur Le Sueur of Minot, North Dakota, Caroline Lowe of Pittsburg, and George Brewer of Girard, the group received a fifty-year charter from the State of Kansas. The new school would offer correspondence courses but would also operate "mines, farms, dairies, orchards, and gardens" in Fort Scott to permit students to work their way through college. Hoffman served as the college's first president, and Eugene V. Debs was elected chancellor in 1913.[15]

The FBI closely monitored socialist activities in southeast Kansas during World War I and took an interest in the new college. An agent's memo described the Brewers as "Radical Socialists" and noted that Caroline Lowe was "formerly identified with the *Appeal* and was assistant County Clerk under the Socialist administration in Crawford County six years ago." The agent added that Fred Warren "was identified with the formation of the Peoples College."[16]

The college's vice-president was Arthur Le Sueur, and his wife, Marion, was head of the English department at the fledgling college. She wrote a textbook on "Workers' English." Emanuel described it as "a revolutionary textbook, the first issued by the college to constitute the proletarian literature, self-inspired and self-produced, true to truth and free from all-ruling class taint, that is to dispel the darkness and ignorance and superstition among the workers." He decided to publish the textbook, thus adding a new genre to his series, the self-help book for all types of endeavors. Le Sueur also adopted some of his classics as textbooks.[17]

The success of his new series led Emanuel to devote more time to book publishing and less to the *New Appeal*. He printed an advertisement in the *New Appeal* asking readers to send $5 and promising to mail them fifty books as they came off the press. This was a sight-unseen proposition, because readers had to trust him that more books would be coming that they would want to read. Five thousand readers responded to his offer, giving him $25,000 for operating capital. He "hurried through the fifty titles (and they were good ones, too, for I haven't believed in trash at any time in my life)" and received many letters expressing satisfaction with the venture. He immediately announced a second batch of fifty titles, called for $5 subscriptions, and again received orders from 5,000 customers. Meanwhile, the first fifty "were selling well" to readers who had not initially subscribed. As a result of this surprising success, he was able to pay off the original owners of the *New Appeal* that year as well as paying back Marcet's $25,000 loan by purchasing a 160-acre farm with a large house at the edge of Girard. Not long after he had 210 titles in the Appeal Pocket Series, he changed the name to "Little Blue Books."[18]

With an expanded list of titles in the Little Blue Book series and, more importantly, "a mailing list large enough to exploit in a substantial way," Emanuel began to expand operations significantly. He prepared a 420-line advertisement to place in the Sunday edition of the *St. Louis Post-Dispatch* for $150. It worked so well he escalated his advertising. He advertised 185 books in the *Leslie's Illustrated Weekly*, *The Nation*, *The New Republic*, *Red Book Magazine*, *Popular Mechanics*, the *New York Call*, the *New York Times*, *Current Opinion*, and the *Independent Outlook* in full-page ads. He had found that this expensive method paid off in the long run, and with the money pouring in he could buy "all kinds of new machinery, hire new authors, have the books set in typescript in Kansas City, enlarge his plant," and "before long" could produce a fantastic 240,000 copies a day if the machines worked a twenty-four-hour shift. This success led Emanuel and Kopelin to think of selling the failing *New Appeal* and concentrating on publishing Little Blue Books.[19]

Emanuel brought a new technique to his project. He admitted that "advertising is of first importance" in his publishing operation. It brought in "a steady stream of new names, the heart of the business side of distributing my publications." Without these fresh names day after day, "the list would soon turn sour. In a few years it would be dead." His theory was simple: if he could spend $1,000 for advertising space and receive back $2,000 in orders, he was "satisfied." If he sold $1 in books, he estimated that 50 cents must be spent in advance to get the purchaser's "attention." He admitted that it hurt when he paid out $1,000 for advertising space and received back only $500 in orders, "but the tail goes with the hide." Once he put a name on his advertising list, "the customer is put through the wringer. He is hit often and hard." Orders usually varied from $5 to $50. One subscriber worked in the Arctic Circle as an agent for a fur company and received mail only once a year, so he usually spent $50 for a year's supply of literature. The average sale was $1.50, and thus it was not a business of "nickels and dimes." He depended on volume for profit, as his margins were small. Most importantly, many contributed names for his list. In addition, all Emanuel needed to do was mention in his *American Freeman* that there was an item he could not locate, and "some generous, devoted reader out there was bound to come up with it."[20]

An FBI file on Emanuel reprinted a *Baltimore Sun* article dated 15 July 1921 which stated that the *Appeal* advertised new publications in various liberal and radical weeklies and in some daily newspapers. The books included *Soviet Constitution, Religion of Capital, Nonpartisan League, Braan's Philosophy, Communist Manifesto, Socialist Quotations, Proletarian Dictatorship, Socialism, Socialistic Articles, Marx v. Tolstoi,* and *Steps toward Socialism.* The editorial concluded that this was "the way in which certain advocates of the baser phases of socialism work to spread their unclean beliefs."[21]

Emanuel began collaborating with Marcet in writing stories for the *Atlantic Monthly.* When they collaborated, Emanuel usually came up with the plot and Marcet filled in the details of style and construction. What each lacked, the other supplied. She depended on his instinct and dramatic flair, and she provided the discipline and detail. They made a great writing pair and signed their productions "Mr. and Mrs. Haldeman-Julius." Marcet wrote Aunt Jane in January 1919 that her life "is such a jumble; banking, farming, babies, plots of stories, potties, rubbers, new dresses for Alice, pints and quarts . . . and heaven knows what all."[22]

In 1919 their story "Dreams and Compound Interest" appeared in the *Atlantic*. It was obviously autobiographical in nature. Janet Graham was the vice-president of a bank, and her husband was a writer. "Years spent with newspapers and magazines" had taught him how to write, and Janet was there to help "kindle" this talent "into flame." The *Atlantic*'s editor liked the story so much he asked for another, and they responded immediately with "Caught." Their hero in this story was Gordon, "the author of still unwritten masterpieces" who came from the East. Soon Gordon's ideas and ambitions were slanted to money-making.[23]

After her paternal grandmother died in April 1919, Marcet still dreamed of moving to the farm in Cedarville, but the stories in the *Atlantic* titillated her visions of writing. One publisher, Lowell Brentano, inquired about the possibility of the pair writing a novel. This sparked their interest, but the growing success of the pocket books interfered. Kopelin did not approve of the new emphasis on book publishing, so Emanuel "got the books" and showed Kopelin that in nine months he had sold $28,000 in books, while in his best year, 1915, Kopelin made $7,000 with the *Appeal to Reason*. Emanuel promised that when his Little Blue Books really began to grow "we should get $100,000 yearly."[24]

In the 15 November 1919 edition of the *New Appeal*, Emanuel announced the beginning of a new publishing program. Fifty new titles were being added to the Appeal Pocket Series, and an old tradition of subscription was being revived. At 25 cents a copy, the new series would sell for $12.50. For those who subscribed to the new series at once, the price would be only $5. Five thousand orders arrived in the first week after the ad appeared.[25]

During the Red Scare, liberals were determined to save the country from the antics of Attorney General A. Mitchell Palmer, who violated many constitutional rights in his fanatical pursuit to enforce the country's war laws. Then, too, the threat of the New York legislature to suspend five properly elected socialists provided the *New Appeal* with great opportunities for socialist propaganda in the early days of 1920. Emanuel traveled to New York City to cover the story firsthand, and his reports dominated the February issues. Meanwhile, the campaign to free Debs continued, with Upton Sinclair writing a special feature on the issue. When the socialists again nominated Debs for the presidency that May, the *Appeal* informed its readers that it would campaign for the candidate because he was unable to do this while incarcerated in Atlanta prison. Debs was the first candidate for the presidency to face this campaign obstacle.[26]

In the election, Debs lost badly to the Republican nominee, Warren Harding, and Kopelin resigned his position as editor of the *New Appeal* prior to its attempted sale to Sinclair. Sinclair was the most prominent and possibly the most probable purchaser of the *Appeal*. That March, Emanuel announced the second series of books for the pocket series. Among the important new fifty titles were *Love Letters from a Portuguese Nun*, *The Socialism of Jesus*, *How to Live 100 Years*, *How to Be an Orator*, *On the Threshold of Sex*, *Rome or Reason*, *What Every Expectant Mother Should Know*, and *Love Letters of Men and Women of Genius*. Emanuel would soon discover that books on sex had great appeal for the American reading public. In May he traveled to California to finalize the sale of the *Appeal to Reason* to Sinclair. "I feel I have put this over wonderfully well," he boasted to Marcet.[27]

Emanuel was desperate to sell the *Appeal*. He told Kopelin that Sinclair "was simply tremendous. He burns up with good ideas"—quite different from his previous evaluation of the author. "Uppy" had agreed not to sell or print books of any kind for five years. He would try to raise the purchase money by asking *Appeal* readers for donations, and Kopelin and Julius would use the *Appeal* meanwhile to support Sinclair in his effort to raise the money from subscribers.[28]

The *Appeal* book department attempted to do its part in meeting the financial crisis by holding a book sale. In July 1920 it announced a reduction in price of one-half on all books. It also offered ten famous sex books for $1 and, for one month only, some titles were reduced to 1 cent, some to 6 cents, and others to 9 cents.[29]

Haldeman and Kopelin would receive $200,000 for the newspaper and retain certain book-publishing machinery (which Emanuel needed for his books and Sinclair did not need for publishing the newspaper). Sinclair agreed to provide them with the *Appeal's* subscription list on a regular basis, including new names, and the option of repurchasing other machinery and the book inventory. Sinclair envisioned his funding to purchase the newspaper coming from special requests to the Appeal Army League.[30]

While in California, Emanuel visited some of his old haunts of the previous decade. At the Goldwyn, Lasky, and Chaplin studios he visited with Charlie Chaplin, who was filming *The Kid*. Also working there was Douglas Fairbanks, whom Emanuel did not "care for . . . at all." Fatty Arbuckle and Thomas Meaghan were present, the latter under the direction of Cecil B. DeMille, who demanded his filming be done five or six times before he would say, "That isn't too bad."

Fairbanks said to Chaplin: "Why is it when the rich sportsmen of the East—the prosperous carpet mill owners and others get out here they always run out to me while when the artists come out they always hunt up you?" Rob Wagner then interjected:

> "Doug, let me tell you a story my friend Stewart Edward White tells in one of his novels. An Easterner, I believe, went to a Western barroom (this was in the old days) and proceeded to do some big talk. He blowed all over the place, getting on the nerves of an old character seated at one of the tables. Finally the old fellow broke in with 'say, if you want to talk big why don't you say elephant?' Rob then added, 'Doug, you rush right in with elephant and you keep yelling elephant until the end. No reserve. No poise, no contrast. Cut out the elephant stuff.'"[31]

Emanuel had more problems with his Walt Whitman booklet. When the Post Office "swooped down with its complaint" and was fortified with a "statement from the United States Attorney," he wrote H. L. Mencken that there was "nothing to do but withdraw the edition," of which he had about eight thousand copies in stock. Emanuel had argued that the Post Office was permitting Mitchell Kinnerly "and other publishers to issue these very same poems." The authorities responded that those editions sold for $2 or more and thus would reach "only the well-to-do," whereas books in the pocket series cost only 10 cents and would be "within the reach of boys and girls of immature mind, and therefore should be suppressed." What an interesting interpretation of "obscenity"! The price differential made Whitman acceptable for rich adults, but obscene for poor children. Emanuel's objective in the pocket series was, of course, to make these classics available to the poor.[32]

Emanuel invited Mencken to visit their farm in Girard "if you ever get out this way." He was certain he could get "some good ideas" from Mencken for the pocket series. He also reminded the Great Debunker that the area's "white mule" was "so much better than the moonshine made in Arkansas." He was sorry that Mencken had been unable to complete the writing of "The Gist of Nietzsche," which would have been "a good title."[33]

Emanuel had forwarded a complete set of pocket series books to Mencken, as well as a copy of the novel *Dust*, which he and Marcet had recently published with Brentano's. Mencken responded that Emanuel had published "a splendid ersatz" library, "which he and his wife were currently enjoying." He believed the range in the pocket series was "astonishing" and that the only thing comparable to it was the famous Richlim Bibliothek, which sold for "20 Pfennig's apiece."[34]

Dust is the story of three generations of Wades struggling to make a living on a farm in Kansas. There are struggles against the dust, which would worsen a decade later in the Dirty Thirties, "the harshness of the lack of money and resources," and the "hard-bitten characters formed by the interplay between the environment and human nature." Marcet also contributed her views on the nature of marriage in the novel. She was upset that the dedication to "S.A.H.," her mother, was omitted, but this proved to be a minor distraction in the general excitement of publishing her first book. Emanuel proudly sent a copy to his parents with a dedication, "To Mother and Father with Deepest Love, Marcet and Emanuel."[35]

Emanuel made several promotional trips for *Dust*, and when he returned from promoting the novel in Chicago, presses for the pocket series were really humming. "Publishing House Now a Gigantic Industry," blared the *Pittsburg Sun* headline. Despite its fame as the home of the *Appeal to Reason*, many people did not know that Girard was the home of "another giant of an industry that is rapidly reaching its maturity under the capable and energetic owner and manager, Emanuel Haldeman-Julius." After just two years of publishing the pocket series, "the clatter of presses has already drowned out the deeper rumbles of the old press which still prints the *New Appeal*."[36]

As the Red Scare swept the nation, subscriptions to the *New Appeal* continued to decline. Newsprint rose in price from 10 cents to 14 cents per pound, the editors were forced to cancel the planned Debs special editions when subscriber funding was not forthcoming. The book department was forced to help, and it slashed the price of books by one-half and announced a new series of "How To" books. In early 1921, Emanuel was able to announce his plans for "The University in Print." He printed the first twelve Blue Books as a "feeler," and when they sold well he decided it was "safe to experiment further." Soon there were 50 titles, then 100, then 150, and by March 1921 he reported a total of 2 million copies of 185 titles had been sold.[37]

By this time Emanuel was reaching a far wider audience with the pocket series through widespread advertising. Full-page ads appeared in magazines and journals announcing the entire list of books at 10 cents each. When the *Literary Digest* ad man wrote in April 1921 that he had never seen the set of books to examine them or their offer, and questioned the use of headlines such as "World's Greatest Masterpieces" and "World's Most Wonderful Books," the journal refused this advertisement. Emanuel angrily accused the publisher of trying to freeze him out because his product was so cheap. He noted that "we are finding it hard to get into the magazines which are published by firms that are in the book publishing business."[38]

The *Sun*, published in Girard's neighboring town of Pittsburg, was fulsome in its praise of Emanuel's publishing program. All 205 titles, the editor noted, were printed in lots of 10,000. When a lot was depleted, 10,000 more copies were printed. An order blank was included in each advertisement, and books were ordered by number, not by title.[39]

After a year of trying to raise the necessary $200,000, Sinclair had not yet bought the *New Appeal*. On 2 July 1921, Emanuel placed a front-page ad in the *New Appeal*: "Save the *Appeal*! It must not suspend!" followed by an ultimatum that it would have to be suspended unless readers produced $25,000. This special plea worked, and in the next issue Emanuel announced that "the people had won!" In August the publishing venture was reorganized into the *New Appeal* and the book-publishing department, with Emanuel as president and Kopelin as secretary-treasurer. Then, on Christmas Day 1921, President Warren Harding released Debs and twenty-three other political prisoners and the *New Appeal* could crow about its successful crusade to free "political prisoners."[40]

With book sales booming, Emanuel needed additional printing capacity. In early 1922 he appealed to readers for a loan at 6 percent, asking for $13,000. He received $15,500. His supporters, he argued, had been fed "on slush and buncombe" but really desired "the very best in the world's literature." He purchased a new Miehle press and immediately campaigned for more loans. The money poured in, and he next purchased a Prefector press, which would enable him double his production capacity. He bought a new folding machine, and the pocket series was now going to every state in the country, as well as orders being filled from China, Japan, India, Ireland, Canada, Mexico, Brazil, and France.[41]

Emanuel had taken a primitive printing operation and changed it into a totally electric printing process. The original machinery he had acquired with the printing plant—one 12 x 18-inch job press—took many hours to produce a single copy of a Blue Book. Now his presses were capable of printing 240,000 books daily with three shifts of workers. This technological revolution meant he could mass-produce and lower his costs, and thus reduce the selling price to 5 cents, or one-fifth of its original price. It also meant that the plant was employing as many as 150 people to handle this mass production during the 1920s, and his payroll became a major factor in Girard's economic life. Although the residents rejected his political ideas and lifestyle, they welcomed his contribution to their economy.[42]

When Sinclair was finally forced to decline becoming editor of the *Appeal* because of lack of reader financial support, Emanuel announced that the newspaper would be replaced by the *Haldeman-Julius Weekly*. Emanuel decided that improvement in mankind would be achieved through "man—not in men, the individual, not the mass." In August 1922 he began an audacious plan: he would publish thirty volumes of Shakespeare for 8 cents a volume. When his plant had produced 250,000 sets of Shakespeare's works he placed advertisements in the *American Magazine*, *Saturday Evening Post*, *Cosmopolitan*, *Review of Reviews*, *Outlook*, the *Nation*, and the *New Republic*, offering all thirty volumes for $2.35. Then the Post Office dropped a bombshell on him. His advertisements were illegal, officials said, because they included a contest for a trip to Europe but were not accompanied by a full explanation of the rules. The ban would not be removed until he agreed to withdraw the contest. Emanuel would have to revise his advertisements, at a cost of $200,000.[43]

Emanuel decided to fight back. He mobilized newspaper support, and the public came to his rescue. The evening *Kansas City Star* surprised him by assisting the mobilization "wonderfully," and the morning *Kansas City Times* gave a full account of the battle. The *St. Louis Post-Dispatch* went even further by editorializing on "A Legal But Bad Ruling," insisting that Emanuel was "doing cultural work of the first magnitude" and calling him "a great businessman and one of the country's greatest educators." Emanuel even mobilized a movement under the auspices of the Girard Chamber of Commerce that voted unanimously to send a letter of protest to Washington. "I knew the public wanted a good show," he informed Marcet, "so I gave it to them." The Post Office finally capitulated to the pressure and telegraphed Emanuel to proceed "with our business in an orderly manner." "Emanuel had gotten mad," and he "enjoyed every minute of the fight."[44]

All this publicity led to increasing demands on Emanuel's time as a speaker. When he traveled to Chicago to address the Book and Play Club, Marcet wrote Jane that she would have a chance to hear him when he came to her city. The committee had asked for either Marcet or Emanuel, and "after some consultation, we decided he should be the one to go." Marcet was not certain this was a wise decision, because "as a dinner guest or at holding center stage at informal gatherings Manuel outclasses me utterly, but when it comes to a formal talk before a formal audience he does not make nearly so good an impression as myself for the simple reason that he *insists* on *reading* whatever he has to say." She added, "If you ever show him this letter I'll die."[45]

Emanuel admitted to Marcet that all was not well with his public speaking. Instead of accepting invitations to speak, he guessed "he could better serve the Republic by remaining at home and tending to my knitting." He could "get by on the lecture platform," but he did not think it was "worth the time and effort." When giving speeches put him behind in his publishing work, he would "spend a frantic half week trying to catch up" and, in the process, make "numerous hasty decisions that cause me no end of worry." He needed to concentrate on his publishing.[46]

In November 1923 a convention of professional journalists asked Emanuel to address their annual meeting at Kansas State Agricultural College. He informed his audience that mail order was the wave of the future for books. More than three-quarters of the American population lived in rural areas or small towns, he said, and they rarely traveled to a city and even more rarely entered a bookstore. Publishers had to find another way to reach this market. He had been reviewing the books in his pocket series, and the unsuccessful ones had been eliminated. Some of the books had been criticized for errors and sloppy editing, so all of them had been reedited to eliminate any errors. The list of 300 titles, he announced, "is now sound."[47]

As a result of the postwar Red Scare, the Ku Klux Klan enjoyed a rebirth in the 1920s. The revived Klan had many more targets than the old; in addition to being anti-black, the new Klan was anti-Catholic, anti-Jewish, anti-alien, anti-anything contrary to the fundamentals of the nation, whatever they decided that happened to be. The new Klan also enjoyed considerable success in many parts of the North, at one time taking control of the Indiana legislature.[48]

In the first issue of the *Haldeman-Julius Weekly*, Emanuel launched an attack against the Klan, describing it as "something slimy which had crept out of the gutter. It represents organized hatred, bigotry, maliciousness, jealousy, and cruelty. It is living proof that America is not a civilized country." Currently, the Klan was for "100 percent Americanism." When they arrived in Canada it would become "100 percent Canadianism." He defended blacks who had been kicked into the gutter, where "this slimy ooze" wanted them to stay. Emanuel was not surprised to hear that the new movement was led by Protestant ministers. Interestingly, for about the first time in his life he had praise for the Catholic Church because of its "sane" perspective on the Klan issue. Of course, the Catholic Church was responding to the attack by the Klan on itself.[49]

In almost all his publications, Emanuel included a picture of himself stylishly dressed in a double-breasted suit, a confident, faint smile in the corners of his mouth. He was surprised when people told him he looked like Edward G. Robinson in this pose. He was a salesman, he informed the public, trying to sell people on the idea of acquiring knowledge. He wanted to sell culture, and to do so he had to associate his books with "position, respectability, money."[50]

His new weekly quickly and easily replaced the old *Appeal to Reason*. He wrote much of each issue, expressing his opinion on whatever popped into his mind, but usually it was connected with a theme or a news item. His column "What the Editor Is Thinking About" often spilled over several pages. His writing was direct, conversational, and covered almost everything, because he knew about almost everything and was rarely without an opinion on any topic. He used the *Weekly* to divulge his publishing plans and, especially, to advertise his books. He soon expanded the paper from four to eight pages and included a column by Upton Sinclair, Julius Nortizen's "New York Letter," and articles by the Arkansas editor and publisher Charles H. Finger. Emanuel also used the *Weekly* to test out various advertisements. This normally included a list of book titles, a price, and an order blank that used numbers rather than titles, which made ordering nearly fool-proof.[51]

In May 1923, Emanuel sought to make the acquaintance of Will Durant for the purpose of signing him to write for the *Weekly*. He heard that the philosopher would be in Kansas City on a certain date, so he drove up there to meet him. He had met Durant during World War I and was impressed with his nontechnical approach to the study of philosophy. Durant, in turn, liked Emanuel's ideas, and he agreed to write a series of essays on Plato, Aristotle, Socrates, Nietzsche, Bacon, Voltaire, Kant, Spinoza, Schopenhauer, Spencer, Dewey, Santayana, and Bertrand Russell. They would be introduced through the pocket series. Eventually they would be collected as the highly successful *Story of Philosophy*.[52]

Emanuel had begun his pocket series with a few classics that were in the public domain, then acquired a few titles on a mixture of topics, and finally bought some titles and paid the authors, not a royalty, but a flat fee of $25 or $50. Selections in the third category were usually based on what the public wanted. This was determined by discussions with mechanics and extending upward through the fringes of the professional classes, or as he put it, "the common people."[53]

In March 1923, Emanuel promised in the *Weekly* that when sales reached the correct height he would be able to lower the price to 5 cents per book. Had sales gone up 500 percent in the test period? He subsequently reported that sales had reached almost 6 million copies, or about 60 percent that month, and as long as the volume of sales justified it, the price would remain at 5 cents. At this point *Publisher's Weekly* announced that Emanuel had built up the greatest publishing business ever in existence, from the standpoint of quantity.[54]

In May 1923 Emanuel wrote the Girard Chamber of Commerce to request a loan for expansion of his facilities. His company owned the lot next to his current plant, and he wanted to construct on it a building measuring 100 by 200 feet. The Truscan Steel Company submitted a bid for $35,000, which would include a heating plant, wiring, and so forth. It was "essential," he insisted, that work on it begin immediately so it could be completed in eighty or ninety days. He was asking the banks of Girard to loan his company this amount for twelve to eighteen months at 6 percent interest, which would begin when his company began to draw on the loan. His present assets were "clear in every sense of the word," but he needed the additional space, and of course, the expansion would mean additional jobs to fill at Girard's largest employer.[55]

In September 1923 he announced in the *Weekly* a new program that would break all previous printing records. Volume would double, he said, from 40,000 to 80,000 books per day. The plant had been expanded, and this meant the addition of a new shift. A new means must be found to help market this massive production, and he proposed Little Blue Book Shoppes as the solution. He had tapped the rural market through advertising in his weekly, and now he needed to expand into the vast urban populations. He proposed that, for a $1,000 franchise fee, an investor could receive an exclusive right to sell Little Blue Books in a particular city for one year, subject to renewal. The investor would receive 33,333 five-cent books for stock, 5,000 circulars, a free front-page ad in the *Weekly*, 300 copies of the publications carrying the ads, a complete list of Haldeman-Julius customers living in that area, and a guaranteed discount of 40 percent on all future Little Blue Book purchases. Each franchise must carry a complete stock of Little Blue Books and could sell no books other than those published by the Haldeman-Julius Company.

Emanuel intended to blanket the nation by making the Little Blue Books available everywhere. In counties that lacked a city with a population of 50,000, one could become an "agent" by purchasing a franchise for $300 to make the books available. Train and bus stations would provide vending machines for the books, and, of course, his mail-order business would make the Little Blue Books accessible everywhere.[56]

He reported to Marcet that, with this money coming in, he had paid all their bills and was "tackling" certain notes at the bank. He believed that he would be completely free of debt by the summer of 1924.[57]

Austin A. Breed of Cincinnati was the first retailer to buy a franchise. His comments on his experience appeared in the *Weekly* on 27 October 1923. Breed's first rule was to have crowds passing by the front window—"no matter how high the rent." His neighborhood was not "tough," nor was it a "toney" one. The store set out two racks of books for enticement, and he thought the stealing was "negligible." The first shipment was already sold out on the first weekend. The franchise concept was so successful that in May 1924 the Haldeman-Julius Company lowered its franchise price to $500, and 16,666 books instead of 33,333. At that time the *Weekly* advertised thirty-nine major cities that still had available franchises.[58]

Roberta Ray, reporter for *Publishers Weekly*, visited Breed's Cincinnati store and observed that Haldeman-Julius, who prided himself on being called "The Henry Ford of Literature," could now claim status as a "Ford-Woolworth" because of "situating the Little Blue Books in a commercial

spectrum between the Model T and the nation's Five-and-Dime Store."
"The store was painted blue inside and out . . . so blue, in fact, that it
becomes a trifle monotonous. A crowd is usually elbowing before to get
a good look at the book titles, and so the purpose of all display windows
has been attained."[59]

By July 1924 there were franchises in New York, Brooklyn, Chicago,
Philadelphia, Detroit, Cleveland, St. Louis, Pittsburgh, Washington
DC, Newark, Cincinnati, Atlanta, Birmingham, Atlantic City, and Montreal. While in Chicago for the opening of a Little Blue Book store he
met Morris Fishbein, editor of the *Journal of the American Medical
Association*. Fishbein was also the author of *Pasteur: The Man and His
Work*, a pocket book in a medical series. The doctor took Emanuel to his
home to meet Harry Hansen, editor of the *Chicago Daily News*. Hansen
promised that his long-overdue manuscript on Carl Sandburg would
soon be ready. Emanuel also met Ben Hecht and decided to add a few
of his titles to the series. Wherever Emanuel traveled, he was ready to
sign up new authors for the Little Blue Book series because the titles
and authors were so ubiquitous.[60]

Emanuel addressed the Writers' Guild meeting at the University of
Missouri convention in May 1923. The relationship between writers
and publishers is supposed to be "a sort of armed neutrality," he told his
listeners, "but this position, I find, is held by those who neither write nor
publish." He was different, he told the group, because he did both, and
he liked "all kinds of writers because I have done all kinds of writing."
Writers write to be read, and his pocket books offered writers "the largest
audience in all the history of literature." From Homer to H. G. Wells, he
insisted, "the art of writing has never been so closely related to the great
multitudes of human beings that read." When a writer got an assignment,
he knew that "the millions of readers of the pocket series are definitely
interested in the subject about which he will write."[61]

The summer of 1924 found Josephine, who now went by "Joey," on
the farm in Cedarville. By this time, Mary Fry and Marcet had not only
resolved the financial problems but had become the best of friends. Marcet's
grandmother had passed away in 1919, and Mary was now taking care of

the family farm. Marcet wrote Mary that it would be good to separate Joey and Alice for a while, because Joey, now a teenager, tended to become too "motherly" with the youngster and was also carrying on "a romance with a Girard boy." Joey was "far behind in her school work," and at Cedarville she "seemed to be trying to catch up." Joey wrote Marcet that they had fun with a Halloween party and that Mary gave a party for Joey and her friends on Christmas night.[62]

Joey was eager to return to Girard the next summer, but she had to wait because Marcet had to have breast cancer surgery. By the end of July 1925, however, Marcet believed she had recovered sufficiently to travel to Dayton, Tennessee, to accompany Emanuel to the Scopes trial. Emanuel was riding high that summer as the pocket series was selling by the hundreds of thousands, and Marcet was feeling so positive about Emanuel that she made an agreement with him that she would come to regret. She turned all her assets over to him, and he promised to pay her $400 weekly for the maintenance of the children and their home. He also put her on salary for the writing she was doing for him. Unfortunately, there was no provision in the agreement for inflation or other exigencies.[63]

After eight years of marriage, Marcet was still capable of evaluating her husband objectively. In 1924 she wrote that he was "a very curious, and at times, baffling bundle of contradictions. . . . Almost but not quite his is a split personality. . . . Altogether I find him one of the most thoughtless, but most consolingly lovable, most exasperatingly egocentric, but pride-stirringly efficient of men."[64]

At a meeting of the National Association of Publishers at the Waldorf on 20 January 1926, Professor Edouard Lindeman of the New York School of Social Research gave an address deploring what he termed the "Penny Classics." Emanuel's response was that his first two Little Blue Books were first issued as pamphlets, just as the first folios of Shakespeare were. He refused to set high prices, as other publishers did, preferring to publish the best literature for the so-called masses. That, he asserted, made him an outcast "in the eyes of these dollar-snatchers."[65]

Activities at the office were beginning to get hectic for Emanuel. In 1925 he announced a new publication venture. Emanuel loved startling headlines, and he created one with this new venture. Harold Ross, one of the founders of the *New Yorker* and the husband of one of Marcet's longtime Girard friends, Jane Grant, published a highly favorable essay in the regular "Profiles" section of the journal. The headline read, "After June 30, the Deluge." In this essay Emanuel told the author that "after June 3, I quit." By this he meant that he would concentrate on his new endeavor, but it sounded more sensational to his followers, suggesting to them that he would quit publishing Little Blue Books.[66]

Emanuel's plan was to start a new company that would publish Big Blue Books. He would charge 50 cents apiece, but, like the Little Blue Books previously, these would be reduced in price to 25 cents once the venture was established and the list grew. Stock at $100 per share would be sold to the public to raise the necessary capital. "Instead of going it alone as he did with the Little Blue books," he explained, "I should allow friends of my work to join with me." This venture meant more work for him, but he had recruited Lloyd E. Smith as an assistant. In addition, in early May 1926 he had introduced Joseph McCabe to his reading audience. McCabe was a former monk and a leading agnostic and freethinker from London. Emanuel was now ready to expand his list of offerings in these categories, and McCabe could supply numerous manuscripts.[67]

Emanuel seemed constantly to have difficulty supporting his family financially, and at this point Marcet was also facing a money crisis. She had to pay $125 to replace the kitchen stove, and she had racked up more than the usual bills during the Christmas season. She felt compelled to write Emanuel for a $300 loan. She promised to repay it at $50 weekly. The miserly Emanuel would demonstrate more than once his unwillingness to provide her with assistance beyond what they agreed to in 1925, but this necessity for the kitchen would appear to fall under the category of maintaining the family household. On the other hand, he apparently had no qualms about paying $6,309 for a custom Lincoln Coupe in May 1926. Four hundred dollars weekly seemed like a fabulous sum, but the Haldeman-Juliuses had an extravagant lifestyle with exotic foods, numerous guests, and expensive tastes.[68]

Part of this lifestyle included Emanuel's unique demands. At his office or at home, "except for the teary-eyed outbursts of belly laughter among friends or relatives," according to Marcet, Emanuel was all work, preoccupied with ideas and writing. He never hummed, or whistled, or sang, but seemed to be in a perpetual state of "opaque thoughtfulness" or could block out his surroundings or other people. Money, Emanuel admitted, "came easily—almost too easily. I never have to give much thought to money." He was totally engrossed in his books, his publications. Money was always easily available to him during the Roaring Twenties, because he owned "a lot of presses that turn out millions of little books that sell at the price that Wrigley charges for his gum." Marcet, at the same time, often was hard pressed to make ends meet on the amount Emanuel gave her.[69]

Marcet felt a strong ambivalence toward her husband. Obviously, he was domineering and selfish, yet she deeply loved him and respected his abilities. Her sheltered early life in Girard, her puritanical sense of duty, and her feeling of intellectual inferiority toward Emanuel translated into a need of purpose and approval in her life. Like Aunt Jane, Marcet, while enjoying "a strong liberal and liberated personality," also possessed a fragile psyche. As she once wrote Emanuel, "Honey . . . everyone admires you so—and justly. You are the most wonderful man I know—because you are gifted in so many ways." She loved and respected him so deeply that she could never deny him anything, no matter how badly he hurt her.[70]

While his marriage was beginning to unravel, Emanuel was quite busy bringing to fruition his *Quarterly*, which he considered his publishing masterpiece. Getting it ready for a fall 1926 publication "was a demanding task." He was ready to spare no effort to ensure its success and asked several of his favorite authors—Joseph McCabe, Nelson Antrim Crawford, Clement Wood—to submit pieces for it. It was to be "the biggest, the most worthwhile thing I ever did." It was an attractive production on fine-grade, egg-shell paper, well illustrated with photographs and sketches and featuring articles by Marcet, Goldberg, McCabe, Crawford, and Wood. This would be "the crowning glory" of his publishing career.[71]

During the Roaring Twenties, Tennessee was one of several southern states that enacted various laws prohibited the teaching of the theory of evolution in public schools. High school biology teacher and football coach

John Scopes of Dayton offered to test the law as sort of a joke among friends, but when he was arrested in May 1925 it became very serious. William Jennings Bryan came to Dayton to lead the prosecution, while Clarence Darrow appeared for the defense. Soon the entire nation's attention was focused on this tiny mountain town, with both sides inflaming their supporters. Calling the case "Superstition versus Science in the Hills of Tennessee," Emanuel wrote in the *Weekly* that Scopes was being "lynched" and that Judge John T. Ralston was "the director of mob law," "the avowed enemy of science and education," and "the brazen tool of the Bryans who seek to crush scientific knowledge and progress."[72]

The Haldeman-Juliuses were frustrated because one of the jurors could not read or write. The other eleven were in their box only three hours for the first week, and freely admitted they knew nothing about the theory of evolution. Darrow brought in "nationally known experts" on evolution, but Judge Ralston refused to allow them to testify on the grounds that the law against teaching the theory of evolution was not on trial. Scopes had admitted he broke the law by teaching the theory of evolution in a public school. Bryan refused to be educated and, instead, offered himself as a renowned expert on the Bible. Darrow decided to take advantage of this expertise and put him on the stand. Bryan believed in a literal interpretation of the Bible, and Darrow got him to state that God punished the serpent by forcing him to crawl around on his belly as a punishment. Darrow then asked him the obvious question: How did the snake get around before that edict? The state's attorney general was quoted as saying that Scopes "does not deserve a chance because he taught doctrine that contradicted the Bible." Darrow noted that his only possibility for victory lay in appealing the verdict to a higher court. The state was determined this would not happen ,and when the trial was over, Scopes paid his fine of $100 and that was the end of it.[73]

Marcet wrote an account of her reaction to the trial, and a Clinton, Oklahoma, lawyer composed a response to her essay. He considered her article "intensely interesting" and "one of the best pieces of writing I have ever read. It is in many ways a masterpiece." But he believed she "spoiled that excellent Scopes write-up by your prejudice and ignorance of courts and judges." The writer thought she was too impressed with Darrow, who did no more in the trial than "any Tennessee lawyer of good standing could not have duplicated." Darrow was "a brilliant lawyer," the attorney noted, but he "didn't have a chance to show it in the Scopes case."[74]

Following the trial, the Haldeman-Juliuses invited Darrow and his wife to the farm in Girard. Marcet had heard about the celebrated defense attorney when she visited Hull House as a little girl. Now she was entertaining the great man and his wife in her home. After several conversations she concluded that he sounded like "a mellow pessimist, yet an optimist by nature, edged with scornful wit. Three of his witticisms were burned in her memory: if you take the bunk out of people, what do you have left? You can Fordize literature but you can't Fordize intelligence; and to anyone who asked him if he thought right was on his side—what is right but power?"[75]

Yet there was a practical side to the man. When in a courtroom in the mountains of Tennessee, she noted, his "trousers hung loosely and were not too well pressed, while his galluses were very much in evidence." It was swelteringly hot, and his sleeves were often rolled up before the judge adjourned the session to the courtyard lawn. Darrow easily adjusted to the Haldeman-Julius routine in their home, and the children enjoyed his lovable qualities.

Marcet saw Darrow in action again in Detroit a year later when he defended Henry Sweet, who was accused of murder in helping his brother, Dr. Ossian H. Sweet, defend his house from attacks in a predominantly white neighborhood. The Sweets "and a number of other Negroes" were charged with murder. A previous trial had resulted in a hung jury. Darrow lined up some key people for Marcet to interview for background and suggested she stay in the same hotel at which he and his wife were registered. Nine-year-old Alice stayed with her during the trial. Here in Detroit she saw a completely different Darrow from the lawyer in Dayton. In Tennessee he was ready to do battle with the cosmopolitan lawyers of the big city. Here he showed Marcet "what an adroit master of all the tactics of a legal battle" he was. She concluded that he was at his best when he was "fighting for someone's liberty or life," and the result in this case was "a sweeping victory" for the Sweets and their friends. Walter White, assistant secretary of the National Association for the Advancement of Colored People, wrote her that she had presented "a magnificent pen picture" of the trial.

Upton Sinclair was another visitor to the farm who was unfamiliar to Marcet, so Emanuel gave her his manuscript for *The Brass Check* so she could become familiar with his writing style. By the time she finished it she was fascinated with the author. She knew he was a socialist, but she had no insight into his abilities as a social critic. Reading *The Brass Check* was "a revelation" to her where "the theme of social justice illuminated it like a flame." She "realized with a stab of pain how helpless anyone is when in the grip of wealthy and powerful newspapers." This roused her to something like a fury of sympathy "for the victims of captive journalism." Thus Marcet was eager to greet Sinclair when he visited so that she could acquire firsthand impressions of him.

She found him the easiest of persons to entertain, "so gracious that one was aware, not of graciousness but merely of ease." At that time the Haldeman-Juliuses were building a pond in their pasture. The intent was to keep the neighborhood youngsters busy with swimming during the summer months and with skating parties in the winter. Sinclair gave them some insight on how better to approach the task, then "with a twinkle in his eye" asked if they were on good terms with their neighbors. If not, come summer and the mosquitoes the pond would attract, both the children and the Haldeman-Juliuses "might all be in high disfavor." Sinclair's practical social mind saw the menace of the mosquitoes as the outstanding question in the situation. As a result of his warning, "at the right moment each summer we pour oil on the water" to kill the mosquitoes.[76]

Charles Finger of Fayetteville, Arkansas, publisher of the magazine *All's Well*, had once described Emanuel as follows:

In shirtsleeves, he sits at a desk, and the desk is littered with a constantly changing mass of papers—constantly changing because there is a never-ending stream of girls and men coming and going, bringing and taking letters, checks, proofs, books, pictures. So the picture of Julius as a pleasantly smiling young man in faultless attire, the picture of the advertisements is altogether misleading. . . . He is constantly in motion. . . . His business has burst through the shell as a chick will break through the egg.[77]

Finger was also a guest at the farm that evening. He fancied himself something of an English squire to the point that one could hear "the youiching of the hounds and the sounding of the horns and the clinking of tankards of ale when 'Squire' Finger hove in sight." Finger was always a gentleman, but "with more than a suspicion of bluster and bluntness in his manner when slightly aroused." The duel of words between Finger and Sinclair that evening was not memorable, but Finger made allusion to his adventures in Patagonia, which gave him an excuse to extol the greatness of the English Empire. This, of course, provoked an outburst from Sinclair, whose "manner in argument is quiet, controlled, and rapier-like." Marcet concluded that, of the two, Sinclair had "thought out his position far more carefully than Finger had," and the former quickly turned the conversation to socialism. Then, the clash with "the individualism of Finger was even more resounding."

Sometime later Sinclair wired Marcet, requesting she accompany him to Boston. He was then embroiled with authorities there over his novel dealing with the Sacco-Vanzetti case. She was unable to accept his invitation, though, because she was on another assignment for the Haldeman-Julius establishment. When she went on tour in Russia later, Sinclair almost overwhelmed her letters of introduction to Russians, as he was the "most widely read foreign author" there. Marcet believed Sinclair was a great pamphleteer, ranking with Voltaire, Swift, and Paine. Because Emanuel preferred to call him "Uppy, the entire Haldeman-Julius family casually adopted" the nickname.[78]

In the spring of 1927 the Haldeman-Juliuses drove some fifty miles to Chanute to hear the opera star Lawrence Tibbett sing in concert. This was a special treat for Emanuel, as music, according to Marcet, was "his finest, truest bond with life. Its strains seemed to knit up within him all the elements of his character and desire, bringing them into harmony." Tibbett "satisfied his tone hunger," Marcet reported, because he was "the romantic hero of grand opera, an impudent gamin and a rollicking laborer." A family friend invited them to an informal after-concert dinner where Tibbett was the guest of honor. He and Emanuel soon discovered they had much in common—an appreciation of both music and books. Soon the question arose, why not go over to the farm? Several carloads of fun-lovers were soon on their way. Marcet had the foresight to call Joey and warn her of the impending invasion.

After a "few highballs circulated" everyone was merry, but no one appeared to be intoxicated. The recreation room had a stage at one end that the children used for their shows. Joey was with Tibbett when he picked up one of the half-covers of a butter churn. Tibbett's accompanist caught the gaiety of the moment and accompanied them on the piano while Tibbett and Joey staged an impromptu Dutch-like dance to the sport of butter. This noise, of course, wakened the neighborhood, as it did a flock of geese, and the group saluted the dawn as they often did. All guests trooped down to the barn, which was fragrant with hay and the smell of cows and horses. Tibbett and others tried to chin themselves on low-hung rafters. Finally Marcet got them all in bed, where they slept until 11:00 when she and the cook prepared a hearty breakfast of eggs, bacon, and butter "all from our own farm, which vanished steadily." Too often an artist's personality changes when away from the floodlights, but in Tibbett's case he proved to be as charming in his romp in the barn and his "dance of mischief" on the little stage as on the large stage and "his voice range out gloriously across our fields and pasture."[79]

Just before her trip to Russia, Marcet met Anna Louis Strong, Caroline A. Lowe had told Marcet about her. Caroline, a former teacher, was a lawyer and a recruiter for the Socialist Party in southeast Kansas and Oklahoma. Strong and Lowe had known each other in Washington State, where they both had opposed World War I. Lowe had arranged for Strong to come to Pittsburg State University to lecture on the Soviet Union. She had lived in Moscow during the Revolution, and upon John Reed's death she had become the chief interpreter of the Soviet Union to the American people. That day Strong talked of Leon Trotsky as "the biggest man I have ever met anywhere." She was able to convince this southeast Kansas audience that this struggling Soviet government had great possibilities. The next day Caroline and Anna came to Girard for lunch. Marcet's discussions with Strong helped convince her that she should visit Russia and make up her own mind about the Soviet system through personal observation. Strong was a founder and currently an editor of the *Moscow News*, an English-language newspaper, and was a major contact for Marcet on her trip to the Soviet Union.[80]

Nelson Antrim Crawford was another prominent Kansan befriended by Emanuel. Crawford early decided on a career in the Episcopal priesthood, but his first love proved to be literature, and eventually he taught English and journalism at Kansas State Agricultural College. He met the Haldeman-Juliuses at a meeting of the Kansas Authors Club in 1920. Emanuel quickly recruited him to edit several Little Blue Books of poetry. In 1924 President Calvin Coolidge appointed William Jardine, president of Kansas State Agricultural College, as secretary of the Department of Agriculture, and Jardine named Crawford as the department's first director of public information. At this point Crawford asked one of his students, Muriel Shaver, to marry him, and they invited a handful of friends, including the Haldeman-Juliuses, to the wedding in Kansas City in 1925. The great agnostic found the church service confusing. "It's incredible," Emanuel announced to Marcet. "What does he [Antrim] see in all that rigmarole, that mumbo-jumbo, that witch doctor business." How could it "bamboozle a brilliant fellow like Crawford?" Antrim accepted their bottle of Scotch as a wedding present, then the couple raced back to Manhattan, he to finish teaching for the semester, she to complete her degree. The couple then moved to the nation's capital, along with Milton Eisenhower, to take up their appointive duties under Secretary Jardine. Crawford could soon count H. L. Mencken among his literary admirers when the latter's *American Mercury* carried a shortened version of *A Man of Learning* as well as several of his short stories.

In July 1925, following the Scopes trial, Emanuel and Marcet traveled to New York City for a vacation. While there they had dinner with Jane Grant, an old friend of Marcet's from Girard, and her husband, Harold Ross, one of the founders of the *New Yorker*. Emanuel also met with M.

Lincoln Schuster of the publishing firm Simon and Schuster. This firm gained notoriety and success early in the decade of the 1920s by exploiting the crossword puzzle craze that swept the country with a book of puzzles. The two had lunch at the Breevort, and Schuster told Emanuel he was not interested in mass production of books but only in producing a few good ones. He asked Emanuel for book suggestions, and he recommended bringing out a good, well-written history of philosophy. Who is to write it? "There are not many Will Durants," Emanuel responded. The more Emanuel thought about Schuster's query, the more he was convinced Durant was the writer they sought. How about printing Durant's fifteen Little Blue Books on philosophy as one volume? Schuster liked the idea, and one year later *The Story of Philosophy* appeared. It proved to be a bestseller. Durant wrote Emanuel:

> I owe you two great debts: first, you took the initial chance on me and had the unprecedented courage of putting philosophy into a maga-zine and into your booklets and second that you secured Simon and Schuster as publishers of my book. They have done a fine job; and like yourself they have turned out to be not merely publishers, but scholars and friends.[81]

It is hard to believe that Marcet and Emanuel undertook all this activity only a few months after Marcet had undergone a serious operation for breast cancer. That it was serious is indicated in a note to Alice and Henry regarding it. "If anything should happen to mother," she wrote, "remember nothing is so hard as it seems, and that to be kind and tender to others is the whole secret of happiness. Bo-Peep."[82]

Before they left for Dayton, her operation prompted the couple to write new wills. Marcet left the Cedarville farm to Alice and Henry and to any other children born to her, "share and share alike." This sharing included her husband, over and above a $30,000 equity or interest that belonged to her children, because she had already conveyed to Emanuel a good deal of her estate. The Girard farm she left to her husband and children. Because she had already given Emanuel a good deal of money, she left her bonds, securities, and cash to Alice and Henry. But she left any furniture, jewels, china, silver, and other personal effects to her husband and children, "share and share alike." Emanuel's will left all his property, real and personal, to Marcet and appointed her as his estate's executor. He also consented to pay her $100 weekly for maintenance of the home and family and all real and personal taxes on the farm at Girard. He agreed to pay all outstanding notes and obligations of Marcet made prior to the agreement. She resolved her financial problem by becoming completely dependent on Emanuel, something she would come to regret deeply during the Great Depression.[83]

On 30 July 1925, his thirty-sixth birthday, Emanuel took a moment to reflect on his life. He had "health, wealth, two country homes, three cars, two beautiful children, success as a publisher, editor, and writer, and my name in the papers." It was wonderful to be married to Marcet, and he would marry her all over again because it was great to have such a woman who was "so everlastingly ready to forget herself for the children and their father." But he was tired of being perpetually in debt. With such high sales one would think his financial sheet would be in good shape, but with his tiny profit margin he had to keep running to stand still financially. With his franchise sales, however, he hoped to pay off all accumulated debts and some of the notes at the bank.[84]

Louis Kopelin had been dissatisfied with Emanuel's dominance of their financial relationship for some time. He had shared in the satisfaction and rewards of the book department, but his opinions were listened to less and less every year. He had watched his *Appeal* slowly die, to be replaced with the *Haldeman-Julius Weekly* under the editorship of Emanuel, and he now found himself in the position of business manager. With Marcet no longer active in the bank, Kopelin and Oscar Shaeffer sold their shares in the bank to the rival bank in Girard, thus, in effect, creating a merger. This ended the Haldeman banking interests in Girard in the fall of 1925. Emanuel used Marcet's assets to buy Kopelin's interest in the Haldeman-Julius Company. Kopelin left Girard for New York City where he could ply his expertise in editing. Again, Emanuel found himself as sole owner and manager of the Haldeman-Julius Company.[85]

While they resolved their financial differences, Marcet and Emanuel faced a more basic problem than money. When they got married they had agreed not to interfere with each other's personal lives. The difficulty lay in Emanuel having an eye that tended to stray toward members of the opposite sex, especially the pretty ones.

His great pleasure in life was to race through the countryside in his custom-built Lincoln coupe with its black and orange wheels. He also loved to motor 120 miles to Kansas City to spend the night with a lady friend in conversation, good food, and the theater. Or to Joplin or Tulsa. But after eight years of marriage and these weekend flings, Emanuel was forced to cast an ever wider net to find women to take on these trips. He seemed to be exercising his prerogative more and more frequently, and when it was with Girard women it was causing increasing embarrassment for Marcet in her hometown, discreet as he might try to be. Local pundits came to believe he relished sex much like they enjoyed a good cup of coffee. As his reputation as a womanizer grew, she was becoming less and less willing to abide by their marriage agreement. "Never one to be denied anything he really wanted, Manuel demanded his absolute freedom at any cost as he went along his merry way."[86]

Finally, she wrote him in desperation in May 1924:

Manuel, there is just one thing I want to say to you and I want to say it just as simply as possible. You have your own life to live and must decide for yourself—as I must—what is right or wrong. I don't want to hamper you or make you feel tied in any way and—if you want me to—I am going to stay with you through everything. But, dear, I think you will understand that I cannot keep my own self-respect if I let you come to me from other women or caress me with the thought in my mind that even so you caress young girls. I should be no better than the fast women themselves and by sanctioning the others I should be truly culpable.

Maybe, Emanuel, you feel that you have put all this behind you. Maybe in your heart there are only deep regrets. If this is so, you will find in mine only forgiveness and love. You don't need to say so in words, dear. Or you don't need to say that you want to feel perfectly free—perhaps your very soul needs that sense of utter freedom. I can understand that, Emanuel, and I am not judging you—believe me.

But I cannot and will not share you. My humiliation in my own eyes, and in the eyes of Alice and Henry later, would be too profound. I could not bear it. I am proud, Emanuel, and already I have suffered past belief. I have burned and bled with the consciousness of insult and outrage. But that is that. . . .

I will wait for you, my darling—a year, five years, the rest of my life, until you are quite tired of all the others, of variety itself and of unripe youth, until you long for me with a deep aching hunger for the peace and comfort that a man can find, Emanuel, only in his wife. If ever you do come to me again it must be with a pledge in your heart of hearts that never again will you be unfaithful to me.

Meanwhile I shall try, in all sincerity, not to criticize you for whatever you do—for love comes and goes and cannot be bound by promises—nor even created by earnest wish. It is not your fault if you have lost yours for me.

And I know that you have deep—and perhaps just—resentments of your own. I can only say that whereas last year I was planning to spend—to make bills and debt, since the first day of 1924 my one unfaltering determination and effort has been to catch up—to pay my bills and debts.

Yet full of resentments and mutual mistrust as we are, aren't we both big enough—and wise enough—to cast aside all recriminations—even in thought? I, for one, Emanuel, intend on the eve of our ninth year of marriage to gather together all my precious, beautiful memories of you—and they are so many—and to cleanse my heart of all lurking grudges.[87]

We do not know Emanuel's reaction to this ultimatum, but it was probably one of indifference or disdain, as he took her for granted and refused to reform himself.

By this time Emanuel had developed the following daily procedure: Each morning, after thumbing through bundles of mail orders piled on the big office desk, he would hurry into his office, slam the door, sprawl on his couch, and devour the *Wall Street Journal* and the *New York Times*. He demanded industry and accuracy from his employees. Known to be a firm disciplinarian, he tolerated no nonsense, and scuttlebutt was that he would fire you at the drop of a hat. As success eased the pressures, he became more relaxed and compassionate toward his employees. Smitten with self-importance brought about by national reputation, and not without vanity, he seemingly developed an imperious air that did not sit well with the humble folk of Girard, who stood in schoolboy awe of him; yet they disliked him for no valid reason except that he was an upstart from back east who had married the richest girl in town. The fact that his publishing business had turned Girard from a third-class Post Office into a first-class one with door-to-door delivery was unappreciatively taken for granted.

His office was a noisy, busy place, so he made certain at home that he enjoyed lots of peace and quiet. There was no doubt that he dominated the household. Usually rising at 7:30 on weekdays, he would turn on his record player to alert the cook to begin preparing his breakfast. Then he would shave and shower to the accompaniment of classical music. Then breakfast and off to work. He arrived in the driveway at 5:00 p.m. sharp, and all noise must then cease and all playmates scatter for home. Dinner was downstairs with the family gathered around the dinner table that Aunt Jane had given the two for a wedding present.

The library was his sanctuary, and others could intrude only upon invitation. Involved in their own friends and affairs, Emanuel and Marcet could pursue their own interests. He enjoyed a challenging game of chess in the evening or a game of Parcheesi with Alice or an inspection of Henry's projects. He enjoyed horseback riding until a horse fell on him and broke his leg. His love of animals precluded enjoying hunting or fishing.

Emanuel was well aware of his stunning national reputation as a great publisher of books, and he gloried in it. But people did things his way, including family.

FIG. 1. Emanuel Haldeman-Julius at the typewriter, 1925. Coll 13, B9, F449, Emanuel Haldeman-Julius Collection, Axe Library, Pittsburg State University, Pittsburg, Kansas.

FIGS. 2 & 3. Emanuel and Marcet Haldeman–Julius. Coll 13, B9, F452,
Emanuel Haldeman-Julius Collection, Axe Library, Pittsburg State University,
Pittsburg, Kansas.

FIG. 4. Emanuel Haldeman-Julius and his Little Blue Books, 1947. Coll 13, B9, F450, Emanuel Haldeman-Julius Collection, Axe Library, Pittsburg State University, Pittsburg, Kansas.

FIG. 5. Emanuel Haldeman-Julius. Coll 13, B9, F449, Emanuel Haldeman-Julius Collection, Axe Library, Pittsburg State University, Pittsburg, Kansas.

FIG. 6. Emanuel and his sister Rose. Coll 13, B9, F450, Emanuel Haldeman-Julius Collection, Axe Library, Pittsburg State University, Pittsburg, Kansas.

FIG. 7. Haldeman-Julius home in Girard, Kansas. Photo courtesy Marilyn Lee, 2013.

FIG. 8. Swimming pool where Emanuel was found dead. Photo courtesy Marilyn Lee, 2013.

FIG. 9. Building in downtown Girard that Emanuel Haldeman-Julius first used for his publishing operation. Photo courtesy Marilyn Lee, 2013.

5

A CORNUCOPIA OF BOOKS AND EVENTS, 1923–1928

Emanuel had a "hospital" for "sick" books where he "doctored" them back to healthy ones, sometimes for content, often merely for title change. Theophile Gautier's *Golden Fleece* was one of the first to go to the hospital. Emanuel changed its title to *The Quest for a Blonde Mistress*, which was quite descriptive of the content. Under its old title it sold 6,000 copies in 1925; the next year, with its new title, it sold 50,000. Molière's play *Les precious ridicules* was translated to *The Ridiculous Women* and sold well. Jack London's *Tales of the White Silence* was helped immensely when the title was altered to *Tales of the Big Snow*. *The King Enjoys Himself* sold 8,000 copies, but when the title was changed to *None But the King Shall Enjoy This Woman*, sales jumped to 34,000. Likewise, Wilde's *Pen Pencil and Poison* sold 5,000 copies, but with its new title, *The Story of a Notorious Criminal*, sales rocketed to 15,800. Clement Wood's *Casanova and His Lovers* should have been a bestseller, but it was not until its title was changed to *Casanova, History's Greatest Lover*. Emanuel had two recommendations for editors: first, make the title descriptive of the book, and second, make the title distinctive. A number of books surprised Emanuel along the way. Marcet's *Story of a Southern Lynching* became a top seller, as did Leo Markum's *A Dictionary of Geographic Names*.

Some writers were disturbed over Emanuel's propensity for changing titles of books. A writer for the *San Francisco Argonaut* considered this as "effrontery," "vulgarity," and "indifference to the standards of common honesty." He recommended that Emanuel change the title of his *The*

First One Hundred Million to *Sewer Sex for the First One Hundred Million Morons*, since this would make it sell like "hotcakes."

Then there were Emanuel's books. "For years," he admitted, "it's been a standard joke around the office that any book carrying my name is bound to be a poor seller." "It was true," he said, he had written a series for years for the *American Freeman* titled "Questions and Answers" on a multitude of topics. He gathered these essays of thirteen years into twenty-seven volumes with the same title, and they never sold well. In fact, he had to give sets away as a premium for those subscribing to the *American Freeman*. He had printed 5,500 copies of each volume, and "after about thirteen years there are still copies of them in stock."[1]

The Little Blue Books he wrote were not spectacular sellers either, but that did not "discourage" him, since he wrote because he liked "to do the work and thumbs down from the public can't deter me." Someday he hoped to find the formula for writing a bestseller, but until then he had "to be content with small editions of my own works." Then, a person in the press room production records completed an up-to-date analysis on the sales of his fifty-three titles in the Little Blue Book series and found that 1,273,500 copies had been sold!

In February 1923, in an address to the Kansas City Advertising Club, Emanuel revealed some of his plans for the future. He wanted to make science, history, art, and literature in the pocket series "simple and interesting" to the average person. Why shouldn't the evolution of life be as interesting as a baseball game? Why couldn't those remote themes and personalities be introduced into the thinking of the common man? "I wish to bring the great thoughts and discoveries and artistic creations and significant personalities of all ages," he said, "realistically into the life of the common man of today."[2]

Radio was just beginning to be introduced to Americans, and Emanuel wanted to build a broadcasting station in Girard. His agenda called for lectures in all fields of human knowledge and activity, such as music and news. Especially valuable, he thought, "would be the information on the 'march of science.'" Unfortunately, as it turned out, his publishing business kept him so busy he never had time to develop this medium.[3]

Emanuel also explained his ideas to Charles Finger of Fayetteville, Arkansas. He dreamed of developing a department for motion pictures, but his more immediate goal was to establish a giant correspondence school. He would offer the public courses "with the padding" knocked out. Commercial correspondence schools invariably "loaded" their courses, he wrote, because "they were 'out to make money.'" His courses would disseminate only "knowledge and culture" to the masses.

In March 1923, in the *Haldeman-Julius Weekly*, Emanuel announced good news to his reading public. During January and February he had advertised all titles in the pocket series for 5 cents—for one-month-only as a test. He wanted to lower his prices, but only if his sales volume was high and he could still "make a reasonable profit." He later reported that his special resulted in almost 600 percent increase in sales and the company sold "almost six million books" during 1923. Henceforth their price would be 5 cents as long as the sales for each volume justified this price.[4]

As Emanuel commissioned new authors to write expressly for the pocket series, it soon became a medium by which original works could be offered to the public at a low price. This development was good for the authors, who were paid a flat sum, usually $50 per volume, as well as the readers.

Henry C. Vedder of the Crozier Theological Seminary pleased Emanuel immensely when he wrote:

This wild idea of a people's university of culture made available to all through books that are as good as they are cheap, not only arouses one's admiration for this man who conceived it and has already carried it so far towards realization, but inspires one with new faith and trust in the people, who have so whole heartedly responded.[5]

Pierre Loving added his adulation following a visit with the Haldeman-Juliuses:

During that delightful period when I was your guest I was gnawed every day by the misgiving that I was not . . . fulfilling my part as the honored guest. Your own spate of anecdote, wit and after-dinner chat positively embarrassed me—I was so impressed and over-awed that I never even hoped to emulate it. Certainly, during those lovely six weeks I spent with you in the middle of your Kansas prairie, I was envying you steadily. . . . But I assure you I felt decidedly second fiddle to your urbane achievement.[6]

The year 1926 was a banner one for the company, as the list of Little Blue Books jumped from 900 to 1,200, and 200 books were sent to the morgue and replaced. Most manuscripts only took about two months to write, because the authors were already familiar with the topic. When a completed manuscript was sent to Girard, Emanuel read it at once. If it was acceptable, the author was paid immediately. The manuscript was typeset in Kansas City, Missouri, in eight-point type, which allows 35 lines per page in a 3½ x 5-inch book of sixty-four pages, and the galleys were read and corrected there. It was returned for further corrections and then mailed to the author for a final reading. The plates arrived in Girard by freight, ready for printing, and after being printed and bound they were boxed, shelved, and warehoused by number. Fifty complimentary copies were sent to the author. For those books to be copyrighted, Emanuel filled out the proper forms and sent two copies to the National Archives.

All orders required a minimum number of twenty books for $1.[7] Book orders arrived in Girard, averaging 2,500 requests daily, and women sorted the letters by state. This made it easier later in zoning the Parcel Post labels. Other women worked in pairs, with the first one calling out the remittance and type, whether check, cash, or stamps, and the second verifying this. The orders were checked with the remittance and then zoned, a process requiring fifteen to forty workers, depending on the amount of business. Some workers were space-fillers, making sure the pigeon-holes were always full of books, and the others checked for errors of omission or commission. The books were packaged in corrugated cardboard boxes of various sizes, then on to the mailers.[8]

At this time Emanuel used six presses, four folding machines, two stitchers, two trimmers, and a "guillotine" for separating books printed in pairs. His plant also had machinery for other publishing work, such as the Big Blue Book series, his various magazines, office forms, order blanks, and circulars. This included five additional presses, two more folders, a foot-powered stapler, a perforator, a cutter, and a baler to prepare waste paper for sale. Like Henry Ford, Emanuel opened his plant for public tours. The editor of the *Girard Press* reported a 1927 "open house" in which Emanuel and his employees explained their unique processes of publishing.[9]

At this point in his book-publishing career, Emanuel decided to describe his reasoning for his previous special sales, which had garnered much criticism in the past. The Little Blue Book series, he explained, had been in an experimental state from the beginning, that is, they were fighting "for real commercial success" for their first eight years. Now, as 1928 opened, the period for time-limited sales had passed.[10]

The type of sale that gives a definite closing date was used for books that were being closed out and replaced. In 1919 the Little Blue Books were sold for 25 cents, then at five for $1, then for 10 cents. This last reduction meant that sales would need to double. At the same time, the initial expense of putting a new title on the list had to be diffused over a wider distribution of the books. The cost for each book would remain the same until newer and more automatic machinery could be used. If the turnover was twice as rapid as before, the unit could be content with a smaller margin of profit on the larger volume of business.[11]

The problem Emanuel faced was attracting more buyers at the five-cent price while at the same time putting pressure on his printing capacity to keep manufacturing costs down. This meant producing an ever increasingly attractive product. Slowly he learned what his market of readers wanted and, over a ten-year period, he gave it to them. It is much easier to attract sales from a list of 1,200 titles than from one of 500, but to increase the list like this required "sensational advertising." In the nine years of publishing the Little Blue Books series, nearly 2,000 titles were in print at one time or another. If merely exposed to the advertisement of a product, people would take their time to decide to purchase, so he needed to set a deadline by which the purchaser would have to decide. This sales technique, which many critics did not like, galvanized the buyer into action.[12]

Emanuel's task was to discover the correct ratio between selling price, cost of manufacturing, and choices of titles. This he had slowly uncovered, and by 1928 could offer the series permanently at 5 cents with his newly expanded list. Now his task was to prepare new catalogs and new advertising copy. Special advertising was no longer necessary, although he continued to do it on occasion.[13]

Back at the ranch, Marcet wrote her daughter in June 1929 that she had taken Henry to Pittsburg for his music lessons. She was convinced his teacher was capable. "It's not his fault that Joey won't work and Henry hasn't any natural musical ability," she told Alice. She also noted that she believed Emanuel was wrong about Joey's voice. "She has a voice far above the average. It has a really lovely quality"[14]

The following month, Emanuel wrote Alice that when he was in Pittsburg and the Fourth of July was approaching, he bought "a large bag of fireworks for Henry. A glorious mixture. A little of everything." When he carried the bag into the house, "Marcet thought it was a bag of pretzels and Henry thought it was full of sandwiches. Imagine his surprise when he saw that it was full of the best fireworks he had ever seen in all his life, and that it was intended for him alone. He was happy and gave me a warm hug, which made me feel very good."[15]

Marcet wrote Alice soon after this that John Gunn had come home drunk again. Emanuel had told a handyman to call a taxi to take him home. John disappeared before the taxi arrived, and everyone was fearful he "might get mixed up in the machinery and eventually rolled out between the leaves of a Little Blue Book." Aunt Ruthie Bob was visiting from California and talked "turkey" with Josephine about her future—"in the nicest, sweetest way." Ruthie Bob was "a crack stenographer," and after she graduated from Spalding's Commercial College, a prominent secretarial school in Kansas City, she could go to work anywhere. The six-month course cost $60, and Marcet thought it would be a bargain and promised Josephine she would pay for it. But, she added, she was "not going to put any more money into either dancing or singing for Josephine." If Josephine and her current heartthrob, Aubrey Rosell, "were smart he would stay right here until she finishes her course [at Spalding's] and then she can support herself and maybe help him." Marcet was surprised that "Josephine seemed to take to the idea," but she was afraid the youngster might "blunder" to Chicago or New York City looking for work.[16]

In mid-July, Joey's natural father, Mr. Wettstein, arrived at the farm to ask Marcet for money. He "pretended" he wanted it to go see Maggie, his wife, who had been in a home for the feeble-minded for four years. Marcet informed him in no uncertain terms that there would be "no money-dealings between you and us." She wrote to Alice that "it was all I could do from turning over that last threatening letter he wrote to your father to the Postal Authorities and that if he wanted to stay out of the penn [*sic*], he had better not write or phone any more such messages." All during Ruthie Bob's visit, Marcet was sick and nauseated from food poisoning. It was not until 20 July, and again on 1 August, that Emanuel reported to Alice that her mother was recovering from the food poisoning. The Haldeman-Juliuses soon were greatly preoccupied with Josephine's decision not to attend Spalding's but to announce her companionate marriage to Aubrey, who worked in her father's plant.[17]

Through his reading, Emanuel managed to keep abreast of current events. In 1927 he read of a judge in Colorado, Ben B. Lindsey, who was proposing new thinking on marriage and divorce, and he assigned him to write his account in a Little Blue Book. Then he dispatched Marcet to Denver to explore further the thinking of Judge Lindsey of the Juvenile and Family Affairs Court in that city. His thinking impressed Marcet profoundly, and she, in turn, wrote a Little Blue Book on the topic in 1927, titled *Why I Believe in Companionate Marriage.*

Judge Lindsey had handled many cases in which couples believed that divorce was the only way they could resolve their marital problems. Boys eighteen years of age and girls sixteen were ready physically and emotionally for sex, but societal mores said no, you must wait until this was sanctified by marriage and the man is prepared to support a home and family financially after completing high school. This meant, in many cases, completing a college degree and establishing a career. Meanwhile, legally one could give the young couple no advice on contraception, which at that time was primitive at best. Judge Lindsey proposed that society accept two types of marriages: a companionate one, in which the couple had no plan to have children and in which neither assumed any financial responsibility for the other. Then, when they were prepared financially and otherwise, they would be licensed to conclude a family marriage, where they would be responsible for each other and for their children.[18]

Marcet had considerable contact with young women in their late teens in the tri-state area. She knew how they thought and what they thought, and she agreed with Judge Lindsey that companionate marriage was a solution to the problems these young people faced while maturing. During the Roaring Twenties there was an alarming increase in the rate of divorce, which society also frowned upon, and she thought the judge was proposing a perfectly logical solution.

State laws varied greatly regarding the dissemination of information about contraception, child support, and similar issues, and companionate marriage would help to resolve these variances. If there were no children, the couple might live out their lives in companionate marriage. If there were children, the couple could take the next step of family marriage. Those who objected that this would legalize what society regarded as illegal sex would be answered that young people will experiment in any case. In experiencing companionate marriage, couples could go to a certain location in a large city and receive explicit information about sex. This could prevent the conception of an unwanted child or a sordid and dangerous abortion.

Marcet knew from talking to many young people that a large proportion had premarital sex. Young people were interested in sex, just as they were interested in religion, future vocations, attitude toward war, and, for college students, football. These youth were "essentially idealistic and high minded," but some young men expressed the preference of abstaining from sex with their loved one and having brief and passing alliances with "a more common type of girl" who offered and expected nothing beyond the moment. Even if the union did not turn out to be permanent, there were many present-day couples in which one of the partners had been married and divorced. Many had had sex prior to their current marriage. Was there a difference between these unconventional unions and a companionate marriage, beyond the fact that the latter would be legal? Any church that countenanced divorce should condone companionate marriage. The latter would be more lasting than those made under society's current rigid code. In addition, it would not place undue financial burdens on young people not yet ready to assume them. Companionate marriage was the answer, Marcet believed, for the changing economic conditions in which women were men's economic competitors. A healthy, childless woman was just as capable of supporting herself as was a man.

Marcet was deeply puzzled that current laws against the distribution of contraceptive advice or equipment "are allowed to stand for usually women get whatever they make up their minds they are entitled to have." Women certainly had a right to information to help them control their own bodies. Everyone whom Marcet discussed the subject with, of whatever religious persuasion, believed in and used contraceptive measures.

In 1927, Josephine was a beautiful young woman with all the thoughts and desires associated with a healthy seventeen-year-old. When she had become close to Aubrey Rosell, whom her parents regarded as unacceptable, they had sent her to live in Cedarville for a year. She had also had a flirtatious affair with Leburn Guy, who had worked at her father's plant but was fired for "raising too much 'hell.'" The bookkeeper told him he could return to work the next summer, because then he would have more "horse sense and would know when to go to bed." Meanwhile, Leburn had obtained "a much better position with the Associated Press in Wellington [Kansas]."[19]

With Aubrey at the University of Kansas, the Haldeman-Juliuses began paying more attention to higher education in the state, especially when Marcet discovered that schools were discriminating against black students. Emanuel wrote an editorial on the "color line" at KU, and Chancellor E. H. Lindley responded to it. The Department of Physical Education prohibited African American students from using the swimming pool yet required them to complete a swimming class for graduation. It was pointed out to the chancellor that this was not only illegal but "educationally and socially unwise." The chancellor responded that he had heard about the issue from "another distinguished Kansan, Mr. William Allen

White," the editor of the *Emporia Gazette*. His protest was "alcohol for your acid." Lindley was unhappy over the segregation issue, not only at the University of Kansas but in "the country at large." Black students were not getting "the full measure of their rights." This problem had increased because of the recent influx of black students from Oklahoma and Missouri, whose state universities would not admit them. Emanuel used an article in *Crisis* as a basis for his attack on the University of Kansas. Lindley noted that blacks enjoyed equality in the classrooms and laboratories "and have agreed to limit themselves to a rather large section of the cafeteria" where friendly whites also may come. This restriction was practiced in all Kansas state schools.[20] The University of Kansas ranked high academically at this time nationwide and was pioneering in "social reform and uplift." Numerous social injustices occurred every day at the university under Chancellor Lindley although one of his boasts was that he "comes from abolitionists stock." He did not state how this ancestral heritage justified his attitudes toward race. Lindley concluded with the observation that he had "long been a friend of your Blue Books, usually carrying some with me when I travel."[21]

The dean at Hays State Teachers College responded to an inquiry from "Margaret" that the school had no "Negro" students. Walter Burr at Kansas State Agricultural College informed Marcet that he made "absolutely no distinctions in my regard for persons on a racial basis." He was increasingly coming around to the opinion that "if every individual will attend well to his own business and quit trying to save society by some patent nostrum of his own, and quit trying to boost his own organization or other interests by stirring up questions of antipathies, society will get along very well, and gradually solve her own problems."[22]

In Crawford County, the officials at Columbus High School refused to play against the Girard football team, because they included two black players on their roster. Girard's superintendent of schools, Walter Walleck, "refused to submit to this insolence." The Haldeman-Juliuses commended Walleck's attitude and wrote a letter to the editor of the *Pittsburg Headlight* that race relations at the University of Kansas was "deplorable," blacks could not receive the last two years of their education at the School of

Medicine and both Physical Education and Fine Arts "discriminate grossly" against them. As long as F. C. Allen, the present director of athletics and physical education at KU, remains there, "race prejudice will increase and not grow less." In Emporia, "colored girls" were alone, for instance, in receiving unfair treatment.[23]

Marcet had an experience with racial segregation when she visited Little Rock at this time to cover the race riots there for Emanuel. She took a public bus to the penitentiary to interview an inmate. She seated herself on a long seat at the back. Whites on the bus were seated together while blacks stood up. Two black girls eyed Marcet's long bench, then Marcet, and she invited them to sit with her. Instantly a white man ordered them to stand up. "She asked us to sit," the girls protested, but they stood up. She apologized to the girls but heard the man loudly say "nigger lover" as he left. A few blocks later a police car stopped the bus. A policeman and the white man got on, and the officer ordered Marcet to take a seat up front with the white people. The white man followed her repeating the insults until she stopped him with a sharp "That's enough!" The two white men got off the bus, and the trip was resumed.[24]

The Haldeman-Juliuses faced a far greater crisis than segregation when the companionate marriage of Aubrey and Josephine was announced. Aubrey was the son of a Girard merchant and a sophomore at the University of Kansas, while Joey soon would be a senior in high school at Girard. Aubrey had to work his way through college, and in the summer of 1927 he signed on to work on a freighter bound for ports in northern Europe. He thought of becoming a lawyer and considered remaining on the East Coast and enrolling at Columbia University. Joey could not stand the thought of being that far away from him and persuaded Emanuel to give him a job at the plant. That way he could save his money for school and they could be together.

Joey expressed her typical teenage frustrations with adults in a letter to Aubrey:

I have tried to forget my surroundings and my unhappiness. I will be eighteen in September and I feel fully competent to take care of

myself. (She) would stick it out for the coming summer but if things
don't take a violent change I am leaving on my birthday. I am tired of
dodging E. H-Js footsteps, Alice's laziness and dominance, Henry's
deep love, Mother's wishes, scoldings, and my old parents. I am tired
of life—sick of it. I want to throw what is left of me to the four winds.
I want to live hard, fast, and recklessly.[25]

Marcet wrote Joey in February 1928, saying that she approved her
attending high school in Lawrence while Aubrey enrolled at the university. She could go tuition-free and receive all credits from Girard High
School and thus graduate in 1928. Emanuel "growled a good deal," but
left it up to Marcet to decide and he sent Aubrey an extra $5. Marcet
suggested to Joey that he might send "a bill like that" occasionally. She
encouraged Joey to dance professionally when she could but she begged
her to have "no more lies and deceptions." All the "heartaches" everyone
had gone through could have been avoided if Joey had been "sweet and
tender and frank in the first place." Marcet had attempted to follow the
developing romance but Joey, a typical teenage girl, was sometimes evasive
and occasionally lied when it suited her purpose. The young couple had
discussed their situation and decided to live together in Lawrence while
attending school.[26]

Once Aubrey returned to Girard in 1928, events moved rapidly and
by early November the two were planning details of their marriage.
For a number of reasons they soon determined it would be a companionate marriage and the news quickly spread across Kansas and the
nation. Emanuel always enjoyed publicity and he soon had more than
he wanted. First of all, with the blessing of their parents, the youngsters
were quite amenable. Second, Marcet had just written her Blue Book
on the topic and it was on the minds of the public. Finally, Emanuel
was beginning to develop political ambitions and, following the lead of
William Allen White of the *Emporia Gazette* and a leading Republican
figure, Republican editors across Kansas saw the possibility of giving
Emanuel some bad publicity and damage his political plans if they
publicized Joey and Aubrey's decision.

The *Kansas City Star* announced its support of the Haldeman-Juliuses for the companionate marriage, and Emanuel promised publicly to provide for Joey until Aubrey completed his education. Always eager to accept any kind of publicity, he suggested that the major problem of young people was an economic one and this type of marriage was a viable answer. If a child was forthcoming and their love continued, the companionate marriage would turn into a regular one. Marcet, of course, was completely supportive of the young couple's plans. The next day the *New York Times* elaborated on Marcet's views, quoting her as saying that Joey and Aubrey were "acting wisely and will find their greatest growth in the same, time-honored, if ever changing institution" of marriage. She added that she hoped their experience would "be an encouragement to other young people to do the same."[27]

The wedding was set for Thanksgiving Day in Kansas City with Rev. L. M. Burkhead officiating. The hotel in Girard was deluged with requests for rooms from out of state reporters, especially California, and this alarmed Marcet who saw the possibility of the affair becoming a national circus. She consulted with everyone involved and the decision was made to advance the wedding two days. Marcet explained to the press that "a girl's wedding is too solemn a moment to be marred by a sensational atmosphere. Frankly, we will not have it." Of course, the phrases "till death do us part," "obey," and all references to God were eliminated, but otherwise, the ceremony was the standard one.[28]

The following day Judge Lindsey sent the couple a telegram of congratulations. He said he was sending a letter also that would arrive on Thanksgiving Day extending his congratulations again and suggesting that if the marriage should not work out, "do not frame up the lies, frauds, and collusions with or against each other as is done in 90 percent of our divorce cases . . . but insist in your honesty on a divorce by mutual consent." Instead of accepting the judge's advice, "many Americans felt that the marriage had caused them and the country a great hurt." Many of the nation's purists compared this marriage to free love. As usual, there were always many who were willing and anxious to impose their beliefs on others.[29]

Marcet's attempt to prevent a circus failed. After the wedding, reporters continued to rummage around Girard until they discovered Joey had been adopted. To preclude damage to the youngsters, the Haldeman-Juliuses consulted with the Wettsteins and foolishly decided to claim Joey as their natural daughter. There was at least one problem with this course of action: Joey was almost eighteen and Marcet and Emanuel had been married only eleven years. But they concocted the incredible story that when Marcet was a student at Bryn Mawr they fell in love and moved to New York City where they lived in the same apartment building. Marcet's parents opposed their marriage and they could not afford it anyway. In 1910 Josephine was born in a house of friends and they raised her until she was adopted in 1918 to give companionship to Alice. This fantasy merely spurred reporters to "greater endeavors." Judge Lindsey finally stepped in and explained that the Haldeman-Juliuses concocted the story out of love for Josephine and to protect her, the story was "meant to help and to correct and not to injure." Emanuel explained that "a lie that sprang from a heart full of love for one's daughter and my wife and I ask the public to see it in that light." Reverend John W. Bradbury of Kansas City's Bales Baptist Church waxed indignant, saying "I regard such men as Ben B. Lindsey, E. Haldeman-Julius, and the Reverend C. M. Burkhead as fostering a human relationship unsanctioned by God and infamously degrading to the participants."[30]

The press had a heyday. Reporters dug up many of Emanuel's extramarital affairs and exaggerated them, making life uncomfortable for him. Citizens of Girard became so hostile to him that he threatened to move his publishing plant to Freeport, Illinois. He and Marcet decided to be remarried and Reverend Burkhead performed the ceremony in his church in Kansas City on 3 December 1927. It took time for the small town hostility to die down but eventually citizens began speaking to him again. City leaders realized how important his business was to the town and they soon relented and elected him president of their chamber of commerce.[31]

Joey had some musical talent and attempted to obtain employment as a dancer and singer. Marcet wrote Joey that the Haldeman-Juliuses viewed the situation as being that Joey was very pretty, knew how to wear clothes well, and was a dancer with years of training so she was worth $1,000 weekly to a knowledgeable manager. "Everybody," she noted, was eager to pay to see the "companionate" bride. High school was now in her past, according to Marcet but her problem was she had "absolutely no judgment." Whenever she "opens her mouth in an interview, she says exactly the wrong thing." For instance, she said she wanted to stay in Lawrence to make money. As a result, the Haldeman-Juliuses received a telegram from Washington and a statement from the Hearst press asking if Josephine had recalled their marriage. On the other hand, Aubrey was "clear and concise and truthful—all at the same time." Marcet and Emanuel concluded that Aubrey should become her manager and take advantage of her ability plus all the good publicity they had garnered as a result of their companionate marriage.[32]

The youngsters ended up in Los Angeles broke, with Aubrey working at a "big skating rink" and Joey looking for her big dancing break in either "the stage or movie work." She asked Marcet to ask two of her friends in Girard to write her, as "it is at times extremely lonesome for me." Eventually they had to return to Girard, where Joey went to work for her father and Aubrey's father employed him in his creamery. Joey did not have a "lived happily ever after" ending. Over twenty years later, the couple divorced and Joey remarried and moved to New York City. She returned only once to Girard, and that was to attend Marcet's funeral.[33]

Emanuel decided in February 1929 that it was time to clean up some of his publications. The *Haldeman-Julius Quarterly* became the *American Parade*, and the *Haldeman-Julius Monthly* became the *Debunker*. The new *Parade* would avoid sensationalism and concentrate on "a quiet dignity." He announced a contest to rename the *Weekly* but when none were forthcoming that he liked he renamed it the *American Freeman*. He remained the editor but now listed the contributing editors. Each front page was divided into two parts and then continued on other pages as necessary, much resembling his old *Life and Letters*, with the concentration on larger issues.[34]

In early November, Emanuel received a letter from Paris. Fagnani deplored the new *Debunker* and *American Parade*. "What does this metamorphosis into a *rag* mean?" he demanded, "Were they (the previous titles) not paying well in their respectable dress?"

> The original *Parade* was a fine magazine, the original *Debunker* was a pleasure to handle and a delight to read. I have put up with the form of the *Freeman* because of long association from the days of the *Appeal to Reason* but I refuse the eye cracking task of reading more of this poorly printed wide-column unmanageable output of your formerly beautiful presswork.

It was former Haldeman-Julius writer Louis Adamic, though, who was the most cutting of all. Emanuel considered *First Hundred Million* to be worthy of shelf room along with the Lynd's *Middletown*. But Adamic implied that Emanuel had built a "great democracy of books" by trickery. Haldeman-Julius had rigged his vote by encouraging his voters to support unpopular books. He did this by switching titles and promising more than he delivered, and he did this time and again. He had learned this technique by working on Wayland's *Appeal to Reason*.[35]

Emanuel insisted he wanted to get out of the publishing business and had been negotiating the sale of his company. He wanted to get out of publishing and spend the rest of his life writing. The Bernarr McFadden Publications of New York City appeared to be the most promising prospect. The company was deeply involved in publishing mass-circulation publications. Emanuel traveled to New York City in January 1929 to talk to the McFadden interests. Upon his return to Girard, he listed his assets of 12,000,000 Little Blue Books in stock at a cost of 1 cent each; the real estate was worth $156,000; the plates of 1,500 titles in the series at $200 per title amounted to $300,000; mailing lists, materials inventory, and good will brought the price tag to $750,000. The McFadden interests believed this total was too high. The 12,000,000 books would be costly to liquidate. His plant and equipment estimate exceeded replacement costs, and many of the titles were slow movers that needed to be replaced. What would his reaction be to determining if they could arrive at "a trading basis"? Emanuel responded that his price was not negotiable.[36]

Emanuel wrote to Mayer Dvorkin at McFadden that he believed the two parties could come to an agreement. "Give me your figure," he urged, and "if we are not too far apart I will come for the final conference. But I do not intend to dispose of this property at any sort of distress evaluation, for this enterprise is a going concern and in no way in alarming circumstances." The deal subsequently fell through, but Emanuel was not upset. He could advertise extensively and bring the company back into financial control. He was forced to merge the *American Parade* with the *Debunker*.[37]

Marcet wrote Emanuel on their thirteenth anniversary that, at forty, he was "famous and justly so." She expressed the hope that they could travel in the next decade and that he could "get out from all the oppressive strain." But the pace continued, and he had little time to think in his "squirrel cage."[38]

They were at work on their second novel. This one was rooted in her experience in reporting on the lynching of an African American and covering the trial of J. Frank Norris, the Baptist preacher who had killed a person in his church study. Emanuel wrote the publishers that they were "satisfied with everything except one thing—the title. Marcet can't see 'Dixie.' We are both for 'Violence' without the exclamation point. We are not going to start a revolution, but we are on our knees begging you to surrender on that one point."[39]

Violence, published by Simon and Schuster in 1928, is more a sociological study than a novel. It indicts a southern society, proving that justice in the South depends on the color of one's skin. The Reverend Jordan is described as a "fighting parson" by his supporters, and Skip Early, the sixteen-year-old African American boy, is presented as a victim of circumstances. In a moment of terror he murders the white girl he seduced—or did the girl seduce him? The girl, "a promiscuous experimenter," set up a sort of boudoir in the belfry of the Methodist church "where she dispenses her favors." The contrast between the jury's acquittal of the preacher and the mob's lynching of Skip Early provides the format for the novel.[40]

Emanuel's *Big American Parade* was in bookstores by October 1929. In this novel he lauded the fast-paced society of the 1920s. There was "a new freedom" produced by the automobile, by the movies with their new code in morals, and by jazz music. Life moved so rapidly that one had no time to reflect. Life was short at best. Those who were not with the crowd were bored so the lesson was to stay with the crowd. America was great because of its material power and Haldeman-Julius had no sympathy for those who protested this materialism. Albert Chinz reviewed it for the *Mercure France* and wrote that the book accurately mirrored "American reading tastes, national culture, mob aspirations, and motives."[41]

Also in 1929, Emanuel published his *magnum opus* on bunk. In almost 500 pages, *The Outline of Bunk* presents a skeptical attitude toward the topic. He defined it as "a short, sharp, pointed and puissant word that . . . is the most forcible term of criticism and contempt that can be applied to any statement of opinion. . . . When we say that anything is "bunk," we mean that it does not make good sense. Bunk is poor reasoning . . . or no attempt to reason at all. Religion, he believed, is the highest form of bunk in history, hiding its foul designs under the impenetrable fog of "mysticism, supernaturalism, fear and emotion."[42]

The book provided under one cover the principal concepts of Haldeman-Julius's typical approach to American life. It was a wide-ranging attack on bunk by one who was profoundly convinced of the righteousness of his crusade. Religion, he believed, was the supreme bunk of history, followed by public opinion and war. He regarded all attempts to explain life on the basis of subconscious, primitive personality, mysticism, romanticism, or idealism as bunk. The *New York World* concluded that *Bunk* believes that anyone who would "sell pills of wisdom in the form of Little Blue Books knows his business." Much of this criticism, of course, was an expression of jealousy.

In *The Big American Parade*, Haldeman-Julius captured American life in the Roaring Twenties with his penetrating eye. The reader is both an actor and an observer, sensing confusion, whirled by kaleidoscopic events that are uncontrollable. The events are a rich and swiftly moving materialism that is sweeping aside the narrow Puritanism that had long dominated American life. His America was one that had undergone remarkable change.

All this occurred in the context of the nation watching in horror and fascination the debacle that took place on Wall Street in October 1929.

Emanuel was in New York City at the time and witnessed his financial destruction first hand. Since 1927 the nation had been engaged in a hysteria of speculation on the stock market. This was rooted in the purchase of stocks on margin, which ran as high as 50 percent. That is, when you purchased a $100 stock, you paid $50 and borrowed $50 for the margin. This way your portfolio money went twice as far. The problem was the bank you borrowed from kept the stock as security. If the price dropped too far, the bank would sell the stock, keep their money and give the purchaser the remainder, if any. That this was a speculator's market is shown by the fact that these margin loans rose from $3.3 billion to $8 billion from 1927 to 1929. When this bubble burst in October 1929 the value of shares on the New York Stock Exchange plummeted from $87 billion to $19 billion in March 1933. This drastic drop ruined many speculators, such as Haldeman-Julius, and ushered in the worst depression in American history.

On 7 November, Emanuel wrote Marcet that he "must start all over again. Three weeks ago we faced independence, freedom from business, travel, happiness." He admitted he had himself to blame for this debacle. "I thought I was market wise. I wasn't," he wrote from the Algonquin Hotel in New York City. He lost everything, holding on only to the plant, "$2,500 in cash, my health, my readiness to begin over—and a deeper and stronger love for you and the children."

When you realize the plant has not operated for three months and that there has been practically no advertising and absolutely no promotion by direct mail, it is plain that the Little Blue Books are vital & strong. The proofs are in the receipts. They have been running around $500 per day right along, which means daylight is in sight. The bank failure cost the plant $5000 instead of $3000. This loss and all bills payable are to be taken care of out of the receipts. In a month I will be out of the red. Frank can prove this to you. And when we begin again I will stand at the wheel and make the plant produce as it did before. I feel confident, and I know you will stand by me. You always do. I know I have failed you in many ways but *not* in all ways. During the next year I ask you to do one thing about money—keep within $150 per week.[43]

6

THE GREAT DEPRESSION, 1928–1938

The Haldeman-Juliuses suffered from a problem common to millions of Americans during the Great Depression, differing only in degree: the lack of sufficient funds to meet the daily requirements of living as they were accustomed to. The average wage was $1 daily for those who found work, so the distinguishing point is that it would be difficult for those working people for whom he was publishing the Little Blue Books to understand why Marcet would encounter stress in making her household budget function on $150 per week.

According to Sue Haney, his secretary, Emanuel had to curtail his life-style considerably. First, he was forced to cut staff, keeping key employees by giving them part-time work doing odd jobs, using every means possible to keep a few dollars in their pockets. His ostentatious Lincoln was relegated to the storehouse, too expensive to operate. It was replaced by "a black and tan Ford" coupe so he could continue his pleasurable rides through the countryside.[1]

During the plush 1920s he had enjoyed expensive cigars, but he soon switched to ten-centers, then to the smelly five-centers. He was too stubborn to admit any sign of defeat, keeping a sign on his desk that read "This, Too, Shall Pass Away." It was not until 1938 that the publishing business began to recover. A new generation of readers was emerging then, and his advertising began to be effective again. He was paying off his debts, and he had most of his old crew back in the publishing plant. Most importantly, to speed the recovery he had to sacrifice his trips to his beloved New York

City, which he never saw again. He maintained contact with old friends but insisted he was going to remain in Girard and observed that "I am content. If the world wishes to see me, let it come here."[2]

Emanuel wrote to Marcet sometime in the fall of 1930 that the future looked bleak for the Haldeman-Julius Publishing Company. "Receipts are scraping bottom again," he said. "Debts are piling up higher than ever and I don't have a dime to my name." He would pursue the stalling strategy on debts, but he believed they were facing "a real crisis" and "a bust up" was near. In attempting to persuade Marcet to hold down her expenses, of course, he could not present an air of optimism.[3]

Some way or another, he managed to finance a trip to the West Coast for Alice that year to visit relatives she had never seen, as well as an extended trip to Russia for Marcet the following year. Marcet's trip, however, was undertaken to collect royalties, and the visit fairly well paid for itself. Their novels *Dust* and *Violence* had been translated into Russian by Peter Ochremenko. The Russian government did not permit any of its currency to leave the country. The only way to enjoy the royalties, then, was to go to Russia and spend the money there.

At this time the Tom Mooney case was again making headlines. Mooney, born in 1882, was the son of a coal miner and Knights of Labor organizer. He became a radical labor organizer for the Industrial Workers of the World (IWW) and became friends with "Big Bill" Haywood, Mother Jones, and Elizabeth Gurley Flynn. He soon gained the reputation of a "dynamiter," as this was the preferred weapon of the more radical IWWs.

Tom, his wife, Rena, and Warren Billings had been tried for bombing a Preparedness Day Parade in San Francisco in 1916. Amid a carnival atmosphere of lynch-mob rule, Tom and Warren were found guilty. One witness claimed that her "astral body" was present at the scene of the crime and thus her testimony was unassailable. Later there were recantations of testimony, new evidence, and other developments to demonstrate that the verdict was unsubstantiated. Mooney and Billings were sentenced to hang, but President Woodrow Wilson and a presidential investigating committee were unable to discover much evidence of their guilt, and the president persuaded Governor William Stevens to reduce their sentences to life imprisonment. Mooney proved to be a model prisoner in the prison hospital, attempting, unsuccessfully, to convert his fellow convicts to socialism.

By 1930 there was a good deal of public support to pardon the two men. Emanuel sent his crack reporter to California to cover the story, and Marcet spent two weeks interviewing Mooney at San Quentin, Billings in Folsom Prison, and the governor of California. Marcet found that the Merchants, Manufacturers, and Employers Association of Stockton had been determined to crush the IWW and decided the best way to do this was to send Mooney and other labor leaders to prison. Long after the trial, it was discovered, through recanted testimony, new evidence, and delayed confessions, that the association's campaign to "frame" the accused had been successful. J. J. Emerson, for instance, after he was arrested for carrying a suitcase of dynamite, confessed to having plotted to plant dynamite on Mooney.[4]

During her interviews, Marcet discovered that Mooney and Billings had to be tried separately, because Billings had received a prison sentence in 1914 and was thus a convicted felon. Therefore, Billings had to apply to the state supreme court for a pardon, whereas Mooney, a first-time offender, would receive his pardon from the governor. If Billings filed for a pardon with the court and was rejected, he could never file again "unless new evidence arose." Marcet convinced the two that "it is so much easier to persuade one man to do the right thing than to convince a group like the California supreme court." As a result, Mooney and Billings agreed that Mooney must apply to the governor and receive a pardon first, and then Billings could make his singular appeal.[5]

Marcet also found out that, through the years, leaders of organized labor did not want Mooney to be pardoned, because he was a political embarrassment to them with his "dynamiter" reputation. She sympathized with Mooney and admitted that "never have I come in contact with a more moving, dramatic story than Tom Mooney's."[6]

Marcet later wrote Jane Addams "in strict confidence" that the day after she arrived in San Francisco, the state supreme court's chief justice told Vic Larsen, a reporter for the *San Francisco Call Bulletin*, that the state supreme court had decided on Mooney's innocence, but of course "this fact could not be released until the governor had officially signed the pardon." There were things about the case and the way Mooney was illegally convicted that she could not "put in my articles."[7] It was not until 1939 that California's liberal Democratic governor, Cuthbert Olson, pardoned Mooney. His twenty-three years in prison had taken a toll on his health, though, and he died in a San Francisco hospital on 6 March 1942, at age fifty-nine. Billings was also released in 1939 but was not pardoned until 1961.

In the early 1930s, Marcet and Emanuel "motored" to Kansas City occasionally. On one occasion they did so to meet Sinclair Lewis. Emanuel and "Red" Lewis were good friends. Marcet told Emanuel many times she too was a friend of the author's, but she thought it never registered. Emanuel was like Alice in this, she concluded, because "they seemed to think that before they adorned her life it was more or less a blank." Marcet had taught Lewis "to play his first love scenes in the theatre" in Montreal. When Emanuel met "Red" that evening he said, "I want you to meet Marcet." Lewis looked at Emanuel "in a quizzical way, then at me," and exclaimed, "*Meet* her! I know Marcet." He swept her into his arms and "gave me a kiss full on the lips." "I have her trained," Emanuel informed Lewis later that evening. The author looked at him with amusement and responded, "*You* think you have Marcet trained? Like hell you have." Lewis spent the rest of the evening sitting on the arm of Marcet's chair, kissing her occasionally. She watched Emanuel for his reaction but saw nothing. She wondered if it was because Lewis's behavior that evening was similar to how Emanuel behaved around other women.[8]

Meanwhile, Alice was reporting occasionally to her parents about her trip to the West Coast. Marcet wrote Jane Addams that she was sending Alice to California. Alice was doing well in school, making all A's except in sewing and writing, in which she received B's. She always made the honor roll, and she received keen competition from Nelson King, the son of a Presbyterian preacher, and Kenneth Cox, a physician's son. The three were always at the head of their classes. Intelligence tests showed Alice at age sixteen (she was twelve) and Henry at age ten (his actual age). Alice also took part in several extracurricular activities, such as Glee Club, basketball, Camp Fire Girls, and all the "honors." She had recently won the Declamation contest, although she did not prepare for it until the morning of the event." She was a well-rounded, dependable, capable girl.[9]

Alice's actions, though, occasionally caused her father "considerable worry and perplexity." She failed to make her 11:00 curfew one night, and he was fretting. Where is she, he demanded to know, and Marcet replied that she was at the skating rink. "But it is closed now. Does she have the car?" "It is and she has," responded Marcet. Alice arrived a few minutes later, and Emanuel "upbraided" her for fifteen minutes. At one point she responded, "Oh, Daddy, don't be so old-fashioned." Marcet got the impression that Alice was giving her father "a most unlikely story." She came to Marcet's bedroom, exclaiming "Whew, how antiquated Daddy is. It took me all this time to get him calmed down. For a man who takes the position he does on sex—he doesn't know what a laugh he is to me." Marcet concluded that Alice was "going to be more difficult to guide than Josephine because in some ways she is so much more clever." Marcet knew that Alice loved her father. There was "very little about her father that she does not know good, bad or indifferent. She admires and loves him, criticizes him and laughs at him. He can't put anything over on her." Alice also told her mother that she loved being around boys but she would never do "you know what" with one of them.[10]

"Daddy" received a card from Alice when she visited the Royal Gorge in Colorado. In his reply, he called this "a wonderful experience" and told her he had just seen "a wonderful picture called 'All Quiet on the Western Front.'" He enclosed a dollar for her to go and see the movie, and asked her to write him her response to it. Children were taught "patriotic bunk" in school, he said, and the movie demonstrated "how harmful" were "these destructive doctrines." Marcet noted that Emanuel attended the movies "four or five times a week" and found "sweet relaxation there"; he would even sit "tranquilly through astonishingly trashy talkies," but he especially enjoyed good movies.[11]

In July, Marcet thanked Alice for the "lovely lavender cigarette holder" she sent from San Francisco. Emanuel had not yet received his gift of "a redwood pipe" as the mail had arrived that day after he went to work.

She also said that Louis Adamic had just written an article for *Outlook* in which he accused Haldeman-Julius Publications of running a "racket" and of Emanuel meeting "bunk with bunk." Marcet had been very busy with her Mooney articles, but she felt a need to write an open letter to *Outlook* correcting these two misconceptions. Adamic was just getting even with Emanuel for having "rejected the last three or four of his articles," she asserted. Emanuel reported that "yesterday . . . I had to lay off 45 employees. That leaves a staff of 50."[12]

Alice went to Cedarville the following summer, and Marcet and Henry had Emanuel to themselves. Several times he took them to Pittsburg or Joplin for a movie, and occasionally he let Henry drive. After one such trip with dinner at Maxwells in Joplin, they came home. It was a "gay, warmly friendly trip," Marcet reported to Alice, and she and Henry went to bed "happy and tired." After a while, "Daddy came to the door and wanted me to go up to his room." Marcet refused, and he "waxed in his sweetest way" and the two went up to the "big room." They were "cuddled up" asleep with a cool breeze when Henry woke up and found himself alone. He called Marcet down, and she returned to her room.[13]

In early October 1930, Emanuel decided to declare war on President Herbert Hoover over his lack of activity in combating the Depression. He began by calling the president "fatuous." Perhaps the Great Engineer was not "the most ignorant man who has sat in the White House," Emanuel observed, but "he looks fatuous, he talks fatuously, and he conducts himself with an unmistakable air and effect of fatuousness." Perhaps Hoover was not to blame for bringing on the Depression, but the ideal of economic individualism that he "worships fatuously" brought on the Wall Street crash. As conditions worsened periodically, Hoover issued pronouncements that things were improving. "He has met bad conditions by denying them." Critics began insisting that prosperity was just "Hoovering" around the corner.[14]

The next week he renewed his attack by noting that Hoover's wealth of an estimated $10 million "removes him from the possibility of real sympathy with the masses of the American people." Hoover had made his millions through his career as a mining engineer in the Far East, by public service in Belgium relief in World War I, and as secretary of commerce during the 1920s. "He has never given a hint that he has the slightest understanding of modern social problems," Emanuel charged, but instead has revealed "in politics, at least, a petty mind." Hoover was quite aware, Emanuel was convinced, "of the widespread dislike with which he is regarded by the American people." His only public policy or goal was to be renominated and reelected in 1932.[15]

After Hoover addressed the American Bankers Association, in which he delivered his message "Don't Lower Your Standard of Living" to the millions of unemployed, Emanuel added the nickname "Hoover the Brazen." The millions who felt the strain and privation of these "wonderful" difficult economic conditions, Emanuel urged facetiously, "ought to join Hoover in exclamations of elations and awe and pride over the beautiful spectacle of enforced idleness and poverty!" The millions who were suffering "are merely sharpening and refining their appetites so that they can better imagine how good cake would taste if they had the cake."[16]

In early 1931, Emanuel's tone of attacks on Hoover became more aggressive, more strident, more shrill. He began to expose the details of how Hoover had acquired his millions. In 1901, Chang Yen-Mao, director of mines for the Chinese empire, had asked the London firm of Bewick, Moreing and Company to recommend a mining engineer to assist in the management of Chinese mines. The company suggested Hoover, as he was operating some of their Australian mining properties. Hoover was not literally managing the mines, but controlling the finances of the properties and selling their stocks to the public. In other words, he would represent his British company rather than the Chinese government if he had to choose between the two. During the chaotic conditions of the Boxer Rebellion of 1900–1901, it was suggested that these Chinese mines might be better protected in the hands of the British. The Chinese government sought loans and other financial assistance, and in the process of financing this endeavor, Moreing and company and Hoover cheated the Chinese. As a result, Chang traveled to London to bring suit against the Bewick company.

The *Mining Manual* and the *Mining Year Book* of 1905 showed Hoover as directing several mining companies, which he subsequently raided as he had done to the Chinese mines. Hoover told David Starr Jordan, president of Stanford University, Hoover's alma mater, that he was receiving $5,000 a year as a mining expert and $95,000 yearly as a financial expert. This was his pay for watering the stock of the Chinese mines he was representing, the Chinese Engineering Company. Chang was made "the picturesque and tragic personal victim." He testified that Hoover had offered him 50,000 shares of watered stock in the mining company but he had refused them. The English judge ruled he could not order the English company to make restitution of 425,000 shares of stock to the Chinese, but that "undoubtedly fraud had been perpetuated in that the terms of the memorandum had not been carried out by Bewick," which he subsequently ordered done. Hoover continued his questionable mining deals until World War I interrupted and thus amassed a considerable fortune. Hoover had the support of Wall Street as secretary of commerce and later as president because the financiers deemed him the supreme promoter of capitalism.

The *American Freeman* planned to send Marcet to Washington DC for six significant interviews: Senator George Norris on the power trust; Senator William Borah on the question of official recognition of the Soviet Union; Senator Robert La Follette on the burning issue of the farm problem; interviews and research on "Hooverism" to strengthen the crusade against President Hoover; the financial control of the banking house of Morgan; and the issue of Italian Fascism under the dictator Benito Mussolini. The journal would undertake this venture, though, only if "loyal readers" sent in two thousand "clubs of four subs" at 25 cents per subscription, with each running for twenty-five weeks.[17]

Apparently, the required number of subscriptions failed to materialize, as Marcet's investigations were limited to an exposure of the American Bond and Mortgage Company of Chicago. William J. Moore, president of the company, headed up a "ring" that had close ties to senators, representatives, cabinet members, and Vice-President Charles Curtis of Kansas. The ring would sell bonds backed by real estate and promotional schemes on hotels and apartment houses, which they would juggle through holding companies and trusteeships. The Mayflower in Washington DC was one of these hotels. Curtis paid an astonishing $5.35 daily for an eleven-room apartment suite, the same one Harry Sinclair had paid $150 a day for during his trial for contempt of the U.S. Senate in the Teapot Dome scandal. This was the payoff to the vice-president for his "valuable personal and political aid" to the grafters. The *American Freeman* suggested that, at this point, Charles Curtis was preparing to abandon Hoover and run for the open Senate seat in Kansas, a place "where he could do no wrong." Moore's shady deal stretched from Maine to Florida. The "notorious" ex-convict Al Gross was part of this financial group. He had assisted the "Curtis for President" club in 1928 with its headquarters in the Mayflower hotel. In "the last six months" a federal investigation of the schemes had been under way, but with no results. Marcet questioned if Curtis had a hand in "the cloak of silence" over this inquiry.[18]

Emanuel was particularly interested in exposing any of Curtis's nefarious activities, because he planned to run against him for one of the Senate seats in 1932—as the Kansas editors had predicted during the "companionate marriage" episode. Emanuel opened his campaign with a speech in Fort Scott challenging Curtis to explain his role in the hotel bond scandal. The *American Freeman* also telegraphed Curtis to request his response to its story. Curtis declined, being content to give a statement to newspaper reporters that his hotel bill was "not Mr. Haldeman-Julius's business."[19]

Following the hotel bond scandal exposé, Harold Moore, William's son, filed a $500,000 libel suit against the *American Freeman* in a Chicago court. The suit included the statement that the name of Vice-President Charles Curtis had been used "in a defamatory manner." Emanuel thought it strange that Curtis was involved in the lawsuit, rather than "the Moore ring" simply bringing its suit against the journal, and wondered why there was a delay of two and a half months between the publication of the story on 9 May and the suit in July. Clarence Darrow, Emanuel announced, would represent the *American Freeman* in the case.[20]

In August 1931, Emanuel observed that his candidacy "has excited, perplexed, and worried the orthodox newspapers and editors of Kansas." He concluded that the Curtis forces wanted to "dodge" the real issues by focusing on the *Freeman* attack. The "conventional" newspapers in the state were using "veins of ridicule of heated opposition, of intense and many-sided prejudice, and serious but polite remonstrance and debate but are afraid of his candidacy and its ability to arouse the ire of voters against current economic conditions." They were also pressing the "companionate marriage" issue, taking advantage of the adverse publicity that Joey and Aubrey had generated. His candidacy "has given old party leaders the biggest scare in years." He concluded that political issues were driving the libel suit.[21]

The *Freeman* was ready with further disclosures on the Moore family. In 1927 the Moores had convinced investors to purchase $5 million of the American Bond and Mortgage Company's sinking fund. This was in addition to the company's millions "sunk in their mortgage bond schemes." At that time, however, the Moores knew their company "was on the rocks and drifting to a smash." With the company "rushing to bankruptcy," a meeting was called of officers and directors of the company in Chicago, where "its desperate situation was revealed." The following year the company ordered its salesmen to cease selling their debenture bonds and preferred stock in New York City. Finally, in September 1931 a federal grand jury indicted the American Bond and Mortgage Company for using the U.S. mails to defraud investors. It was "freely admitted" in Boston that the revelations of the *American Freeman* "had quite a great deal to do in forcing the government, long hampered by mysterious higher-up influences, at last to bow to the fact that this rotten case required action."

Meanwhile, financial problems forced Emanuel to combine the *Debunker* with the *Freeman* to cut his publishing expenses. The *Debunker* had been running in the red since December 1929 with a deficit of "about $500 per month." This, combined with a weekly deficit of $105 for the *Freeman*, "causes a drain which must be stopped at once." This combination would result in a deficit of slightly over $100 weekly. The company needed to increase *Freeman* subscribers to 50,000 "at once." In the interim, the *Freeman* would have to fulfill the subscriber obligations for the *Debunker*.[22]

Marcet's trip to the Soviet Union was fast approaching. Jane Addams wrote that she was unable to help Marcet with names of people in Russia, as she did not know anyone "now directly connected with the Collective Farm movement, although I had friends among the Pioneers." She noted that the Gregory Yaroses were in Moscow and, while he was not a communist, his wife was and their daughter had been one "for long years."[23]

Marcet had trouble getting her passport updated when she discovered that Crawford County had no record of her birth. When contents were moved from the old courthouse to the new one, all records for her birth year were lost. She had to ask old friends to testify that she had been born. Then she had to have passport photos made. When she watched the court clerk paste on her photo, she thought she was finished, but no, a woman's citizenship was determined by her husband's, so she also had to prove that Emanuel was a U.S. citizen. Total cost was $10. Usually one had to wait two or three weeks for the passport to clear the hurdles, and she was scheduled to sail before then, so she had to arrange for the procedure to be expedited by a friend in Washington DC and mailed to her in New York City.[24]

On her way to New York City she stopped at Josephine and Aubrey's apartment in Chicago. "My best friend" Mary Fry was also there with other friends and relatives to wish her bon voyage. Marcet reported further to Mary while on board the *Aquitania*. Aunt Jane was "horrified" that she was traveling third class with a *Daily Worker* group of communist reporters. Marcet had insisted on this arrangement herself, though, hoping to broaden her acquaintances as much as possible so she would be invited into the homes of Russian friends and relatives. She cautioned Mary to write Henry "twice a week," while Alice would be "all right" while she was gone.[25]

Supporters and opponents alike were engrossed in Marcet's description of her trip and of the Russian system. Idealists—male and female, young and old—were especially entranced over the social and economic experiment taking place in the Soviet Union. Malcolm Cowley spoke for these people of what the Russians were attempting:

All through the 1930s the Soviet Union was a second fatherland for millions of people in other countries, including our own. It was the land where men and women were sacrificing themselves to create a new civilization, not for Russia alone, but for the world. It was not so much a nation, in the eyes of Western radicals, as it was an ideal, a faith and an international hope of salvation.[26]

Marcet reported that the Finns were quite skeptical of anyone going to or coming from Russia. The groups she was with were supportive of the Soviet Union, and the Finns were hostile because they were afraid their workers would be "stirred" to follow the lead of Soviet workers and revolt. The train they took from Finland had the berths made up—three decks in each compartment. The space between the walls and the berths was so narrow you had to "sidle" through the car. She visited a collective farm near Moscow. Stalin's picture hung on the office wall, and a half-dozen men, neatly dressed like farmers in the American Midwest, were working at clerical jobs. The vegetable farm consisted of 407 hectares (about 1,000 acres), farmed by 233 families with 120 horses to do the work while the collective awaited its turn to acquire tractors. Those who were dissatisfied with the collective had left, and those who remained believed it would be "the greatest misfortune" to have to leave the group. Once a year the members elected a board of seven directors, three from the office and four from the fields.[27]

A week later Marcet reported from Red Square, where the fourteenth anniversary of the October Revolution had just been celebrated. "Long Live the World October," read banners everywhere in Russian, English, German, and "other languages." The celebration included two paid days off for workers. "Festival was in the air," she wrote, but "under the gaiety there was something deeper." The present generation did not take their favored status for granted "and savored it to the full." Line after line of khaki-clad soldiers with pale green helmets marched into the square. Amid a clatter of hoofs, Kliment Voroshilov, commander of the Red Army, rode past the troops while the military band played "the ever-stirring 'International.'" Voroshilov dismounted and delivered an address describing how every young peasant and worker must serve a year in the army. Next in line came the "osoaviachim," boys and girls in their teens and early twenties, each carrying a gun they had been trained to use, no two dressed alike. Then came the cavalry, tanks, trucks, armored cars. It took one hour and twenty minutes for all this military display to pass. "It was an unforgettable experience," she observed.[28]

Marcet concluded her tour with a visit to Ukraine, a thousand miles south of Moscow. She was invited to stay with a Russian family there and met with people who had been collectivized. When farmers actually lived together, she learned, it was a commune; when they owned their homes but had livestock and farms in common, it was a "kolhoz," or collective farm. There were no fences, but an elderly man from the collective tended the cattle. There were "acres and acres of wheat." Occasionally there was a hay meadow and cows and huts in a village with chickens and small gardens. In the early years of the revolution, the communists tried to enforce collectivization but discovered force did not work with the Russian people, so currently they admitted a man to a collective farm only if he wanted to join and believed it best for him and the others in the collective for him to do so.[29]

Marcet observed that the Soviets used a card system for purchases. Category A-1 encompassed all collective and industrial workers, B-1 included all men and women in light industry, including teachers, writers, and professionals; category B-2 included office and factory clerks, housewives, guides, and interpreters. Children had special cards. They all paid the same amount for purchases, but the difference came in the amounts one could purchase. Bread and sugar could be obtained plentifully, bread by the day and sugar by the month. Those in categories 1 and 2 were allowed a quarter of a pound of tea a month. Russians, she wrote, drank tea like Americans drank Coca-Cola. Those in category 1 could also purchase herring, olive oil, barley, and a pound of butter monthly. A special order form from one's union or place of employment was required for shoes. Shoes at the cooperative store cost 10–15 rubles, compared with 50 rubles at the commercial store.[30]

Caroline Lowe wrote Marcet that "we are all reading your articles with great interest." Marcet, she said, was much better prepared to write them after her visit was extended for "several weeks," rather than the two she had originally planned. Either John Gunn or Mary Fry had told her that Marcet had written that "if it were not for your family you would be glad to remain in Russia indefinitely." Emanuel telegraphed Marcet when she landed in New York City of his happiness over her "safe return" and said that her articles had been "ideally fitted to the papers." He was "thinking seriously" of sending her to China and India.[31]

Emanuel returned to his quest of denouncing the president. The editors of the *American Freeman* warned Hoover of their intention to publish a special edition in December 1931 devoted to his financial and business record. They enclosed a set of proofs for him to peruse, stating that if anything was untrue they did not wish to print it, whereas if the story was true, they insisted on the right to publish anything they could prove "as absolutely true." Hoover ignored their open letter.[32]

The charges this time were extended to Hoover engaging in "slave trading" by transporting Chinese coolies to South Africa to work in the gold mines. Bewick, Moreing and Company, of course, owned or controlled many of these mines. After the Boer uprising in 1902, mine owners in South Africa no longer had an endless supply of cheap black labor and sought other sources. At that point, 50 cents daily no longer attracted native labor in this dangerous work that killed 71.25 per 1,000 yearly. To prevent white labor from taking over the work and organizing to force higher wages and better working conditions, Chinese coolie labor provided a good alternative because they would gladly work for 25 cents per day.[33]

To receive approval for this scheme from the South African legislature and the British Parliament, Alfred Lyttleton told Parliament that the wage scale would be 50 cents per day and that the coolies would be permitted to bring their wives and children and live in "garden cities" where they could grow fruit and vegetables. Actually, they lived in compounds enclosed like prisons. Two thousand coolies were herded into a half-acre compound with twenty per hut. Flogging and torture were used on those who tried to escape. Workers were returned home after three years. In case of death, the relatives were paid $50. Their families were left in China, and the "slaves" were barred from holding property or practicing a trade in Africa. Hoover's contract called for $10 per slave and $25 for shipping them to South Africa, and giving him a lucrative monopoly on the traffic.[34]

This sordid story was revealed in the trial of Anthony Rowe, an associate of Hoover's in the company. An ex-convict, he and Hoover violated the rules of the Moreing Company, which directed that speculation in mining companies should be done in the name of the company, not as an individual partner. The pair violated the rule by speculating secretly in the shares of the company's Great Fingall mine. Hoover, the "engineer" partner, and Rowe, the secretary of the company, received all information about the mine by cable. Based on inside tips, the two secretly bought up Great Fingall shares, a procedure revealed by a director named Robinson. Rowe fled to Canada but was captured and extradited to England, where he stood trial and was sentenced to ten years in prison. Six days before Rowe was extradited, Hoover sailed for Australia on "a business trip and was unable to be reached."[35]

Retribution from the Hoover administration over these adverse stories was swift. It had denied U.S. mailing privileges to the *Organized Farmer*, a Minnesota newspaper that had reprinted the *Freeman* version. Hoover called an executive meeting over the issue, at which an official from the U.S. Attorney General's office "stated positively that the *Freeman* could not be suppressed legally." Hoover could not sue because the action would have to take place in Kansas, where state law provided that truth could be used as a defense. A Post Office official suggested denying mailing privileges, and this was accepted. The usual procedure was to require the accused one week's detailed analysis of its subscriptions. In this case, the *Freeman* had to provide three weeks of information. Officials were using the Minnesota instance as a test case. If the newspaper was at fault, it would have to pay 1 cent per subscriber, or $500, which would put the *Freeman* out of business.[36]

In exposing this scandal, the *Freeman*'s subscription list grew from 32,792 on 2 January to 45,802 on 13 February, but the Post Office figures were 46,000 and 57,000 for the same dates, because officials were counting gift subscriptions along with current permanent ones. Subscribers should notify the newspaper henceforth which were gift subscriptions, because the *Freeman*, of course, could not accurately count its subscriptions without this information. The editors intended to use the crisis to expand its

subscription list by appealing to readers to contribute to its defense and
to send in gift subscriptions.[37]

In this same issue the editors reprinted the story of Arthur Train's article
in *Collier*'s on 20 February 1932 in defense of Hoover, but the editors did
not mention the *Freeman* story. A New York lawyer and novelist, Train
was actually answering similar charges against Hoover in a book by John
Harnell titled *The Strange Career of Mr. Hoover under Two Flags*. Train's
article came after the *Freeman*'s circulation jumped to 300,000 with the
special Hoover story.[38]

Postal officials chose to punish the editor of the *Freeman* by suppress-
ing the offending article and fining him for the next two issues after the
Hoover story. All copies of the issue were sent to the dead letter office in
Washington DC and were destroyed. This occurred after the Haldeman-
Julius Company had spent $700 to mail it to subscribers. With the two
anti-Hoover stories, this amounted to a $1,400 loss to mail the copies. As
a result of this action, the company was forced to cut publication of the
Freeman to twice monthly. On 15 October, President Hoover announced
in a speech that the author of the statement that he dealt in enslaved coolie
labor had retracted that "lie." Emanuel denied that anyone connected
with the story had retracted anything and offered $10,000 to anyone who
could prove that anyone had retracted anything. There were no takers. In
all this ballyhoo, of course, Emanuel had his name splashed on the front
pages of newspapers across the nation, which he loved.[39]

Several important elections were held in November 1932. First of
all, Franklin D. Roosevelt crushed Hoover's attempt at reelection by
a vote of 23 million to 16 million. For a vacant Senate seat from Kansas, Emanuel had announced over a year previously he would accept the
nomination of either major party for the post. Neither the Democrats
nor the Republicans would endorse this radical, of course, so he ran as a
socialist. Prior to the election, Emanuel offered to "throw the dice" with
opponents Democrat George McGill and Republican Ben Paulen. "By
this economic and sensible throw of the dice," he assured them, "the
nitwit voters stand a chance of getting a real statesman like myself in
Washington." His offer was declined.[40]

Clinton W. Gilbert, a nationally syndicated columnist, reported that Emanuel, "publisher of 5¢ books, formerly a Sociologist and certainly a radical," was doing well in his campaign. "If the election were held today [July 17, 1931] he would beat all opponents." W. G. Clugston, a well-known Kansas political analyst, said he had interviewed conservative Republicans and leading farmers who told him that if economic improvements did not come before the next election, Emanuel would become "a real factor."[41]

The Roosevelt landslide carried McGill into office with 45.7 percent of the vote; Paulen won 42 percent, and Emanuel came in a poor third with 12.3 percent. John R. Brinkley, the notorious "goat gland" doctor, ran again as an Independent for governor in this election. By winning he hoped to be able to pack the state medical board with supporters and retrieve his medical license, which had recently been revoked. Brinkley used his radio station effectively, and during the campaign he went from town to town on his Ammunition Train No. 1 (a truck with sides that let down like a tailgate) using an amplifier to promise voters free textbooks, a lake in every county, and hundreds of miles of paved roads. He also used Marcet's article on Curtis and the American Bond and Mortgage Company, but all to no avail, as Alf Landon easily defeated him. Following the election the circulation of the *Freeman* headed down, falling to 36,061 by mid-December.[42]

Emanuel condemned the rise of Nazis to power in Germany after receiving a detailed report on the German situation from Cornelius Vanderbilt Jr. following the Hitler "revolution." This Vanderbilt was "a noted traveler" who had visited Emanuel a year earlier and wrote him from Paris on 7 April 1933. He reported Germany as preparing for war "five years or more hence." A German cabinet member told him Hitler had 866,000 men in the Stahlhelm, 100,000 in the Reichswehr, 60,000 stormtroopers (for domestic riots), and 150,000 special private police. The French secret service was estimating 3.6 million "trained manpower" in Germany. Vanderbilt had "chatted" with Hitler and interviewed "almost everyone of importance there."

Vanderbilt had witnessed no atrocities, but German authorities informed him that the Jews "must be persecuted, and the French punished."

Germans blamed the United States for the humiliating Treaty of Versailles and were boycotting Woolworths, Ford, and other American companies. He concluded that Germany was "no place for American tourists" and that "the longer diplomatic representation takes [for the Nazi government] the stronger we make the position of America with these rash partisans."[43]

Emanuel editorialized on the Nazi situation in the *Freeman* in January 1934. He labeled Hitler's power "a death grip" on 65 million Germans. The führer was surrounded by "sadists, homosexuals, dope addicts, and murderers." This crazy man had given the civilized world a "spectacle of horror, frenzy, blood lust, perversion, and triumphant medievalism." Hitler, Emanuel believed, "belongs in an insane asylum," but instead he controls "the most populous country in Central and Western Europe." Hitler came to power, Emanuel noted accurately, by having Goering "burn the Reichstag" in February 1933 and blaming Jewish conspirators for the arson. They then pursued pogroms against the Jews, driving them out of German courts, schools, hospitals, and the universities. Hitler hounded, tortured, and murdered thousands of communist leaders, and slaughtered pacifists. Socialist leaders were killed, imprisoned, or exiled. He exiled Albert Einstein because he was a Jew. He had "murdered every manifestation of democracy" in Germany.[44]

The Nazis further inflamed world public opinion against them when, in November 1938, they initiated a pogrom against Jews. Targeting Jewish shops, they smashed display windows, leaving sidewalks littered with broken glass. It was referred to as the "Reich Crystal Night." Stormtroopers looted and burned Jewish houses and apartments everywhere in coordinated attacks.

Meanwhile, back in Kansas, Emanuel's monetary woes continued, which in turn, meant financial problems for Marcet. She listed the *New Appeal* as worth $125,000 in the new will she made in 1934. In this will, her lawyer emphasized rights of courtesy, under which, if the wife does not wish "her husband to participate in the equivalent to the wife's dower rights, her wishes prevail." Under the terms of their 1925 agreement, the attorney declared, Emanuel had "already received far more of the estate than he would be entitled to through Courtesy," and thus he had waived that right. The attorney informed Marcet that he resented "a great deal the highly unnecessary suffering to which you have been subjected" and found it deplorable that "a man's philosophy should have such a duality that his published views as to important relationships should be so different from his own. . . . Our mutual friend has so many qualities that I do like, but certainly this is a defect in his whole being." By November, her lawyer saw no alternative to solving her problems with Emanuel "except legal action."[45]

The agreement she and Emanuel made for her to operate the household never had sufficient funding for her expenses in running a large house with constant guests; in addition, he frequently was so stretched financially that he could not meet this obligation fully. Marcet had the farm in Cedarville, but it certainly was not a paying proposition in these depressed conditions. Henry adored Mary Fry and often spent time with her in Cedarville. Sometimes he spent the school year with Mary, costing Marcet $25 monthly for his care and tuition for the schools there. These straitened circumstances were further accentuated when extortionists threatened Emanuel, Alice, and Henry unless they received $50,000. Henry was in Cedarville, and Emanuel took Alice to stay with relatives in Kansas City while he moved from place to place. On 11 December 1933 the extortionists were exposed and Emanuel and Alice returned home.[46]

Marcet was enduring major financial stress. Following the national banking crisis, she wrote Alice that Emanuel owed her $150. She felt this was "ominous." "If he had felt friendly, he would have given [me] some—or at least so it seems to me." Marcet was certain he was concealing something. When servants George and Leroy cleaned his library they told Marcet they had seen deposit slips from Philadelphia, Baltimore, and Topeka banks. "I am glad if he is salting something down for himself," she wrote Alice, "but if true, he is not so pushed as he often wants us to think—as, for instance, at this moment."[47]

Marcet had been estranged from Emanuel since January 1932. She spent five months in Cedarville but felt compelled to return to Girard for Christmas. She had been able, she wrote Alice, to be her "genuine self" in

Cedarville. She thought she brought out Emanuel's worse traits—and vice versa—when they were around each other. She noted that Henry loved his father sincerely and that she was happy that Alice and her father were "drawing near together." By late 1932 Emanuel had cut her household budget by two-thirds, paying her $50 weekly. But the declining profitability of the *Freeman*, which was practically his only income, forced him to suspend two weeks' allowance during the banking crisis of March 1933 when Roosevelt was inaugurated. That May he was forced financially to cut the *Freeman* to a monthly.[48]

Emanuel and Marcet were constantly growing farther apart. He was living in his office, and in June 1933 she wrote him a note, observing that it was not "fair to Alice" to make her "an oral messenger between us." Marcet, Henry, and Alice "deeply wish you would come home," she wrote. They turned down his bed every night and set his place at the table every evening. "I am hoping this little change of routine and food has done you good," she continued, and "when you return, both the farm and ourselves will wear a more agreeable aspect to you." This was not to be, and their relations worsened.[49]

In December 1933 Marcet finally filed suit against Emanuel, charging "extreme cruelty": he was being "vexatious" toward her and "sought to discommodate her." That June he had become angry with the way Alice was dancing with a friend and he left home for a week, then made this arrangement permanent. In addition, he had "lived lavishly, unstinted, and beyond his means all with the view and intent on his part of wrongfully squandering and concealing his wealth." She further charged in her suit that in August 1932, without notice to her, he had dissolved the *New Appeal* company, resolved all its debts with creditors, and reorganized the company into a new one. Her one share of stock, she argued, gave her legal rights to a knowledge of company affairs. She was fighting to gain possession of the Haldeman-Julius Publishing Company in order to protect it from ruin so the children would eventually inherit it. The judge set alimony at $75 per week until a permanent settlement was achieved. Emanuel, of course, denied living lavishly. That June the judge ordered him to pay Marcet's attorney $3,000. But between January and June the couple adjusted their tangled financial and personal affairs, and on Marcet's motion the judge dismissed the case "without prejudice."[50]

Emanuel had driven to the farm and asked her to go for a ride. They drove to Fort Scott for "coffee and sardines" and talked for almost four hours. She made sure he understood "how deeply I love him and always will," but she also made clear why she must have the plant in her name. She believed that "a real rapprochement had been achieved" that day. The next day, though, his lawyer appeared in the office of her attorney and offered for Emanuel to turn the plant over to her, leave town, "and get an editorial job somewhere else—simply that." He had made the point to her that the judge did not like him and, because she was a woman, he "would not get a fair deal." Marcet, of course, wanted the "status quo ante bellum," but with the plant in her name.[51]

A few days later they reached "a tentative agreement." He would sign over the publishing plant and she would lease it to him for $75 a week, with increased rent if economic conditions improved. This would return the situation to where it was before the suit, except the plant would be in her name to safeguard for the children. She believed the struggle had been "well worth while." Emanuel, however, did not feel responsible for her lawyers' fees and offered to pay only $200, rather than their bill for $5,000. The following month her lawyers drew up a payment arrangement that Emanuel accepted. The couple, however, never truly reconciled after this, especially as Emanuel felt betrayed over the lawyers' fees and refused to be mollified.[52]

Shortly afterward, Emanuel wrote his old friend Isaac Goldberg about the legal tangle. "It took a suit to find out that I was really hard up," he said, adding that the only ones who won, as usual, were the attorneys. Then he noted that, in addition to "money trouble," there was "woman trouble too." There was also "man trouble" that he failed to mention.[53]

John Gunn had been a fierce supporter from the day Emanuel arrived in Girard. During the Depression, John had continued to work on the *Liberty Encyclopedia*, a collection of essays on radicals, but as economic conditions worsened he developed a drinking problem and Emanuel decided he had to terminate his old friend. John could not perform on the job as he should, and under the present economic conditions the plant could not afford free riders. John responded with a plea for toleration. He pointed out he did his drinking on weekends when it did not affect his work. He was drinking in Emanuel's home, but as Marcet's invited guest. He quoted what Emanuel said in *The Great American Parade*:

If the conditions of society demand that we live together agreeably, they also demand toleration of contrasting points of view, unlike habits, individual tastes the last degree of conceivable moral freedom. We cannot justly take offense at what is called a "bad example." We have no right to complain save when we are practically, personally injured, when there is a real interference with our own freedom.

John also pleaded to finish the *Liberty Encyclopedia* he was working hard to complete. To no avail; he remained fired.[54] Marcet wrote Emanuel that she was "crushed." He replied:

I don't want to continue this argument. I have been more than fair. John isn't able to hold down a job, because, as you said yesterday he's a pathological case. . . . I am sick and tired of having you interfere with the plant's operation. I am doing my best to save it, and will, if left alone. If I'm not, we will all go down in ruin, for we are still in a terrible jam. Don't forget that the home is mortgaged, that debts are sky high—and there is only one way to work out—through letting me alone so I can get this plant producing again.

From his office, Emanuel wrote that "until I get assurances that I will not be heckled and badgered any more, I plan to stay down here." Getting in the last word, Marcet offered "no assurances that I will refrain from protesting against injustice or pleading for mercy will be forthcoming."[55]

Conditions during the Depression led Marcet and John to become alcoholics, and even led Emanuel to drink to excess at times. For years Marcet "had gone on drinking sprees." In August 1933 she drove Mary's car from Cedarville to Monroe, Wisconsin, where "she had a few drinks" at a café. The police stopped her for driving "the wrong way around the courthouse, and for backing into a light post." She resisted arrest and was fined $15. She told authorities she did much literary work "and drank a little beer to relax and get away from her strenuous work." Marcet was concerned over the resultant publicity, especially after the Associated Press picked up the story. Mary was convinced that "Marcet's constant worry over money caused her to overindulge."[56]

During 1934, Emanuel was having one of his "periodic love flings," which again infuriated Marcet, but this time she decided to respond. John Gunn, a longtime friend of Marcet's, became her "emotional stay." She empathized with his drinking problem. Soon he moved into the house, and they lived together, and drank together.

In September 1934, Alice started classes at the University of Kansas. Marcet told her that Emanuel had promised, no matter what happened, that he would always contribute $15 weekly toward Alice's education at the university. "Always send your love to him when you write," Marcet cautioned. By this time Emanuel had been forced to cut the *Freeman* to a monthly and to make it a question-and-answer newspaper. It was "a peculiar way to run a paper," he admitted, but he was able to keep it going in this manner, despite the Depression.[57]

In the summer of 1935, on Emanuel's forty-sixth birthday, Marcet sent her congratulations in a telegram. Aunt Jane had died that May, and Marcet had traveled to Cedarville for her memorial service. Emanuel replied with a thank-you for remembering his birthday and described his activities. He was still the whole show at Haldeman-Julius Publications, and the *Freeman* was supporting the family. Writing for the journal "kept him from long fits of depression," he admitted. The circulation was down to 25,000, but these numbers constituted "a loyal following." On her forty-eighth birthday, Marcet treated herself to a thorough physical examination. For some time she had suffered pains around her heart, the area of the operation for cancer in 1925. It was not recurring cancer this time, however, but her heart that was in trouble. She asked Alice to tell no one, including Emanuel, because people might get the notion to try and collect debts she owed.[58]

A crisis came in February 1936 during what Marcet called "a hellish week." Emanuel called her to report that he had a letter from a

Pittsburg lawyer with a bill of hers for $4.76. He told Marcet he would pay it out of her weekly money. She indignantly replied that she would pay it off at $1 weekly. "You would have thought it was for $400 rather than $4," she said. In the Roaring Twenties, $400 was an easy profit on weekly sales of Little Blue Books, but in the 1930s a $4 debt seemed as imposing as a $400 debt.

A relative wrote Marcet about marking Jane's gravesite. She thought "a very plain and simple marker . . . with . . . the inscription JANE ADD- AMS OF HULL HOUSE AND THE WOMEN'S LEAGUE FOR PEACE AND FREEDOM" with dates would be sufficient. She wanted Marcet's approval of this. She also passed along the rumor that the State of Illinois was planning for a marker for Jane at Cedarville in the form of a state park, or simply a monument to Jane, provided Marcet would sell the homestead. She mentioned Marcet's borrowing $1,000 from Jane and said that the estate lawyer wanted to know about arrangements for repayment. Finally, the relative had heard rumors of Marcet having burned "family records and some of Aunt Jane's personal effects" in a trunk she had used at Rockford College.[59]

Marcet responded that the marker would be fine. Also, she thought Jane's name and dates should be on the "large Addams monument." "Mary and I read with amazement," she replied, "your questions regarding the destruction of the family records." Neither of them had heard "the foolish chatter," but she thought she knew the source of the rumors. Marcet had decided to use the "pleasant, roomy cottage" to live in when she visited Cedarville while the homestead was being rented. She moved what furniture she needed for the smaller house and stored the remainder in the garret of the main house, which is where the trunk most like would be found. Everything regarding letters and trunks that were there when her grandmother died "is here." They saw "no trace of the missing diary you spoke of," however, but were still looking for it. Aseneth told old Mrs. Knowlton (over eighty) that Marcet was cleaning out the garret to make room for storage. "Old Mrs. Knowlton then told Aunt Flora I was burning letters." It was "likely Mrs. Knowlton told her sister," who was visiting. Aunt Flora also told Bertha Bidwell and

Amelia Sears. "The little clique on Stephenson Street have able, lively minds," Marcet wrote, "but pathetically idle ones, so they talk on and on," and the rumors start flying.[60]

At this time, Marcet received an unexpected windfall. A man by the name of Brackett died and left her $3,000 because, he said, he had enjoyed her writings in the Haldeman-Julius Publications over the years and wanted to do something to keep the company functioning. In typical fashion, Marcet turned the entire sum over to her husband. Just as typically, Emanuel accepted it, observing that "I'll be able to breathe for a spell." The windfall quickly disappeared among anxious creditors.[61]

On his forty-seventh birthday, Emanuel wrote Marcet, thanking her for her gift. She was spending more and more time in Cedarville, finding life there more pleasant than at Girard. She found her nostalgia for the past growing, her interest in her family history consuming more and more of her time. As her hopes for a meaningful marriage dimmed, she turned increasingly to the past for sustenance. The old homestead, with its beautiful Georgian house built by her maternal grandfather, John Addams, was full of memories for her. John Addams's writing desk, attached to the living room wall, was all that remained of the furniture, and while in Cedarville she used it constantly, writing letters, paying bills, looking back at the lives of her forebears. On 20 October 1938 she wrote a letter to Alice that included the Addams family tree for nine generations, emphasizing the family's constant dedication to the land.[62]

Beyond survival, the Haldeman-Julius family interests for the remainder of the decade centered around the adventures of Alice and Henry in college in Lawrence. In early August 1936, before classes started, Alice wrote "Bo-Peep" that she was uncertain if she "could skrew [sic] up the courage" to talk to her father about school. "I know he will give me the rock bottom talk," but when the question arises, "he'll kick in with as much as he can." Emanuel's mail that day brought in only $8, but he "doesn't seem so *worried* as he should be if he was in as deep as his letter to you said." Alice was beginning to believe Marcet was correct in insisting that Emanuel was "poor mouthing" more than he should. She thought perhaps she should start a college chest, like a hope chest. She decided the wise course was to get "Daddy" to pay for her room in Lawrence and get her clothes and other necessities "all at once."[63]

That October, in a letter to her mother, Alice referred to John Gunn's termination at the plant. John had "in a sense brought it upon himself by "too frequent indulgence," yet he had produced "a well-written and comprehensive beginning of a good encyclopedia." On the other hand, "when a horse throws you off," you have to get back on again. Likewise, when a man starts a job "he wants to finish it." It was logical that Gunn would want to finish the encyclopedia. Mercy and justice, she concluded, just do not fit "practically" into the capitalist system. "Daddy should come home," she concluded, John should go back to work and cut out such heavy drinking, "and you should be allowed the security of a united family."[64]

Emanuel again described his financial woes to Marcet early the next year. He noted that although the plant was "actually making money right now," he was burdened with paying off some debts and stalling other creditors. He owed $9,000 on the *Freeman* and settled that debt for $3,000. He was paying "Rippey" his $4,200 in daily installments, "sometimes as little as $5," but there was also a bill for $1,100 for paper and an invoice of $360 for envelopes. He was paying off the remaining noteholders, especially manuscript readers, in $10 monthly installments, "and there hasn't been a squawk." He held out the enticement that Marcet should get back to writing. He still heard from readers "who want to know when you are going to return to your writing," and it would mean "easily" $100 monthly, which she could certainly use.[65]

Alice wrote her father in February 1935, during her second semester at the university, to thank him for "the five-spot." Shops were beginning to show "little things for spring," and she planned to go shopping. She would spend "the $5 for purses and hats and things that look well with last year's suit." Spring fever had captured her. "The fever may mean love-making for some, but for me it's a new bonnet." She, along with three thousand others, had just heard a concert conducted by Karl Krueger, who "so gracefully gave two encores that he won the whole audience." She believed that being able to attend concerts like this was "one big advantage in going to a large school."[66]

A few days later, in another letter to her father, Alice returned to the subject of how important clothes are to a woman. She was sure Bo-Peep would throw up her hands and say, "Al's got enough dresses . . . wait until they wear out. But the funny thing is they don't wear out. They go out of style and season." She was thinking of taking up tennis "and thus regain what I may of my girlish figure." She reported on an earthquake she had slept through. The university's seismograph "was out of order, so they don't know how much of a shock we got . . . and did Californians snicker over our little quiverings!"[67]

Emanuel wrote that he had read her essay on the topic of the horse and believed "it was a good piece of perfect portraiture"—high praise indeed from the master editor. He thought she could become "a first-rate novelist" if she wanted to. If she would write a 60,000-word novel he would pay her $100, and if he found it publishable he would increase the stipend to $400. He knew this was a lot of money, "and Alice loved money (a characteristic of this family)." She responded immediately. She was greatly enthused with this proposal and "even tried to knock off a couple of paragraphs before my noon class." Then she considered she had no plot nor time to work on it with all her college pressures. She promised to think about doing a novel and thanked him again for the $5. The "greenbacks" are "so tangible."[68]

Around this time, Alice told Marcet she needed eyeglasses. She could not "bear the thought of causing you any more expense," so she wrote "Daddy." He sent her $14 to pay for them. "It is marvelous how they do help," she concluded. After wearing them, she realized "how important it was to have them right away. . . . I guess I have been suffering from eye strain and didn't know it . . . and when I found out about it, they became an imperative item." She admitted she was receiving B's in four classes but A's in music and political parties. She was not sure about "Paleo."[69]

In her senior year she enrolled in a Shakespeare course and asked Marcet to ask Emanuel if they had *King Lear* in a Little Blue Book. "It would save having to buy a more expensive copy." She had to carry eighteen hours the last semester to graduate, with twelve in junior- and senior-level classes.[70]

Emanuel wrote his friend Isaac Goldberg in June 1935. He could not resist bragging a little about his printing business. He had sold 200 million Little Blue Books and about 50 million of the other books. Sales had reached a peak in 1929, a bad low in 1932, and a slow recovery since then, and he thought he would be "on higher ground in about two years." He noted that Girard was the smallest First Class Post Office in the country. With its population it should be Fourth or perhaps Third Class, but his publishing company bought $150,000 annually in postage, plus $60,000 in stamps received from customers. The office provided home delivery, as in First Class cities, and had kept all its employees, because "they believed they would be needed before long." The *Freeman*'s circulation was 25,000, but he expected it "to reach 100,000 in about two years." Emanuel believed he could have been "10 times as big if I had let myself publish the kind of trash one finds in a McFadden publication." He never wanted to go "much beyond my 1929 volume."[71]

In early 1936 he was negotiating with the Lewis Copeland Company to republish some of his Little Blue Books. "*The Autobiography of a Pimp* sounds like a swell book," Copeland wrote him, and if it was still in manuscript form he "would try to place it here for you with a publisher." Emanuel, of course, would receive "the regular royalty." He expected "some real business" from the clothbound books based on Little Blue Books. Their idea was to combine several Little Blue Books on related subjects into one complete clothbound book. The work would then be published by low-priced trade publishers. Instead of the usual royalties, Emanuel insisted on $1,000 as an advance on royalties, which Copeland managed to raise by unstinted effort. Copeland had yet to receive any compensation for his efforts. He failed to understand Emanuel's position. The books involved would each sell from 50,000 to 100,000 copies and, while not as successful as Durant's *The Story of Philosophy*, would certainly produce cash royalties "for many years." Now was the time for Emanuel to decide what he wanted to, do as "the publishers are planning their fall books." Emanuel agreed to the offer.[72]

Emanuel wrote Marcet on 5 January, "as ever, with love," that he was happy that she had the farm "well in hand." It would be "nice if it really became productive." Farming generally was not productive during the Great Depression, and Marcet spent much time and some money trying to save the old homestead out of sentimental reasons. He reported the plant "running smoothly," although all cash "goes to pay the bills." He still had to meet the tax bills for the farm and the plant, but "I believe I will get it all handled OK." He reported great difficulty "getting the money Copeland owes me." Copeland still owed him $500, and "I had to keep at him $5 at a time." He concluded, "I don't think the great Lewis is burning up New York."[73]

The next year Emanuel handled William J. Fielding's *Shackles of the Supernatural*. Fielding had submitted the manuscript to thirteen American publishers and one in London, all of which had rejected it within a year. Emanuel told him, "You did what I feared—wrote a masterpiece that simply has to be published, even though it will mean financial losses for the publisher." He was currently "strapped for money" and estimated the loss at $500. Thus he would accept the manuscript for $200 plus "an additional free shipment of 200 copies of the book." He made no suggestion for what an author should do with 200 copies of his book, but Fielding, out of desperation, accepted the offer in January 1938. He noted that he had "put so much sweat and blood and indignation and loving tenderness" into the manuscript that he could "never hope to be reimbursed in money for the effort."[74]

In early 1938, during her final year at the University of Kansas, Alice reported typing a paper for Henry, who was now also at the university. She spent much of the night on it and then had to do her own class work. She added a perceptive paragraph on her father when writing to Marcet:

> Don't you pay any attention to the nasty things Haldeman-Julius said. . . . [I]t is easy to see he is afraid . . . of how good business is . . . and if you find out how things are going good you'll want more money. What I can't understand is how you can even consider the things he says . . . [he's] crazy, conceited, etc. . . . he's simply repeating the things that he subconsciously knows are wrong with himself, and he hates you because you are just the opposite. . . . [I]f anyone is crazy

he is, and no one but a colossal egotist could tell anyone with so much substantial character about them such as you have, the things that he doesn't even come halfway up to them. . . . He's just a piece of glass battering itself against solid diamond . . . and the sparks fly from the weaker substance.[75]

Henry also wrote his mother from the university. He had talked to his rhetoric professor and gave her a long song-and-dance about how, after a long talk with "Daddy and you about the plant," he decided he wanted to combine "my research theme and this one, into one long theme of 5,000 words." "Last night" on the train he wrote 900 words and then about 900 more "this afternoon." The fact that he had something to show his professor is what "made it so easy," and the "actual truth" was that he was really interested in writing about the plant. He could only "thank God" he had read his father's *First Hundred Million* before talking to her. She was "all het up" about Wayland, so he would probably "make a third of the theme about him."[76]

The early Depression years were difficult ones for Emanuel: he was plagued by creditors, was sued for libel in 1931, had the Post Office ban an issue of the *American Freeman* in 1932, and was sued for negligence in a car wreck that killed a young woman from Joplin in 1932. In addition, he found himself involved in a second lawsuit with the quack Norman Baker, this time for $500,000. Baker ran a mail-order business for batteries and alarm clocks. More importantly, he experimented with medicine. One day he discovered a paste used to take knots off the shins of horses. This was quite similar to the "Hoxie" cure for cancer that originated in Taylorsville, Illinois, and he hyped it as a cure for cancer. Baker also published a magazine called *The Naked Truth*, owned the café TNT, a service station named TNT in Muscatine, Iowa, and a low-wattage radio station, TNT, to advertise his "cure" for cancer. Tragically, many people invested millions in his "cancer cure" rather than seeking legitimate medical help. Emanuel exposed his "quackery," and Baker sued.[77]

In his suit, Baker charged that the articles in the *Freeman* describing his "cure" were libelous. Emanuel had asserted that Baker was a medical quack. Emanuel used the suit to go to his reading public again for financial help. He dispensed with his "question and answer" format and filled the *Freeman* with material on Baker's methods and his legal attack. Emanuel established a fund, calling it the Defense Fund, and by the end of the year had received more than $1,500 in contributions. The suit resulted in Baker's being jailed for practicing medicine without a license. After he was released he moved to Arkansas, where John Brinkley was practicing. Emanuel was completely vindicated, and he had an additional $1,500 he had not anticipated.[78]

RESURRECTION, 1938–1951

Despite a national downturn in 1937, Emanuel's business experienced an upturn during the year. After eight years of struggling to pay the bills, his publishing career had reached its nadir in 1936. Business was slow, and the small number of titles between 1936 and 1938 accentuated this sluggishness. The publishing world seemed to turn around in 1937 as consumers began to spend some of their money on cheap books. It began to rebound noticeably in 1938 when Emanuel started issuing some new titles. But progress was slow going. In 1936 he published *The Autobiography of a Pimp*. "Don't miss the confession of a real pimp," warned the *American Freeman*. Mr. Haldeman-Julius "told me to tell the truth candidly, fearlessly, honestly. I obeyed his instructions to the letter," reported the author.[1] He followed this with *The Modern Sex Book*, with its table of contents:

My Husband is impotent—what shall I do?
How to keep your virginity
How to get a Man
How all women can become passionate
How to cure the jitters
The bad girl's handbook
Sex and the whip (flagellation)

This was accompanied by an advertisement for *The Autobiography of a Madame*. In January 1937 he followed with *Aphrodisiacs and Anti-Aphrodisiacs*. Then came a series called "Wild Women in History." His old sales techniques still worked as long as people had some money to spend. The auto industry was recovering, although in the throes of sit-down strikes and being unionized. People were buying cars, why not Little Blue Books? But things had changed in the publishing world since the 1920s as paperbacks now were larger and more attractive. There was a considerable increase in the costs of ink, paper, and other supplies.[2]

In January 1938, Emanuel began a campaign to raise the circulation of the *Freeman* from 28,000 to 50,000. In March he boasted that his exposure of Baker's quackery had led to Baker's indictment for practicing medicine without a license. By June his deficit fund stood at $2,600 and the *Freeman* circulation at 38,000. In January he had changed the name of the Defense Fund to the Deficit Fund and pled for donations. The page soliciting money for his deficit also contained a cartoon of a hardworking editor sitting at a desk, writing for the *American Freeman*. Behind the editor was a wall titled "Deficit Fund" and an ominous cloud of Fascism, Bigotry, Lies, Prejudice, and the Baker lawsuit. At the base of the wall was the proverbial wolf, crouched with fangs bared.[3]

In March 1938, Alice reported to her father that "just about 13 more weeks and I'll be all through school." She graduated from the University of Kansas that spring and went to Chicago to search for a job. Emanuel responded that she seemed "well located. Now let's see you get a nice, pleasant, well-paying job! If there is no luck, do as you say—come home where you will be received royally."[4]

Henry was not so fortunate. In the fall of 1938, at the end of his first semester at the University of Kansas, he received F's in German and comparative anatomy. Emanuel was furious, storming at Marcet that "he's just a failure. Your boy's a failure." Unable to take any of the blame himself, he concluded it was Marcet's fault because she allowed him to have a car, which "he wastes time in," and because he "drinks too much," which Emanuel decided Henry had learned from his mother. Marcet urged Henry to "buckle down" and get to work. After her struggles to finance Alice's higher education, she was happy Emanuel was providing $15 per week to keep Henry in the university, in addition to paying his tuition and fees.[5]

Marcet felt sorry for Henry, but she also empathized with Emanuel, worried that Henry's troubles would embitter him further. She wrote her son that "it is just tragic that the one time your father does what was really right by one of his family, that one member should make him feel his efforts are not worthwhile. It makes me heartsick."[6]

Henry's problem was that he had an average IQ but was the son of a famous publisher. Everyone expected so much of him, especially his father. Alice's graduation from the university surely had an impact on him. She was no longer there to encourage him, praise him when needed and scold when necessary, or do his typing for him. In any case, he failed to meet the university's academic standards and had to abandon his goal of a earning a college degree. In 1939 he was forced to seek employment in the harsh world of depressed economic conditions.

In 1939 the Haldeman-Julius Company received an interesting proposal from the O. D. Jennings Company: selling Little Blue Books through vending machines. The company's attorney believed it would be "far more orderly between you and the company in lieu of the half-dozen documents that now compose the understanding between you." The company had invested $10,000 "in our initial order for a half-million Little Blue Books." Twelve years later, Emanuel described the machine as "big as a juke-box, with all kinds of chromium and neon lights." He witnessed "about 200 of these machines" go out from coast to coast, and "they did well." The one at Thirty-Fourth Street and Broadway in New York City was especially successful in selling books. But each machine cost $149.50, and people "identified the machine with a slot machine and expected to hit the jackpot or something."[7]

Emanuel received more than he bargained for during a nocturnal visit to Joplin one evening in the fall of 1938. His car collided with another, and a young woman in the other car was killed. Emanuel's passenger, Dorothy LeSorge, filed suit for $3,000 for injuries she suffered during the collision. In public testimony he admitted having two whiskies at a nightclub where he picked up LeSorge. They were driving to another nightclub when he swerved into the path of an oncoming car.[8]

Marcet had written the Child Placement Bureau in Kansas City,

Missouri, in April 1939 that she and Emanuel were "seriously considering taking into our home and hearts" a refugee child from Germany, Austria-Hungary, or Czechoslovakia. She asked for further information, "as there are many things to be thought over carefully before we take such a grave step." This was not to be, as Marcet was suffering from a serious medical problem. Her last medical checkup, in June 1935, had revealed a major heart weakness, and as her health continued to deteriorate she experienced a good deal of suffering. In May 1939 she endured a massive heart attack and was confined to bed rest, which she found extremely difficult, as she had always been quite active. She rallied and occasionally could write to her children.[9]

Marcet died in Girard on 13 February 1941 of a coronary embolism—a blocked blood vessel in her heart. She was memorialized two days later with a secular funeral and then cremation. As a freethinker, she wanted a "funeral service devoid of ideology." Several paragraphs from the Little Blue Book *Funeral Services without Theology* were read at the service. The poem "Debtor," by Sara Teasdale, was read:

> So long as my spirit still
> Is glad of breath
> And life lifts its plume of pride
> In the dark face of death;
> While I am conscious still
> Of love and fame,
> Keeping my head too high
> For the years to tame,
> How can I quarrel with fate
> Since I can see
> I am a debtor to life,
> Not life to me?

Marcet had marked in the margin, "This is exactly the way I feel."[10]

John Gunn wrote a eulogy for her, and it was read at the service by a family friend.

Every man is led or misled in a way peculiar to himself. Of no one could these words of Goethe be more truly spoken than of Marcet Haldeman-Julius. Today, for us, they may serve as an insight both sad and proud, to the poignancy of a life whose flame was too brilliant, whose radiance for others was given at the expense of its own self-consuming, and whose soft, farewell gleam was hastened by the unbearable warmth and light of its rare intensity. For it was by the peculiar fitness of her nature that Marcet was led to embrace with an intense yet fluid eagerness, the beauty, the passion, the struggle, the pain and joy of life; while she was misled—or too swiftly led—in that the greatness of her spirit broke itself upon the reefs of a life that mingled the majestic storm with all the loveliness and the longing that even the strongest mortals can scarcely endure, or can endure for only a little while. Marcet loved men and women and horses and dogs . . . and it will also be remembered that Marcet loved herself least. That is why others loved her so much.

Messages of condolence poured into Girard from over the world.[11]

Milton H. Bledsoe wrote for the black newspaper of Kansas City, the *Call*, about her work on behalf of African Americans, calling her "a militant white woman" and saying that her passing "meant the loss of a real friend." She not only believed that "Negroes should have economic and civic privileges but advocated social equality based on education and social fitness instead of skin pigmentation. . . . Whatever improvement has been made at the Jayhawk school in the treatment of colored students can be credited to the courageous will of Mrs. Haldeman-Julius and her family." He wrote that "their interest in building up an interracial movement for the purpose of getting equal rights for Negro students at the Kansas temple of learning should not be forgotten by Kansans."[12]

A few years earlier, Marcet had written Josephine that she wanted her ashes to be scattered from the brow of a hill overlooking Cedar Creek to the cemetery where she would have a marker. "I want to feel that I shall become a part of the woods," she wrote, "the hills, the streams, the rocks and the good, clean earth."[13]

Marcet had been ill for so long that her death was more a blessing than a shock. True to his nature, Emanuel took this as an opportunity to mix nostalgia with the selling of books. The *American Freeman* soon carried an advertisement for the Marcet's collected works. For $1.95 one could purchase the entire set of fourteen "large-size volumes" and eight Little Blue Books she had written. "Needless to say," Emanuel wrote, "this will mean a complete absence of profit." The purpose was to enable "her old and new admirers to become owners of fresh copies of her warm-hearted, absorbing, timely, progressive writings."[14]

The duties of Emanuel's secretary, Sue Haney, included protecting him from marriage-minded women once he was a widower. One asked to see him at the office. Sue "got rid of her," but she "took [Emanuel] by surprise" one evening while he sat alone in his big house. When he answered the door, he let her know he was not interested. She shoved her foot in the open doorway, and he "kicked it out and slammed the door shut." He then had chain fasteners put on every outside door.[15]

An admirer from New Orleans began courting him by sending him a large painting of a bowl of peonies she had painted for him, and then another, and another, dedicated to "Haldeman—Julius, the humorist, sage, word painter, wit, mollified Boccaccio, gentleman." She next attacked his stomach, sending strawberries in the winter, mushrooms and "other Southern delicacies" in the summertime, interspersed with interjections of passionate poetry. "It was getting to the point where we could hardly wait for the next mail," Sue admitted. "Meanwhile," Sue and Emanuel had gotten married on 15 November 1941 in Webb City, a suburb of Joplin, Missouri. When Emanuel "foolishly" mentioned in the *American Freeman* that he had married, the "goodies" suddenly stopped coming.[16]

Sue gave readers an intimate look at some of Haldeman-Julius's personal traits as she saw them. He had a penchant for privacy and took his daily lunch alone. He liked to have a family dinner. He was a charming and entertaining host. At 7:30 on weekday mornings he would turn on his record player to alert the cook to begin preparing his breakfast, then shave to the music of Chopin and shower to Beethoven or Caruso. He enjoyed a challenging game of chess but had no hobbies except reading and writing. "As far back as he could remember, he had been a sort of loner." He needed to feel the presence of others, but he also needed to be left alone.[17]

Although he never inhaled, Emanuel enjoyed smoking. He did not like cigarettes, because their heat came too close to his mouth. Instead, he preferred a pipe—a meerschaum or even a corncob, and at the plant he usually consumed several expensive cigars daily. Sunday was a day of rest, and on Sunday mornings he was not to be awakened unless a tornado was approaching. He had always been a recluse, first by circumstances, later by necessity, and then by choice. Everyone in the family respected his insistence on isolation unless he chose differently. He loved olives. Someone once noted that if Haldeman-Julius ever had a coat of arms, it should appropriately be an olive branch with green fruit attached. Even his huge, white wolfhound developed a taste for olives.[18]

Emanuel made a living by selling through mail order. He also loved to buy through mail order—Rocky Mountain trout, oysters packed in ice, homemade bread from New Jersey, smoked salmon, western fruits, green turtle soup, clothing from Montgomery Ward. He enjoyed most of all his purchase of an electric incubator for hatching chicks. Sue described the ensuing results:

> After placing the incubator in a small room between his office and the front office, we then scoured the countryside for fresh (fertilized?) eggs to fill it. That accomplished, we turned it on, marked the prospective hatching date on a calendar hanging above it and settled down to wait for the incubation process to pass. Excitedly, we had visions of going into the chicken business as a hobby, knowing nothing at the time of the pit-falls and work involved in that messy chore.
>
> Eventually the red letter day arrived for the chicks to start hatching. Excited as an expectant father, Haldeman-Julius spent most of his day in the hatching room waiting for the first yellow head to emerge limply from its shell. I had to reproach him for opening the incubator so much and allowing the eggs to chill. When at last he did find the first fluffy

yellow chick standing bewildered in the tray, he stood there in total wonder, as though a great miracle had taken place right before his eyes. Gathering the tiny thing gently into his cupped hands, like a happy child he proudly carried it around the plant for all his employees to see.[19]

The *American Freeman* did not cover World War II in any detail. Emanuel obviously hated Hitler, as he indicated when he wrote of the führer's rise to power in the early 1930s, and he supported the Allied cause. But defeating Fascism was not his personal battle. He informed Bertrand Russell early in the war that he had been visited by two FBI agents who informed him that *The Black International* was "offensive to many Catholics and its publication is causing controversy in these difficult times." He promised to stop advertising it to meet this objection and to promote unity in the war effort.[20]

Emanuel found himself in an embarrassing situation when he published Thomas Hardy's *Life's Little Ironies* as a Little Blue Book in 1941. He included a notice of "copyright, 1931, by Haldeman-Julius Company." He immediately heard from Harper & Brothers that they had copyrighted the book in 1894, that copyright was renewed by Hardy in 1922, and that it would not expire until 1950. He could only admit, shame-facedly, that when his company reprinted the title "ten years ago" it was understood that the "British copy we used was in the public domain. Our information at the time had it that many of Hardy's early stories were not copyrighted in the United States." Should his company decide to reprint Hardy in the future, "it would be careful to own the copyright line."[21]

Three days before Marcet died, Emanuel launched a *bookskrieg* of his entire list of 2,000 books. For one month only, one could order as many books as desired and receive a copy of them all for $3, postage paid. Individually, they cost 2.5 cents per copy, plus 1 cent per title for postage and handling. Sex titles led the list, followed by self-improvement.[22]

The famous "radio priest" and editor of *Social Justice*, Father Charles Coughlin of Detroit, had attacked Emanuel in his magazine in June 1941. His essay charged Emanuel with writing Prime Minister Winston Churchill and offering to pay the cost of a half-ton bomb of $1,000, plus $100 in gasoline, to drop it on Hitler's "habitat." Coughlin suggested that, instead of sending a bomb, Emanuel should load his pockets with "some of his choice moronic booklets," fly them over Berchtesgaden, and jump. "The stench of the literature would asphyxiate Herr Hitler," he wrote, and America would be rid of both. Emanuel was delighted with the resultant publicity and the subsequent rise in circulation of the *Freeman*.[23]

In January 1941, Emanuel resumed his attack on the Catholic Church by insisting it had "always" supported Fascism, from European countries to Father Coughlin's movement in the United States. "Brutalizarianism," he asserted, was consistently blessed by the Vatican. This attack was not new, because Joseph McCabe had long supplied him with Little Blue Books exposing some aspect or other of what he called the Black International: an alliance between Catholicism and Fascism. To Emanuel, the pope was the principal enemy to Americanism.[24]

Father Coughlin immediately responded that Emanuel's publications were "salacious trash" that he palmed off as educational literature. Haldeman-Julius insisted that the church "hierarchy" was promoting a campaign of protest to force the editor of the *Detroit Free Press* to refuse his advertisement for his *bookskrieg*. Emanuel was delighted, because he was receiving not only free publicity but also free advertising worth $1,135. *Free Press* editor John Knight soon thought out his decision more carefully and sent his bill to Emanuel. Emanuel responded that he refused to pay a publisher who accepted "his business—says he doesn't want my filthy money—and then duns me."[25]

Two months later, Emanuel issued a call to arms. He informed readers of the *American Freeman* that Jesuits and other Catholics were ganging up on him. He was "just a little man standing alone" against this tide of prejudice and intolerance. He urged them to renew their subscriptions so he would know he was "not really alone in the campaign." By October subscriptions to the *Freeman* were up to 65,000. His goal was to reach 100,000.[26]

In January 1942, his *bookskrieg* ad appeared in the *Philadelphia Enquirer*. Like the *Free Press*, the *Enquirer* soon apologized to its readers for running the advertisement without "scrutinizing" it more carefully and not eliminating the titles that "might give offense to any of our readers and in particular to those with firm religious convictions." Emanuel used this incident as further evidence of the conspiracy working against him.

The battle continued, with Father Clarence McAuliffe writing in the Catholic weekly, *America*, about "the audacity of this man who dares in this hour of national peril to slander the Catholic church and all religions." While President Roosevelt asked all Americans to offer up a silent prayer daily for victory for the Allied forces, he claimed, Emanuel was "indoc-trinating the American people with fools babel that God is non-existent." Emanuel finally had to capitulate and withdraw the Black International series for the duration of the war.[27]

Following the war, McCabe wrote biographies of Churchill, Stalin, Hitler, Franklin D. Roosevelt, and Chiang Kai-shek, as well as a brief history of the war. This brought to two hundred the number of books the renegade priest had written for Emanuel. The Catholic Church renewed its attack on certain of the Haldeman-Julius Company's books, particularly McCabe's. Emanuel made a significant change in the *American Freeman*'s format in October 1948. On 25 June 1948 the *Catholic Universe Bulletin* of Cleveland, the *Catholic Exponent* of Youngstown, and the *Catholic Chronicle* of Toledo had published an "exposé" of the Little Blue Books, calling them "moral poison" and insisting that Haldeman-Julius was corrupting the minds and morals of the American youth. In October, Emanuel responded in the *Freeman* that he had "never singled out Catholic fundamentalists for attack" but rather fought all "superstition and humbug," whatever its source. For the next year, Emanuel broke precedent by printing cartoons attacking Catholicism in each issue of the *Freeman*.[28]

At the same time, Emanuel was launching an all-out campaign to sell Big Blue Books. In the October 1949 and April 1950 issues of the *American Freeman*, the first four pages were devoted to listing 5½ x 8½ Big Blue Books that were on sale.

Alice had married Carroll W. Smith in October 1942 when he was an ensign in the U.S. Navy. Following his discharge at the end of the war, Smith began writing Little Blue Books for his father-in-law. Emanuel would suggest the topic, and Smith provided the copy. In October 1945, Emanuel started him on a series of books on the states, the first being

Facts You Should Know about Illinois. He also suggested a self-help book on selling real estate, a timely topic for servicing the millions of returning veterans. There was no end to the possibilities here. One could do a series on American rivers, another on mountains, one on American cities. Then came *The Diary of a Bell Boy*, which should be "amusing, wicked, exciting, brittle, cynical, slummy." Smith had never been a bellboy, but neither had Emanuel. "Make it plenty hot. But remember it has to be mailable," he instructed his son-in-law.[29]

Emanuel himself wrote on the subject of the Jews at this time. He attacked the National Conference of Christians and Jews as perpetuating "a gigantic hoax" on American Jews. He regarded Judaism "as foolish and harmful" in the same way that all religions were foolish and harmful. It was the Jewish "genius" that he defended. Jews had made significant contributions, he insisted, to various cultures of the world, and this contribution stemmed from their peculiar "genius" as a race. Thus he hailed the Palestinian Settlement in 1947 with its possibilities of emancipation and elevation of the Middle East nations by example from the State of Israel.[30]

The November 1948 issue of the *American Freeman* carried a large advertisement with the headline "Let Me Help You Make Some Extra Income." His Little Blue Book catalog listed 1,845 titles, and his catalog of larger books contained 735 titles, making a total of 2,580 listings. He had hitherto sold these books through mail order. For $288.30, he would mail you a copy of each of the 2,500 books, a discount of 40 percent. You would be your own boss, setting up the hours you would be available, and use your garage, barn, or a space in your home from which to operate. Participants would be furnished 64-page catalogs of the books. By investing $288.30 in each set, they would receive $480.50 when they were sold. He promised to give book agent number 1 a thousand free books "of my own selection," and agent number 2 would receive 900 books, number 3 would receive 800, and so on. "Act on it today," the ad warned.

In 1948, Emanuel had a run-in with J. Edgar Hover over a pamphlet he published that Clifton Bennett had written, "The FBI—The Basis of an American Police State." J. Edgar disapproved of it. Emanuel agreed that the story was "so full of errors as to make it quite useless to me" and promised he would withdraw it from circulation. This was in July. The following February, J. Edgar followed up with the fact that he had received a letter from a person who had placed an order with Haldeman-Julius Publications and received his order, along with a pamphlet advertising the Bennett article for sale. The FBI director was "amazed" that the item was still being distributed. Haldeman-Julius was caught red-handed and had no response but to pull the offensive publication.[31]

On 20 December 1950, Emanuel drew up a new will. He wanted his funeral to be to be "a simple matter"—no flowers, no music, no mourners, no services, no sermon, and his body closed to public viewing. He wanted to be cremated and desired that his "ashes be buried near the ashes of my first wife" in the cemetery near Cedarville. If this could not be agreed upon by survivors, Sue could decide the location. He left Sue the house in Girard, livestock and implements, and his automobile. He requested that his portrait of himself go to Henry and that the portrait of John H. Addams and baby Marcet go to Alice. All other property would be divided, with half going to Sue, one-fourth each to Alice and Henry, with those three as executors of the will.[32]

The Haldeman-Julius plant was burglarized on the night of 8 February 1948. Raymond and Joseph Lee drove from Pittsburg to Girard about 8:00 p.m., parked their car on the northeast corner of the square, and walked to the plant. They easily passed through a locked door, and Joseph remained at the front door as a lookout. Raymond entered the middle office where the vault was located, "knocked the knob off and forced the door open." He saw "money everywhere in drawers" and placed it in a metal box he found at the plant. Raymond returned to the car while Joseph carried the loot to the nearby Catholic church where Raymond picked him up. They drove home where they divided the money, which totaled $40,218. Emanuel reported the burglary to authorities the next morning, estimating the loss at $40,500. It was not covered by insurance. Raymond later confessed and was brought to trial on one charge of robbery and one of grand larceny. Joseph was then serving a twenty-year sentence in the Missouri penitentiary for "assaulting an officer with intent to kill" in a different criminal episode.[33]

The Internal Revenue Service immediately assigned a grand jury to investigate how Emanuel could have had that much money lying around his office, based on his reported income tax returns. Their records showed that from 1944 through 1947 he had reported a total income of $31,303, whereas the grand jury said it was actually $149,200. Therefore, he owed the federal government $65,000.[34]

Not so, Emanuel responded, because IRS agents had assured him "everything was all right" when he had recently checked his returns. Soon after the robbery, Emanuel's lawyer, Douglas Hudson, advised him that it would be a good idea to check his income tax records to make certain they were complete and accurate. Some errors were discovered and reported to the IRS. When no bill was forthcoming from them, Emanuel assumed the issue was closed.[35]

The difference arose over the donations he had received over the years from supporters for appeals he had made for various causes. He declared he had no intention of evading paying income taxes, there was "never any intent to defraud," but he was mistaken in thinking that he was not required to report "income of that sort." He had his accountants examine his books, and they found he had honored the contract to pay Alice and Henry $25 weekly until a total amount had been paid to them of $25,000 each. Then in 1945 he decided to close the contract with Alice and pay her the difference between the current total of the $25 weekly payments and the $25,000, and he did the same with Henry. This was not an attempt to cheat, because these were legitimate debts dating from when Marcet loaned him money to buy the *Appeal to Reason*, and Alice and Henry were her legal heirs. Emanuel did not keep records during the time he reported he acquired $5,000 in gifts. In 1948 and 1949 he kept records of these gifts and, he insisted, they "confirmed" his claim for earlier gifts. The accountants concluded that he had completed his own income-tax returns and that "they are almost wholly inadequate and do not conform to any standards of reporting."[36]

Milton Rippey of the Harrison-Rippey advertising firm of St. Louis forwarded a character witness letter to federal judge Arthur Mellott, who was in charge of Emanuel's trial. Harrison-Rippey had handled advertising for the Little Blue Books for twenty-six years. During that period, Rippey wrote, Emanuel had made a practice of placing "ideas and ideals above money." In regard to the charge that Emanuel had endorsed and forwarded checks to creditors rather than depositing them, Rippey said that between 1944 and 1947 his company had received U.S. Treasury checks totaling $21,000 from Emanuel, endorsed to his company, to apply on invoices for advertising—"a not uncommon practice, I believe."[37]

Emanuel's lawyer portrayed his client as "a self-educated man" with little knowledge of accounting or business procedures. The fact that he kept $40,000 in a tin can in his office demonstrated he had "no thorough knowledge of business affairs. No one but a writer would do this," Hudson asserted. He reminded the jury that Emanuel had voluntarily disclosed the discrepancies in his tax return and that the IRS had never presented an adjustment for him to pay. He suggested that his client had been "deliberately maneuvered" into a compromise position by the government. The so-called "skim-off" payments to Alice and Henry were legitimate payments to Marcet's heirs for a long-standing loan to buy the *Appeal to Reason*.[38]

On 18 April 1951, after a four-day trial and two days of deliberations, the jury made "an amazing compromise" and found him guilty of income-tax evasion for 1944 and 1947 and innocent for 1945 and 1946. An appeal would be expensive, so Emanuel turned to his tried-and-trusted formula and appealed to supporters for donations to the "defense fund." The judge sentenced him to six months in prison and a fine of $12,500. Emanuel immediately appealed.[39]

A reporter from the *Fort Scott Tribune* found Emanuel after the sentencing and reported "a lonely figure in an inconspicuous corner of a federal building corridor. E. Haldeman-Julius, internationally known Girard book and periodical publisher, stood with his eyes filled with tears after a jury in the United States district court here late yesterday afternoon found him guilty of two of four counts of fraudulent income tax evasion." Asked by the reporter if he had any comment, the stocky, bushy-haired publisher pressed his lips tightly together to stifle a sob and shook his head mutely. He had been so certain, he told Sue, that he would win this "thing."[40]

The nationally syndicated columnist Westbrook Pegler could scarcely wait to gloat. He wrote Emanuel that he had read about his conviction and "as a reporter, I would appreciate an explanation from you of the source of this money. Crap game? Found it on the street, maybe?" A P.S. was added, "Honest to God, this is no gloat. But I *do* have to ask."[41] Surprisingly, Emanuel replied: "You have, of course, a fine chance to kick me in the teeth when I'm down," he wrote, and explained that his plant always "had a cash reserve" that was used to replace machinery, typewriters, and other equipment. While "not strictly according to the methods of certified accountants, it worked," he declared. The company had been accumulating money "for some years" to construct another building on the next lot and repair the old one "when the money was stolen." "If there are any other questions you want to ask about this matter, don't hesitate. I'll come clean."[42]

Pegler, however, was not one to give up so easily in the face of a plausible answer. A Brooklyn supporter of Emanuel sent Haldeman-Julius a clipping for an article in which Pegler lamented the many publications of the Haldeman-Julius Company on freethinking. "Pegler may change the trend and tear McCabe apart," Emanuel wrote in the *Freeman*. Pegler had also condemned L. M. Burkhead, the author of eleven Little Blue Books, including *The Essence of Unitarianism*. Burkhead was the pastor of the Unitarian Church in Kansas City to which Haldeman-Julius belonged, "in the sense that I give it money and attend its meetings frequently." Burkhead had also performed the marriage ceremony for Josephine and Aubrey as well as Marcet and Emanuel's "remarriage. Pegler insisted that Emanuel's opposition to communism was "spiritless" in comparison with his attacks on Catholicism "and a long roster of sects." Emanuel wrote that he was "not ashamed for having brought out the works of Joseph McCabe, Bertrand Russell, Clarence Darrow, Ingersoll, Bradlaugh, Blatchford, Spencer, Brandeis, Yarros, and some others." He also noted that Pegler ignored Little Blue Book 753, *The Essence of Catholicism*, as well as *The Sermon on the Mount*.[43]

Following the trial, Emanuel returned to Girard to wind up his business affairs. His legal conviction had taken the fight out of him and drained him of drive and ambition. He was crushed as never before. He felt no reason now to struggle or to compete. All he wanted to do was to seek quietude and write. He had many "novels, short stories, travel articles, sketches, essays, reviews, etc." that he had dallied over for too long. He advertised his publishing plant for $1 million, one-fourth in cash and the balance in 2 one-half-percent notes. He also advertised in newspapers across the country announcing his retirement and sale of stock of 10 million Little Blue Books.[44]

As Emanuel grew older, he became more nostalgic about his parents, his family, and his boyhood in Philadelphia. He decided to write an autobiography. He also kept his eye on a new brick factory five blocks south of his plant. Someday he wanted to acquire it to publish his journal and recoup his losses, not for the money but for the prestige, to build his self-confidence, to occupy his mind and detach it from his recent humiliation.[45]

He and Sue had made it a rule never to have a drink before 5:00 in the afternoon. Now he began to drink more often, more heavily. Many evenings he would drink himself into a stupor. Sometimes he fell asleep and later would wake up and go to bed. When drinking he would often strike out at things he loved. He once threw a cat into the swimming pool and watched it struggle to get out. He would play roughly with the dogs, so rough he would hurt them. Sue found her glass figurines gone and asked him about them. He said he had thrown them out behind the barn. She found them there, shattered. She was obviously hurt, not over her treasures, but because this kind and gentle man was being consumed by a violence and hatred he so despised in others. His doctor finally told him to limit himself to two drinks a day, but this warning was ignored. He told Sue at this time that "whatever happens, keep that mailing list and don't let anyone have it. It is worth more than anything now."[46]

"When I die," he had written fifteen years earlier, "I want to be in such a condition that the undertaker won't be able to say, 'My, what a pity! Isn't he a healthy looking beast!' I want to be burned out completely. I am jealous of death and shall leave him nothing. He had lived intensely . . . and to satisfy himself."[47]

Emanuel was not a good swimmer, but he would occasionally float around the pool to cool off. He had developed an aversion to deep, cold water and seldom went into the pool, preferring to sit in a chair and watch others swim. Once in the summer of 1951, a friend visited and they decided to take the friend's boat to Farlington Lake. While the others boated, Emanuel sat on a bench next to the water. Two rather plump ladies came and sat on the bench with him. Without warning, they suddenly rose simultaneously, causing the flimsy bench to cata-pult Emanuel into the water. Fortunately, some fellows quickly came and pulled him out; otherwise, he might have drowned. This incident increased his terror of deep water.[48]

In June 1951, a "birthday committee" established to celebrate Emanuel's sixty-second birthday published an open letter in the *American Freeman*. They asked friends to participate in a celebration at Emanuel's home. They described him as "strong and healthy, . . . he had a charming, attractive, helpful wife and . . . lived in a pleasant home." The committee predicted he would "write steadily and well for at least 20 more years."[49]

The day after his birthday, Emanuel relaxed with Sue and some friends at the farm. He had had a swimming pool installed years earlier—not for himself, because he did not know how to swim, but for the family's enter-tainment. The guests swam, they soaked up the sunshine, they chatted. When they left, Emanuel was playing with his dog, Squiggles, and Sue wanted something to eat. It was too hot to cook, so she decided to go to a local restaurant to get some takeout, leaving Emanuel beside the pool. When she returned a few minutes later she found him floating in the pool, face up. She managed to get him out but could not revive him, so she called the sheriff and the county rescue squad. Various attempts to revive him failed. His personal physician, Dr. E. G. Lightfoot, testified he had been treating Emanuel for a heart condition for eighteen months, and at first it was believed he had died of a heart attack, but the county coroner listed the cause of death as drowning.[50]

There were those in Girard who saw conspiracy in everything, and they were certain that a plot by the FBI or some other government agency lay behind his death. Others were positive it was a suicide. When Sue drained the pool later, she saw scratch marks on the film of algae on the sidewalls, indicating Emanuel's struggle against drowning.[51]

In a front-page piece she wrote for the *American Freeman*, Sue recalled the story of her first encounters with Emanuel. She was "a kid in school" when she would stop by the plant on her way home "and hang by her knees on his railing just outside his window" with no words exchanged. When she turned sixteen, she began her employment in his plant. She was "a little frightened of him," but she overcame that in the twenty years she worked for him.[52]

John Gunn's eulogy concerned Emanuel's "artistic but what is sometimes called the continental feeling about life." His three favorite writers were Voltaire, Anatole France, and George Bernard Shaw—Voltaire, the crusader whose pen dripped with satire; France, "hedonistic and cynic, and something of the crusader"; and Shaw, with his "severe intellectual passion for a higher social morality." "Oddly enough," the man who became famous for publishing paperbound books "loved fine bindings and rare editions." But "what was inside the book was most important," and "life was more important still—life, the source and inspiration of it all, the mystery from which all came and to which all returned." Gunn recalled the good old days when he, Emanuel, and Kopelin were engaged in hard work, dreamed their dreams, and shared expectations. Kopelin was killed in an airplane crash in Texas in November 1949. Now Emanuel was dead. "There were countless things we three could talk about," Gunn recalled, "now I wander solitary in the halls of memory, which echo hauntingly as I review the scenes, gestures, words and deeds—the splendid wreckage of that vanished time."[53]

Thirty years before his death, in the novel *Dust*, Emanuel and Marcet wrote of Martin Wade that he had within him "a touch of the poet and the philosopher." "His is a constant, consistent materialism spread over many years. For him we feel pity. . . . With his great potentialities, he was a senseless squirrel caged to the end."

A sudden breeze caught up some of the dust and, whirling it around, let it fall. Martin's life, thought Rose, it was like a handful of dust thrown into God's face and blown back again by the wind to the ground.[54]

Those of a religious persuasion might think that Emanuel had thus composed his own epitaph, but he might just respond, "BUNK."

A friend once asked Emanuel why he enjoyed life. He responded:

I find life worth living, because I enjoy good music, great books, beautiful thoughts of truth and freedom, sane living, warm showers each morning, pleasant home life, charming people, lively talk, exchange of ideas, adventures among the masterpieces left by the world's greatest thinkers, good belly plays of sharp wit and worldly humor, beautiful women, tall glasses of orange juice, fresh trout shipped in from the Rocky Mountains, smoked turkey, slices of salty lox, black bread smeared with home-made butter, freshly manufactured eggs, crisp bacon, slightly burned toast, roast duck, thick steaks, German fried potatoes with hints of onion, lofty poetry, plays, magnificent orchestras, letters dictated by my grandchild, huge stacks of orders for Little Blue Books and my other publications, checks that never bounce, accounts that always pay on the dot, honest, friendly neighbors, litters of pigs, brand new calves, ducklings, lambs, chicks, ample crops of corn, wheat, oats, and sargo, lofts jammed with hay, silos pouring over, newly plowed land, the first green of winter wheat, the rustle of corn that's ready for the cornpicker, cats that beg for food at the back door, dogs that eat well then sleep quietly near the fireplace, oak and walnut logs that burn for hours and make the house smell sweet, the reds and yellows of the elms near my bedroom window in the first chirps of spring, my wife's lovely garden, the house and fields, the reflection of the moon in the duck pond near the house, soft-voiced old people, laughing children, roosters welcoming the dawn, hens clucking, wheat ready for the harvest, milk that was grass five hours ago, reveries before the fire, another highball, the long yawn that says it's time to turn in.[55]

POSTSCRIPT

Henry, now known as Henry J. Haldeman, decided to try and operate the Haldeman-Julius Publishing Company on his own. He had failed at the University of Kansas, was working as a pilot for Slick Airways of Chicago, and lived in Cedarville, but he now moved to Girard and took over the publishing plant. He was highly unsuccessful as a businessman and soon began trafficking in questionably obscene literature. In 1964 a federal district court jury ruled that eight books written by Dr. David Oliver Cauldwell were obscene. These were in a series of Big Blue Books and listed in the company's catalog dating to the time when Emanuel was in charge. With the help of the American Civil Liberties Union, Henry's conviction was overturned on appeal. This conviction, however, frightened his book dealers, and he was forced to lay off employees, leaving him to run the plant machinery by himself. He struggled for ten years until a fire forced him to quit. The aged plant narrowly escaped condemnation in 1976, and in a Fourth of July celebration in 1978 an errant bottle rocket burned the plant to the ground, bringing an end to the Little Blue Books.[56]

EPILOGUE

The American world into which Emanuel Haldeman-Julius was born was filled with the swirl of revolution and reform. The populism of an earlier decade had morphed into the Progressive Era of reform. The age boasted of material abundance, juxtaposed with inequality of wealth, cycles of depression, and joblessness. It was an age primed to accept the ideas of Jane Addams of Hull House in Chicago, the center of the new profession of social work by his wife's aunt—an environment much like the current era of American history. Haldeman-Julius had a unique personality to fit into the culture, and he achieved an enviable position in this environment. His singular achievements in this milieu have been overlooked by historians and literary critics. This book will, I hope, correct that oversight.

Haldeman-Julius was consistently generous to the downtrodden and the abused. His spirited and lengthy defense of Tom Mooney comes to mind immediately. He was convinced that Mooney was denied a fair trial and railroaded to prison, and he used his publications for years to campaign to free him, finally succeeding in 1942. His ardent support of Eugene V. Debs was rooted in his belief that the great socialist provided the answer for America's masses, who were severely depressed.

Throughout his life he was consistent in his love of books and his overwhelming desire to bring them to the masses. He liked to think of himself as a Voltaire, but he demonstrated by his actions that he was actually more of a Barnum. His "Henry Ford–like mass production of books," many believed, debased the literature he loved, but he intended his production for the masses, which, to him, required an elevation of the common man through education. This education would elevate the masses in order for them to achieve their liberation from ignorance.

In his professional life he was always ready for a good fight or campaign. He led the opposition to the Ku Klux Klan, fought censorship of every kind, and opposed bigotry, ignorance, authoritarianism, organized religion of all persuasions. He constantly campaigned for better education, equality for all, and more equitable distribution of wealth.

On the other hand, his views on women were far from enlightened. He considered women inferior to men. They were sex objects for men to enjoy. They were the bearers of the future generations of the race. He loved beautiful women who were good conversationalists. But except for his wife, he asked few of them to write for his Little Blue Books. Women, he believed, should be relegated to opening mail, counting book orders, answering the telephone, cooking, and doing bookkeeping. Marcet was the exception.

It is impossible to write about Emanuel without discussing his wife. He and Marcet were not only bound together by marriage vows and children but also intertwined by their fascination with books and writing. They coauthored books and articles, and she was his special investigative agent. Whenever he needed his best agent to investigate a story, he sent Marcet.

The political story of this couple contains an interesting paradox. When they were married, Marcet was a registered Republican; when she died in 1941 she had become a socialist. At the time of their marriage, Emanuel was a socialist, and when he died, a decade after her, he was a registered Republican.[1]

One cannot help but speculate on Emanuel's father and his reaction to his son's fame. The old man hated machines. What were his thoughts on Emanuel utilizing them to revolutionize the book-publishing industry?

In a broader sense, Haldeman-Julius's entire life can be perceived as both a success and a failure for his immediate family. Marcet needed help with her health problems, with her husband's inadequate household financing, and empathy and personal support in coping with his peccadilloes and selfishness. His children often went without their father's advice and counseling. He was unsuccessful in his personal life but a most enviable success in his publishing career.

Emanuel said he owed much to Chester Wright in learning to write. The editor taught him to lay out his notes, "pull up to a machine and let loose," then read it for spelling and punctuation. This is fast writing, and perhaps good advice for journalists to follow, but it is not necessarily good writing. Marcet learned how to write well, and she was the better writer of the two. Emanuel recognized this when he sent her on reporting trips. He never acquired the skill of really good writing, but he was an outstanding businessman who learned the techniques of advertising and the psychology of appealing to the people's baser instincts, sometimes merely by adjusting the title of a book. The art of psychologically appealing to baser instincts and of advertising were products of the 1920s.

He and Marcet were possibly not pioneers in their thinking about sex and marriage, but in this regard they were certainly leaders of their generation. When a couple had trouble living together, get a divorce, they said, in a period when society still frowned on divorce. They became the center of attention, along with Judge Ben Lindsey, in popularizing the concept of companionate marriage. And they practiced what they preached, not only for themselves but for their children. This concept did not mean so-called free love, as many contemporary Americans believed, but included the practice of birth control and equality in finances and rights.

They were also pioneers in promoting the rights of African Americans on college campuses and elsewhere. Emanuel was one of the first to pub-lish an anthology of black American poetry. He sought out black leaders such as W. E. B. Du Bois and James Weldon Johnson for their views on American society. His suggestion to solve the discrimination blacks received was the gradual process of amalgamation: let the colors merge to form a new race. "We see already," he observed, "the lighter the skin, the lighter the prejudice."[2]

While he was an above-average writer in his own right, Emanuel enjoyed an extraordinary career in publishing. Girard became known as the literary capital of the United States as Little Blue Books were shipped out by the carload to all parts of the Earth. Emanuel discovered two decades before the Kinsey Report that Americans, male and female, were interested in discussing sex. Some of his books on sex were blatantly obscene; others were healthy introductions to badly needed sex education. His books were a vital part of the sexual revolution taking place before, during, and after World War II. It might be an exaggeration that the Little Blue Books played a part in the feminist crusade of the postwar period, but not much. The Haldeman-Julius family would have been in the forefront of the civil rights movement of the postwar era, as they led the movement in higher education decades before this.

Little Blue Books were not the first literary effort aimed at the working class. A decade previously, the Charles H. Kerr Company of Chicago had published seventy-two titles of the Pocket Library of Socialism that were sold at socialist gatherings. What set the Little Blue Books apart was Emanuel's flair for promotion, his adaptation to new trends in publishing, his willingness to modernize his publishing and marketing processes, and, of course, his books' low price.

In terms of quantity, he became the greatest publisher in world history. His record of publishing some 500 million copies of 2,580 titles may never be equaled. By contrast, Dr. Benjamin Spock's *Pocket Book of Baby and Child Care*, one of the most popular books ever published in the United States, sold only 19 million copies. At 3½ x 5 inches and sixty-four pages in length, Emanuel's Little Blue Books could fit in a shirt or back pocket, to be read anytime, anywhere. They were intended to bring culture and education to the masses. "The Voltaire of Kansas," they called him, "The Barnum of Books." He inherited good business instincts from his mother and a fertile imagination from his father and established a Henry Ford–like mass-production machine of in quaint little Girard. This was in addition to his writing and producing weekly, monthly, and quarterly magazines.

Orders poured in from around the world. Maharajas from India, for example, and Haile Selassie of Ethiopia, who ordered grammar books, a rhyming dictionary, two crossword puzzle books, a joke book, and a copy of *What Every Woman Wants to Know*. Little Blue Books accompanied Richard Byrd to the South Pole. Highbrows and lowbrows bought them, ranging from Charlie Chaplin and Gloria Swanson to ditch diggers in

Brooklyn. The curator of libraries at Pittsburg State College sent them with American astronauts on their lunar orbital exploration. Students in the Great Depression could buy fifty secondhand Little Blue Books for a dollar and resell them for 5 cents apiece. Libraries of Little Blue Books were collected in hospitals, penal institutions, Civilian Conservation Corps camps, military barracks.

Haldeman-Julius Publications encouraged and produced the first book for Will Durant. Titles by Henry James, Thomas Hardy, and even Shakespeare, found more readers of the Little Blue Book editions than those of their original publishers.

Emanuel was second only to the U.S. Government Printing Office in the quantity of his publications. Literature and fiction that had stood the test of time, classics almost forgotten, found their way into every hamlet in America, as well as around the world. *Who's Who in America* carried his biography for twenty-six straight years. He was the North American Northcliffe, except that he peddled verities, not trivialities.

It is difficult for the present generation, molded as it is by constant communication, to understand the profound impact Emanuel Haldeman-Julius had on his generation. He knew and observed that his Little Blue Books "had done more to bring education to the masses than any other individual since the invention of printing." These books were consciously directed at "Mr. Average Man," and a nickel could purchase classics of various kinds. Emanuel's imagination led him to conceive of his books as "an agent of popular culture" in order to "'strike a blow' for the freedom of the human mind." "Happiness," he concluded, "was to be achieved primarily through self-betterment, through knowledge of one's own weaknesses and potential." This knowledge had been passed down through the ages by a series of classics with which "Everyman" should be familiar. Reading these would eliminate ignorance and intolerance. This knowledge must be put into circulation through the masses to improve the happiness of mankind.[3]

APPENDIX

Books are listed by title followed by the number of copies sold as of 1928.

Many concern common knowledge:

What Married Women Should Know	112,000
What Married Men Should Know	97,500
What Every Young Man Should Know	95,000
What Every Young Woman Should Know	90,500
What Every Girl Should Know	66,000
What Every Boy Should Know	37,500
What Women Past Forty Should Know	34,000
What Expectant Mothers Should Know	25,000

Some offer more specific information:

Women's Sexual Life	97,000
Men's Sexual Life	78,500
The Physiology of Sex Life	65,500
The Common Sense of Sex	63,000
Freud on Sleep and Sexual Dreams	61,000
Homosexual Life	54,500

Womanhood: Facts of Life for Women	52,500
Manhood: Facts of Life for Men	52,000
Confidential Chats with Wives	47,000
Confidential Chats with Husbands	27,500
The Child's Sexual Life	21,500

Most of Havelock Ellis's Books sold well:

Plain Talks with the Married	60,500
The Love Rights of Women	39,000
Four Essays on Sex	31,000
Eugenics Explained	29,500
Ellis and His Plea for Sane Sex Living	29,500
Women and the New Race	16,000

It was illegal to publish or distribute contraceptive material, but Haldeman-Julius managed to do so anyway:

Modern Aspects of Birth Control	73,000
Debate on Birth Control	27,000

He also published books under the general classification of love:

The Art of Kissing	60,500
How to Love	52,500
Psychology of Love and Hate	52,000
What Is Love (Montaigne)	28,500
Hindu Book of Love (Kama Sutra)	28,000
Psychology of the Affections	22,500
The Art of Courtship	27,500

Then there were the more specialized sex books:

Catholicism and Sex	65,000
Sex Crimes and American Law	39,000
Facts about Sex Rejuvenation	37,500
Phallic (Sex) Elements in Religion	36,000
Sex Obsessions of Saints and Mystics	35,000
Modern Sex Morality	34,500
America and the Sex Impulse	28,000
The Evolution of Sex	25,000
Sex Symbolism	21,500
Genetics for Beginners	21,000

Historically speaking, people believe "the ancients were very wicked":

Prostitution in the Modern World	129,500
Prostitution in the Ancient World	84,500
Prostitution in the Medieval World	73,000
Sex Life in Ancient Greece and Rome	56,000
Mistresses of Today	52,000
Women Who Have Lived for Love	24,000
The Evolution of Marriage	20,000

On marriage as the social sanction the law gives sex:

Why I Believe in Companionate Marriage (Marcet Haldeman-Julius)	64,000
Judge Ben B. Lindsey on Companionate Marriage	60,500
Beginning Married Life Right	52,000

Marriage and Morals in Soviet Russia (*Anna Louis Strong*)	36,000
How to Be Happy Though Married	35,000
How to Avoid Marital Discords	27,000
U.S. Marriage and Divorce Laws	18,500
Marriage vs. Divorce (Debate)	9,000

Books treating women specifically:

How to Know Women (Maeterlinck)	49,000
Mental Differences between Men and Women (*Leo Markin*)	36,000
The Degradation of Women (Joseph McCabe)	27,000
Woman, the Eternal Primitive (*William J. Fielding*)	20,000
The Subjugation of Women (John Stuart Mill)	18,500
Great Women of Antiquity (Clement Wood)	13,500

Readers also were curious about sexual hygiene:

Facts about Venereal Disease	41,500
Facts about Syphilis	36,000

Books on how to win love:

Love Letters of a Portuguese Nun	46,000
How to Write Love Letters	23,000
Letters of a Parisian Actress (Sarah Bernhardt)	21,500
Love Letters of People of Genius	12,000
Love Letters of Abelard and Heloise	10,000

Books of maxims on love:

Jokes about Married Life	45,000
What Men Have Learned about Women	36,000
Best Jokes about Lovers	35,000
Jokes about Kissing	33,000
What French Women Have Learned about Love	29,000
What Women Have Learned about Men	21,500
Love Code of a Parisian Actress (Bernhardt)	17,500
Love from Many Angles	15,000
Maxims of Love (Stendahl)	10,000

Books on famous lovers sold rather well:

Secret Memoirs of a French Royal Mistress (Pompadour)	37,500
Cleopatra and Her Loves	35,000
Casanova: History's Greatest Lover	31,000
Pope Alexander VI and His Loves	25,500
Madame Du Barry: A King's Mistress	25,000
Love Life of a Frenchwoman (George Sand)	22,500
Catherine the Great and Her Lovers	20,000
Wagner's Great Love Affair	18,500
Cellini: Swordsman, Lover, etc.	18,000
Eleonora Duse and D'Annunzio	17,000
Lord Nelson and Lady Hamilton	16,000
Shelley and His Loves	16,000
Lord Byron and His Loves	15,500
Aucussin and Nicolette, Lovers	13,000
Romance That Balzac Lived	10,500

As did famous love stories:

Illicit Lover, and So Forth (Boccaccio)	81,500
One of Cleopatra's Nights (Cautier)	60,000
Tales from Boccaccio's Decameron	57,000
26 Men and a Girl (Gorki)	57,000
French Prostitute's Sacrifice (Maupassant)	15,500
French Tales of Passion and Cruelty	56,000
Tales of Love and Life (Boccaccio)	47,000
Amorous Tales of the Monks	45,000
Quest for a Blonde Mistress (Gautier)	44,000
A Bath, and So Forth (Zola)	42,500
Lustful King Enjoys Himself (Hugo)	42,000
Passion Stories of Many Hues (Gormont)	41,500
None beneath the King Shall Enjoy This Woman (Zorrilla)	38,000
Forbidden Love (Barry Pain)	35,000
Queer Night in Paris (Maupassant)	34,500
A Wife's Confession (Maupassant)	34,000
Mme Tellier's Establishment (Maupassant)	33,500
Night in White Chapel (Maupassant)	33,500
Night Flirtation (Chekov)	33,000
Love's Redemption (Tolstoy)	32,000
Love and Other Tales (Maupassant)	29,000
Mlle Fifi , etc (Maupassant)	25,500
A Study of a Woman (Balzac)	25,000
Artist's Wife (Maupassant)	25,000
The Falcon, etc. (Boccacio)	17,500
Romeo and Juliet (Shakespeare)	14,500
Hedda Gabler (Ibsen)	12,000

Poetry and sex were an interesting mix:

The Harlot's House and Other Poems (Wilde)	41,000
A Nun's Desire and Other Poems (John Davidson)	14,500
Passionate Poems (Swinburne)	14,500
The Vampire and Other Poems (Kipling)	14,000
Love Poems of John Keats	12,000
Courtship of Miles Standish (Longfellow)	9,000

The Little Blue Books always emphasized education.
The annual sales of the University in Print, or the Self-
Improvement list, represent a hunger for self-improvement:

Success Easier Than Failure (E. W. Howe)	38,000
The Secret of Self-Improvement (John Cowper Powys)	36,000
100 Best Books to Read (Powys)	32,000
Facts You Should Know about the Classics (Joseph McCabe)	25,000
Hints on Self-Improvement	24,000
How to Get the Most Out of Reading (Georg Brandes)	17,500
How to Get a Liberal Education (Thomas Huxley)	15,000
How to Enjoy Reading (Isaac Goldberg)	12,000
Art of Reading Constructively (E. Haldeman-Julius)	10,500
How to Choose Books (Thomas Carlyle)	10,000

Seven other Little Blue Books by John Cowper Powys should be added to this list, because Emanuel included them in his high school list of booklets and sold 994,000 of them.

It appears that everyone wanted to improve their English:

How to Improve Your Conversation	77,000
How to Improve Your Vocabulary	76,000
How to Write Letters	53,500
Common Faults in English	47,000
How to Talk and Debate	38,500
How to Argue Logically	33,000
Most Essential English Words	33,000
Grammar Self-Taught	31,000
A Dictionary of American Slang	29,000
Handbook of Useful Phrases	25,000
Spelling Self-Taught	24,000
Punctuation Self-Taught	23,000
Rhetoric Self-Taught	14,000
English Composition Self-Taught	12,000
The Romance of Words	10,500

There was a good deal of interest in learning how to express oneself:

Hints on Public Speaking	46,500
Short-Story Writing for Beginners	36,000
Hints on Writing Short Stories	23,000
How to Write Advertising	20,000
How to Prepare Manuscripts	17,000
Writing for the Market	14,500

Hints on Writing Poetry	11,000
Hints on News Reporting	10,500
How to Write Movie Scenarios	10,000
How to Write One-Act Plays	8,000
How to Write Book Reviews	8,000

Interest in the relatively new field of
psychology was on the upsurge:

How to Psycho-Analyze Yourself	43,000
Psycho-Analysis Explained	38,500
Psychology for Beginners	35,000
Behaviorism: Newest Psychology	25,500
The Puzzle of Personality	21,000
Auto-Suggestion: How It Works	18,500
Psychology of Jung	13,000
Auto-Suggestion and Health	12,000

People also sought knowledge about habits:

How to Break Bad Habits	29,000
How to Form Good Habits	20,000

There was a good deal of interest in health:

Care of Skin and Hair	52,000
Eating for Health (Vitamins)	36,000
Latest Food and Diet Facts	27,000
Everyday Health Rules	22,500
Home Nursing (First Aid)	17,000
Facts about Cancer	15,000

X-Ray, Violet Ray etc.	13,500
Tuberculosis: Causes and Cure	12,000
Diabetes: Cause and Treatment	12,000
Quacks of the Healing Cults	10,000
Truth about "Patent" Medicines	10,000
Childhood Diseases	10,000
How to Take Care of Your Mouth and Teeth	8,000

Books on sports did not sell very well:

How to Teach Yourself to Swim	27,000
How to Play Golf	17,000
Camping: Woodcraft and Wildcraft	15,500
Baseball: How to Play and How to Watch It	15,000
Handbook of Golf Rules	12,000
Helpful Hints for Hikers	10,500
How to Get the Most Out of Recreation	9,000

College courses varied:

Facts to Know about Music	37,000
Psychology for Beginners	35,000
Astronomy Self-Taught	30,500
Facts to Know about Painting	27,500
Outline of U.S. History	25,500
Chemistry Self-Taught	25,500
Facts to Know about Architecture	16,000
Evolution Made Plain	16,000
Physics Self-Taught	14,500
Outline of Economics	14,500
The Weather (Meteorology)	14,000

Botany Self-Taught	13,000
Zoology Self-Taught	12,000
Facts to Know about Sculpture	10,500
Sociology for Beginners	8,000

Most languages, especially French and Spanish, did well:

Spanish Self-Taught	47,000
French Self-Taught	46,500
German Self-Taught	27,500
Italian Self-Taught	21,500
Esperanto Self-Taught (proposed scientific international)	17,500
Latin Self-Taught	10,500

Commercial subjects sold consistently, if not famously:

How to Write Business Letters	37,500
Handbook of Useful Tables	33,000
Typewriting Self-Taught	29,000
Handbook of Legal Forms	28,500
Handbook of Commercial Law	27,000
A Rapid Calculator	24,000
How to Own Your Own Home	17,500
First Aid for Investors	17,000
How to Save Money	16,500
How Wall Street Works	16,000
Arithmetic Self-Taught: Part 2	14,500
Arithmetic Self-Taught: Part 1	12,000
U.S. Commercial Geography	10,000
How to Budget Your Income	10,000

Dictionaries appear to increase in popularity
as civilization grows more complex:

Book of Familiar Quotations	34,500
A Dictionary of Scientific Terms	25,000
Pocket Rhyming Dictionary	23,000
A Dictionary of Musical Terms	21,500
Popular Shakespearian Quotations	17,000
A Dictionary of Biblical Allusions	16,000
International Dictionary of Authors	15,000
A Dictionary of Classical Mythology	13,000
A Dictionary of Geographical Names	10,500
A Dictionary of Sea Names	8,000

One category of books demonstrated
Americans had a sweet tooth:

How to Make All Kinds of Candy	45,000
Simple Recipes for Home Cooking	33,000
How to Make Pies and Pastries	29,000
How to Cook Fish and Meats	21,500
Better Meals for Less Money	17,500
How to Make Ice Cream and Gelatin	16,000
French Cooking for Amateurs	9,500

Music was popular:

Facts You Should Know about Music	37,00
Dictionary of Musical Terms	21,000
How to Learn to Sing	19,000
Story of Rigoletto	16,000
Old Favorite Negro Songs	15,000

Jazz: What It Is and How to Understand It	15,000
Harmony Self-Taught	14,500
Story of Tannhauser	14,500
How to Teach Yourself to Play the Piano	14,000
How to Enjoy Good Music	13,500
Story of Das Rheingold	13,000
Introduction to Wagner's Music	11,000
How to Enjoy Orchestra Music	10,500
Old English Songs	10,500
Gilbert and Sullivan Guidebook	9,000
Great Christian Hymns	3,000

Haldeman-Julius did not believe there would be a demand
for jokes, but when he produced Little Blue Books of
them "they grew promptly into a sizable classification."
The *Popular Jokebook* sold well from the beginning.

Toasts for all Occasions	55,000
Best Jokes of 1926	50,500
Popular Jokebook	37,000
Broadway Wisecracks	29,000
Best College Humor	17,000
Masterpieces of American Humor	16,500
Best Jokes of 1925	15,500
Masterpieces of American Wit	9,000
Humorous Anecdotes	8,000

Ethnic jokes always do well:

Best Jewish Jokes	43,000
Best Negro Jokes	37,500

Best Irish Jokes	37,000
Best Scotch Jokes	34,500
Best American Jokes	16,000
Best Yankee Jokes	16,000

Henry Ford's Model T died in 1927, but the jokes lived on:

Best Jokes about Married Life	45,500
Best Jokes about Lovers	35,000
Best Jokes about Kissing	33,000
Best Hobo Jokes	23,000
Best Ford Jokes	22,500
Best Jokes about Drunks	18,500
Best Rube Jokes	11,000

Brain teasers were popular:

Book of 500 Riddles	53,500
Mathematical Oddities	37,500
Curiosities of Mathematics	35,000
Puzzles and Brain Teasers	33,500
Popular and Amusing Riddles	24,000
Riddle Rhymes	8,000

Books on free thought sold well:

Luther Burbank's Why I Am an Infidel	64,000
Voltaire's Skeptical Essays	25,000
What Can a Free Man Worship? (Bertrand Russell)	24,000
Controversy on Christianity (Ingersoll v. Gladstone)	22,500

Rome or Reason (Ingersoll v. Cardinal Manning)	19,000
Rupert Hughes Ghastly Purpose of the Parables	19,000
What Atheism Means to Me	17,500
Clarence Darrow's Voltaire Lecture	17,500

The Little Blue Book series once contained some ninety volumes of poetry, but this genre did not sell well, as the following demonstrates:

Gunga Din and Other Poems	25,500
A Book of Comic Poems	21,500
Mandalay and Other Poems	19,000
The Vampire and Other Poems	14,500
A Book of Humorous Verse	10,000

Philosophy sold surprisingly well:

Story of Friedrick Nietzche's Philosophy	45,000
Story of Plato's Philosophy	39,000
Story of Anatole France and His Philosophy	32,000
Story of Aristotle's Philosophy	27,000
Story of Arthur Schopenhauer's Philosophy	26,500
Story of Baruch Spinoza's Philosophy	25,500
Story of Francis Bacon's Philosophy	25,500
Story of Immanuel Kant's Philosophy	24,000
Story of Voltaire's Philosophy	24,000
Story of Herbert Spencer's Philosophy	19,000
Story of Mark Twain's Laughing Philosophy	10,500
Story of Ralph Waldo Emerson's Philosophy	8,000
Story of Henri Bergson's Philosophy	8,000

The bestsellers included:

Color of Life and Love	58,000
Art of Reading Constructively	89,500
Art of Digesting Ideas	31,500
Meaning of Success of Life	27,500
A Rational Sex Code	51,500
How We Can Live Happily	55,000
Why I Do Not Fear Death	43,000
An Encyclopedia of Sex	62,500
Herbert Hoover in the White House	38,000
Serious Lessons in President Harding's Case	35,000
The Girl in the Snappy Roadster	71,000
Herbert Hoover's Record before He Became President	36,000

Not a bad total for any of his best-selling authors!

NOTES

ABBREVIATIONS

EHJ   Emanuel Haldeman-Julius

EHJC E. Haldeman-Julius Collection, Axe Library, Pittsburg State University, Pittsburg, Kansas

HJC   Haldeman-Julius Collection, Hale Library, Morse Department of Special Collections, Kansas State University, Manhattan, Kansas

HJFP Haldeman-Julius Family Papers, Daley Library, University of Illinois at Chicago

MHJ   Marcet Haldeman-Julius

PROLOGUE

1. Rogger, *Russia in the Age of Modernisation*, 199–201.

2. Baron, *The Russian Jew*, 44–45.

3. Israel, *The Jews in Russia*, 50–51.

4. Israel, *The Jews in Russia*, 50 (pogrom); Harrison quoted in Baron, *The Russian Jew*, 49.

5. Rogger, *Jewish Policies*, 26–27, 67–68.

6. Rogger, *Jewish Policies*, 56–57. The movie *Fiddler on the Roof* depicts this experience beautifully.

7. Marcet Haldeman, known within the family as Bo-Peep—a nickname dating from her days in show business—detailed the Julius family history to her son, Henry, after talking to David's cousin Rose. MHJ to Henry, 3 June 1935, folder 199, HJFP. Some sources say they lost two children on the voyage. Marcet says one. Honeymoon trip, folder 1, box 3, HJC.

8. Emanuel's birth certificate is in folder 98, HJFP. The doctor managed to spell all their names incorrectly, as Davis, Zena, and Manuel.

9. Folder 2, box 3, HJC.

10. Potts, "The Henry Ford of Literature," 5.
11. Herder, "Education for the Masses," 6.
12. MHJ, "What the Editor's Wife Is Thinking About," Little Blue Book #809, 17–18.
13. Miller, Vogel, and Davis, *Still Philadelphia*, 3–11.

1. FORCES THAT SHAPED HIM

1. Scott, "Little Blue Books," 160.
2. Folder F2, box 3, HJC.
3. Mordell, *World of Haldeman-Julius*, 38–39. This is a compilation of some of Haldeman-Julius's writings.
4. MHJ, "Editor's Wife," 23; E. Haldeman-Julius, "The Color of Life," Ten Cent Pocket Series #72, 67, 89, 116.
5. EHJ, *My First 25 Years*, 15.
6. EHJ, *My First 25 Years*, 32–33.
7. Mordell, *Trailing E. Haldeman-Julius*, 23.
8. Mordell, *Trailing E. Haldeman-Julius*, 14.
9. Mordell, *Trailing E. Haldeman-Julius*, 29–30.
10. Mordell, *World of Haldeman-Julius*, 43–45.
11. EHJ, *My Second 25 Years*, 46.
12. EHJ, *My Second 25 Years*, 47.
13. EHJ, *My Second 25 Years*, 48.
14. Mordell, *World of Haldeman-Julius*, 100–102.
15. Mordell, *World of Haldeman-Julius*, 202.
16. Mordell, *World of Haldeman-Julius*, 201.
17. Mordell, *World of Haldeman-Julius*, 136–39.
18. EHJ, *My Second 25 Years*, 45.
19. EHJ, *My Second 25 Years*, 45.
20. EHJ, *My First 25 Years*, 196–98. Haldeman-Julius reprinted this essay in *My Second 25 Years*, 31–34.
21. Mordell, *World of Haldeman-Julius*, 59–61.
22. Mordell, *World of Haldeman-Julius*, 68–69.
23. EHJ, *My Second 25 Years*, 16.
24. Mordell, *World of Haldeman-Julius*, 48–49.
25. EHJ, *My Second 25 Years*, 66–67.
26. EHJ, *My Second 25 Years*, 68–72.
27. EHJ, *My Second 25 Years*, 72.
28. EHJ, *My Second 25 Years*, 73–74.
29. EHJ, *My Second 25 Years*, 70.
30. EHJ, *My Second 25 Years*, 40–42.

31. Mordell, *World of Haldeman-Julius*, 223.
32. Mordell, *World of Haldeman-Julius*, 84–87.
33. EHJ, *My Second 25 Years*, 37.
34. EHJ, *My Second 25 Years*, 35.
35. EHJ, *My Second 25 Years*, 36.
36. EHJ, *My Second 25 Years*, 43–44.
37. EHJ, *My Second 25 Years*, 41.
38. EHJ, *My Second 25 Years*, 42.
39. EHJ, *My Second 25 Years*, 44.
40. EHJ, *My Second 25 Years*, 42–43.
41. Mordell, *World of Haldeman-Julius*, 148.
42. EHJ, *My Second 25 Years*, 46–47.
43. EHJ, *My Second 25 Years*, 100.
44. EHJ, *My Second 25 Years*, 83–84.
45. EHJ, *My Second 25 Years*, 103.
46. EHJ, *My Second 25 Years*, 51–52.
47. EHJ, *My Second 25 Years*, 17. EHJ wrote this reaction forty-five years later. It would be interesting to know how he reacted when he heard the speech as a boy of fifteen.
48. EHJ, *My Second 25 Years*, 74–82.
49. EHJ, *My First 25 Years*, 37.
50. Mordell, *Trailing E. Haldeman-Julius*, 50–58.
51. Buhle, *Marxism*, 29–40.
52. Mattson, *Upton Sinclair*, 218.
53. Ross, *Socialist Party*, xvii, states that the term *socialism* "has proven notoriously problematic to define." I consider the definition used above to be the most acceptable during Haldeman-Julius's time.
54. EHJ, *My Second 25 Years*, 71 (Ella Reeve), 72 (Kirkpatrick), 54 (Debs).
55. EHJ, *My First 25 Years*, 15.
56. Ginger, *Bending Cross*, 27.
57. Folder 2, box 3, HJC.
58. Folder 2, box 3, HJC.
59. Folder 2, box 3, HJC.

2. THE BECKONING WORLD
1. Cothran, "Little Blue Book Man," 6.
2. Isaac Goldberg quoted in Cothran, "Little Blue Book Man," 6.
3. Harry Golden, foreword to Mordell, *World of Haldeman-Julius*, 23.
4. EHJ, *My First 25 Years*, 39.
5. EHJ, *My First 25 Years*, 38.

6. EHJ, *My First 25 Years*, 39.

7. EHJ, *My First 25 Years*, 40.

8. Ginger, *Bending Cross*, 198; EHJ, *My First 25 Years*, 42–43.

9. EHJ, *My First 25 Years*, 44.

10. EHJ, *My First 25 Years*, 45.

11. Cothran, "Little Blue Book Man," 13.

12. Cothran, "Little Blue Book Man," 20–21.

13. Cothran, "Little Blue Book Man," 14.

14. Cothran, "Little Blue Book Man," 21–22.

15. Cothran, "Little Blue Book Man," 15–16.

16. Cothran, "Little Blue Book Man," 16.

17. EHJ, *My First 25 Years*, 16; Niven, *Carl Sandburg*, 183.

18. EHJ, *My First 25 Years*, 19.

19. EHJ, *My First 25 Years*, 19.

20. EHJ, *My First 25 Years*, 19–20.

21. EHJ, *My First 25 Years*, 21–22.

22. EHJ, *My First 25 Years*, 22.

23. EHJ, *My First 25 Years*, 46.

24. EHJ, *My First 25 Years*, 22–23.

25. EHJ, *My First 25 Years*, 23.

26. EHJ, *My First 25 Years*, 23.

27. London to EHJ, May 21 and June 17, 1913, folder 20, EHJC.

28. EHJ, *My First 25 Years*, 24. Tichi, *Jack London*, 28, 175, verifies that London's racism came from his background. Later in life his views underwent "a major revision."

29. EHJ, *My First 25 Years*, 25.

30. Debs quoted in Shore, *Talkin' Socialism*, 208–9.

31. EHJ, *My First 25 Years*, 26.

32. EHJ, *My First 25 Years*, 27–28.

33. EHJ, *My First 25 Years*, 28.

34. Cothran, "Little Blue Book Man," 30.

35. EHJ, *My First 25 Years*, 29–30.

36. EHJ, *My First 25 Years*, 30.

37. EHJ, *My First 25 Years*, 30.

38. EHJ, *My First 25 Years*, 31.

39. EHJ, *My First 25 Years*, 36.

40. EHJ, *My First 25 Years*, 37.

41. EHJ, *My First 25 Years*, 47.

42. EHJ, *My Second 25 Years*, 13–14.

43. EHJ, *My Second 25 Years*, 13.
44. EHJ, *My Second 25 Years*, 18.
45. EHJ, *My Second 25 Years*, 23.
46. EHJ, *My Second 25 Years*, 37–38.
47. EHJ, *My Second 25 Years*, 18.
48. EHJ, *My Second 25 Years*, 18.
49. EHJ, *My Second 25 Years*, 25.
50. EHJ, *My Second 25 Years*, 30.

3 . GIRARD, KANSAS

1. Lawrence Gronlund to G. C. Clemens, 13 November 1893, Clemens Collection, Kansas State Historical Society, Topeka.
2. Shore, *Talkin' Socialism*, 104–5.
3. Shore, *Talkin' Socialism*, 175.
4. Ginger, *Bending Cross*, 244–46.
5. Shore, *Talkin' Socialism*, 178.
6. Shore, *Talkin' Socialism*, 216–17. Bruce Bielaski, the FBI agent in charge of this case, believed that "the activity of the Government in connection with this investigation . . . had considerable to do with Wayland's suicide." Folder 3, FBI case files, #4415, p. 75, RG 65, National Archives.
7. Lord, *The Good Years*, 306.
8. Tichi, *Jack London*, 138–41.
9. Clark, *Deliver Us from Evil*, is a standard account of this movement.
10. Brinkley, *The Wilderness Warrior*, 783–85.
11. *American Freeman*, November 1951.
12. Folder 3, HJC.
13. MHJ to "Auntie," 11 November 1915, folder 21, HJFP.
14. The will is on file at Crawford County District Court, Girard, Kansas. Alexander Woollcott, a highly respected author, helped perpetuate this myth when he mentioned it in an article in the newly established *New Yorker* in June 1925 ("After June 30, the Deluge").
15. Barrett-Fox, "Feminism, Socialism, and Pragmatism," 18–19.
16. MHJ to Alice, 8 November 1909, folder 15, HJFP.
17. MHJ to Euterpe (nickname of her closest college chum, Winifred Bryher), 12 December 1914, folder 31, HJFP.
18. Sinclair Lewis to MHJ, 22 December 1914, folder 15, HJFP.
19. Obituary, *Girard Press*, 25 March 1915.
20. MHJ to Anna Hostettler Haldeman, 28 July 1915, folder 37, and MHJ to Auntie Jane, 7 April 1916, folder 172, HJFP.

21. MHJ to "Dearest Auntie," 30 January 1916, folder 172, HJFP.

22. MHJ to Jane Addams, 11 March 1915, folder 172, HJFP.

23. MHJ to Jane Addams, 11 March 1915, folder 172, HJFP.

24. MHJ to Grandmother Anna H. H. Addams, 4 November 1915, folder 172, HJFP.

25. MHJ to Grandmother, 11 March 1915, folder 172, HJFP.

26. Alice Haldeman-Julius de Loach, memories of MHJ, 11 August 1977, folder 231, HJFP.

27. MHJ, *Jane Addams*, 1–10. When Marcet decided to marry Emanuel, she made "some slight allusion" to the fact that she—"a conservative in politics"—was marrying a Socialist, but Aunt Jane assured her that she should not worry. "People usually follow their temperaments," she assured her niece, "and I should call you anything but a conservative" (MHJ, *Jane Addams*, 11).

28. MHJ, *Jane Addams*, 21.

29. MHJ to "Dearest Auntie," 1 April 1915, folder 13, HJFP.

30. MHJ to "Dearest Auntie," 29 October 1915, folder 172, HJFP.

31. See Cothran, "Little Blue Book Man," 51–55, for this exchange of letters.

32. Fry, "Generous Spirit," 98.

33. MHJ to Jane Addams, 11 March 1916, folder 172, HJFP.

34. MHJ to Jane Addams, 11 March 1916, folder 172, HJFP. On smoking, see MHJ to Jane Addams, 7 April 1916, folder 172, HJFP.

35. MHJ to Jane Addams, 7 April 1916, folder 172, HJFP.

36. MHJ, *Editor's Wife*, 13–14.

37. The engagement document is in folder 21, and the agreement is in folder 119, HJFP.

38. Perrett, *America in the Twenties*, 160.

39. Cothran, "Little Blue Book Man," 58.

40. Cothran, "Little Blue Book Man," 59.

41. Cothran, "Little Blue Book Man," 60.

42. Petition to Crawford County District Court, folder 106, HJFP; Cothran, "Little Blue Book Man," 63–65. The dates of this correspondence are Jane to MHJ, 15 April, 16 April, and 4 July 1916, and Jane to MHJ, n.d. [ca. July 1916], folder 172, HJFP.

43. EHJ to Chester, 26 September 1916, folder 99, HJFP.

44. Cothran "Little Blue Book Man," 66–67.

45. Weinstein, *Decline of Socialism*, 119–29.

46. *Appeal to Reason*, 21 April 1917.

47. EHJ to "My Dear Walling," 28 July, 11 August 1918, in Brown, "Five Cent Culture," chapter 1, page 2.

48. *Appeal to Reason*, 21 April 1917.

49. Emma Goldman to EHJ, 22 January 1917, folder 60, HJFP.

50. Part of a letter written by MHJ to Jane Addams, n.d., stamped "original owned by the University of Illinois at Chicago," HJFP.

51. MHJ to Jane Addams, n.d., HJFP.

52. Cothran, "Little Blue Book Man," 72–73.

53. Cothran, "Little Blue Book Man," 74–75.

54. MHJ to Jane Addams, 5 September 1917, folder 172, HJFP.

55. EHJ to Nathan, 31 October 1917, folder 113, HJFP.

56. MHJ to Jane Addams, 31 October 1917, folder 113, HJFP.

57. MHJ to Jane Addams, 31 August 1917, folder 172, HJFP.

58. MHJ to Homer, n.d., folder 70, HJFP.

59. This document, dated 19 September 1917, is in folder 252, HJFP.

60. J. I. Sheppard to editor of the *Pittsburg Daily Sun*, 19 July 1918, folder 115, HJFP.

61. Emanuel petitioned his draft board for "Industrial" status on the basis of his work as editor of the *New Appeal*, which was supporting the war effort. Petition, 15 July 1918, folder 115, HJFP.

62. Marcet's affidavit in Stephenson County, Illinois, dated 5 January 1918, folder 115, HJFP.

63. Sheppard to *Pittsburg Daily Sun*, 19 July 1918, folder 115, HJFP.

64. MHJ to "Dearest Auntie," 1 November 1918, file 173, and EHJ to "Dear Johnny," n.d., folder 114, HJFP.

65. MHJ to EHJ, n.d., folder 115, HJFP.

66. Affidavit of EHJ, 27 August 1918, folder 115, HJFP.

67. Affidavit of EHJ, 19 August 1918, folder 115, HJFP.

68. Newton D. Baker to J. I. Sheppard, 27 July 1918, folder 115, HJFP.

69. MHJ to Euterpe, 6 August 1918, folder 71, HJFP.

70. MHJ to Jane Addams, n.d., folder 71, HJFP.

71. EHJ to "Dearest Sweetheart," 28 May 1920, folder 111, HJFP.

72. MHJ to Euterpe, 6 August 1918, folder 71, HJFP.

73. Jane Addams to MHJ, 27 November 1919, folder 21, HJFP.

74. MHJ to Jane Addams, 7 October 1919, folder 21, HJFP. This is another lengthy (17 pp.) handwritten letter. Interestingly, in 1930 Owensby first became a cohort of, then a competitor of, the famous "goat gland" doctor of Milford, Kansas. See Lee, *Bizarre Careers*.

75. MHJ to Jane Addams, 7 October 1919, folder 21, HJFP.

76. MHJ to Jane Addams, 7 October 1919, folder 21, HJFP.

77. MHJ to Jane Addams, 7 October 1919, folder 21, HJFP.

78. MHJ to Euterpe, 8 February 1919, folder 21, HJFP.

79. MHJ to Mother Julius, January 1920, and Esther to MHJ, 6 September 1920, folder 113, HJFP.

4. LITTLE BLUE BOOKS

1. W. T. Raleigh to EHJ, 22 November 1918, folder 113, EHJC.
2. Perrett, *America in the Twenties*, 276.
3. Mordell, *World of Haldeman-Julius*, 28–29.
4. Cothran, "Little Blue Book Man," 96–97.
5. Cothran, "Little Blue Book Man," 98.
6. Cothran, "Little Blue Book Man," 99–101.
7. Shore, *Talkin' Socialism*, 167–71.
8. Scott, "Little Blue Books," 164.
9. Scott, "Little Blue Books," 179.
10. Scott, "Little Blue Books," 164.
11. Herder, "Education for the Masses," 56–57.
12. Schiffrin, *The Business of Books*, 5.
13. Schiffrin, *The Business of Books*, 6, 46–47.
14. Martinek, *Socialism and Print Culture*, 64, 70.
15. Le Sueur, *Crusaders*, 32, 44–45.
16. Folder 3, FBI case file #75981, p. 2, RG 65, National Archives.
17. Le Sueur, *Crusaders*, quote at 45.
18. EHJ, *My First 25 Years*, 13–14.
19. EHJ, *My First 25 Years*, 14.
20. EHJ, *My First 25 Years*, 10–11; S. Haldeman-Julius, "An Intimate Look," 17 ("generous, devoted reader").
21. Folder D, Radical Publications, FBI case file #202600-282, p. 150, RG 65, National Archives.
22. MHJ to Jane Addams, 2 January 1919, folder 172, HJFP.
23. Cothran, "Little Blue Book Man," 108.
24. EHJ to "Dear Precious Sweetheart," n.d., folder 111, HJFP.
25. Cothran, "Little Blue Book Man," 104–5.
26. Cothran, "Little Blue Book Man," 114–17.
27. Cothran, "Little Blue Book Man," 117–18.
28. EHJ to Kopelin, n.d. but probably around May 1920, HJFP.
29. *Appeal to Reason*, 21 August 1920.
30. EHJ to "Dear Precious Sweetheart," n.d., folder 111, HJFP.
31. EHJ to MHJ, [4] May 1920, folder 73, HJFP.
32. EHJ to W. C. Mencken, 4 February 1922, folder 75, EHJC.
33. EHJ to Mencken, 4 February 1922, folder 75, EHJC.
34. EHJ to Mencken, 4 February 1922, folder 75, EHJC.
35. "'Dust' by Mr. and Mrs. Haldeman-Julius: Gritty!" (review at amazon.com). In a lecture at the University of Chicago in May 1922, Stewart Sherman placed the novel

in the company of E. W. Howe's *The Story of a Country Town*, Hamlin Garland's *Main-Travelled Roads*, Edgar Lee Masters's *Spoon River Anthology*, Sherwood Anderson's *Winesburg, Ohio*, and Sinclair Lewis's *Main Street*.

36. *Pittsburg Morning Sun*, 1 May 1921.
37. Cothran, "Little Blue Book Man," 126–30.
38. Cothran, "Little Blue Book Man," 130–32.
39. *New Appeal*, 1 May 1921.
40. Cothran, "Little Blue Book Man," 133–41.
41. *Appeal to Reason*, 27 January, 18 March, 25 April 1922.
42. Herder, "Education for the Masses," 177–80.
43. Cothran, "Little Blue Book Man," 154–56.
44. EHJ to "Dear Precious Sweetheart," n.d., folder 111, HJFP; MHJ to Jane Addams, 17 October 1921, folder 173, HJFP.
45. MHJ to Jane Addams, 17 October 1921, folder 173, HJFP.
46. *Haldeman-Julius Weekly*, 25 April 1924.
47. *Haldeman-Julius Weekly*, 25 November, 16 December 1922.
48. Murray, *Red Scare*, 90–92.
49. *Haldeman-Julius Weekly*, 9 December 1922.
50. Cothran, "Little Blue Book Man," 170–71.
51. Cothran, "Little Blue Book Man," 172–73.
52. Cothran, "Little Blue Book Man," 174–75.
53. Cothran, "Little Blue Book Man," 174–77.
54. *Haldeman-Julius Weekly*, 3 March 1923.
55. EHJ to Girard Chamber of Commerce, 8 May 1923, folder 76, HJFP.
56. *Haldeman-Julius Weekly*, 8 March 1924.
57. EHJ to MHJ, n.d., probably January or February 1924, HJFP.
58. *Haldeman-Julius Weekly*, 27 October 1923, 17 May 1924.
59. Brown, "Five Cent Culture," chapter 4, pp. 131–32.
60. *Haldeman-Julius Weekly*, 26 July 1924.
61. *Haldeman-Julius Weekly*, 26 May 1923.
62. Fry, "Generous Spirit," 123–24.
63. Fry, "Generous Spirit," 125.
64. Quoted in Herder, "Education for the Masses," ix.
65. Folder 25, box 3, HJC.
66. Woollcott, "After June 30, the Deluge," 7–8.
67. Cothran, "Little Blue Book Man," 259–61.
68. Cothran, "Little Blue Book Man," 259–65.
69. Herder, "Education for the Masses," 25, 40–42.
70. Herder, "Education for the Masses," 42–43.

71. Cothran, "Little Blue Book Man," 268–71.
72. *Haldeman-Julius Weekly*, 18 July 1925.
73. *Haldeman-Julius Weekly*, 18 July 1925.
74. Walter S. Mills to MHJ, 13 August 1925, folder 84, HJFP.
75. MHJ, *Famous and Interesting Guests*, 14–20.
76. MHJ, *Famous and Interesting Guests*, 3–8.
77. *Haldeman-Julius Weekly*, 24 March 1923.
78. Mattson, *Upton Sinclair*, notes that friends called him "Uppie" (6).
79. MHJ, *Famous and Interesting Guests*, 9–11.
80. MHJ, *Famous and Interesting Guests*, 28–29.
81. Mordell, *World of Haldeman-Julius*, 30–35. Durant was another of Marcet's "Famous and Interesting Guests at a Kansas Farm."
82. Cothran, "Little Blue Book Man," 237.
83. EHJ to MHJ, n.d., probably January or February 1924, HJFP.
84. Cothran, "Little Blue Book Man," 203.
85. MHJ to Jane Addams, n.d., folder 21, HJFP.
86. S. Haldeman-Julius, "An Intimate Look," 6.
87. MHJ to EHJ, 13 May 1924, folder 111, HJFP.

5. A CORNUCOPIA OF BOOKS AND EVENTS

1. EHJ, *My Second 25 Years*, 102.
2. Reprinted in the *Haldeman-Julius Weekly*, 10 February 1923.
3. John Brinkley developed his radio station, KFKB, in 1922 and was a pioneer in developing radio programming. Emanuel dispatched John Gunn to Milford, Kansas, to study Brinkley's operations, but nothing materialized from this venture. See Lee, *Bizarre Careers*, 62–65, 165.
4. *Haldeman-Julius Weekly*, 24 March 1923.
5. *Haldeman-Julius Weekly*, 19 December 1923.
6. Pierre Loving, Vienna, to EHJ, 25 November 1923, HJFP.
7. EHJ, *First Hundred Million*, 191–93.
8. EHJ, *First Hundred Million*, 194–97.
9. EHJ, *First Hundred Million*, 228–39.
10. EHJ, *First Hundred Million*, 253.
11. EHJ, *First Hundred Million*, 254–55.
12. EHJ, *First Hundred Million*, 256–58.
13. EHJ, *First Hundred Million*, 260–63.
14. MHJ to Alice, 21 June 1929, folder 99, EHJC.
15. EHJ to Alice, 2 July 1929, folder 101, EHJC.
16. MHJ to Alice, n.d., folder 102, EHJC.

17. MHJ to Alice, 16 July 1927, folder 103, EHJC.
18. MHJ, *Why I Believe in Companionate Marriage*.
19. Leburn Guy to "Dearest Josephine," 17 August 1926, folder 87, HJFP.
20. Quote from Barrett-Fox, "Feminism, Socialism, and Pragmatism," 79.
21. E. H. Lindley to EHJ, 30 September 1929, folder 89, EHJC.
22. Walter Burr to MHJ, 14 October 1927 and Floyd B. Lee to MHJ, 31 October 1927, folder 99, EHJC.
23. The Haldeman-Juliuses to *Pittsburg Headlight*, 28 October 1927, folder 91, EHJC.
24. Cothran, "Little Blue Book Man," 284–85.
25. Joey's note to Aubrey is quoted in Cothran, "Little Blue Book Man," 293.
26. MHJ to Joey, 17 February 1928, folder 222, EHJC.
27. *Kansas City Star*, 20 November 1927; *New York Times*, 21 November 1927.
28. *New York Times*, 23 November 1927.
29. Cothran, "Little Blue Book Man," 298.
30. Cothran, "Little Blue Book Man," 299–303; Bradbury quoted in Scott, "Little Blue Books," 169.
31. Folder 10, box 3, HJC.
32. MHJ to Aubrey and Joey, 22 February 1928, folder 255, EHJC.
33. EHJ to Mr. Swancara, 13 June 1949, folder 205, EHJC.
34. Cothran, "Little Blue Book Man," 334–35.
35. Cothran, "Little Blue Book Man," 345–48.
36. Cothran, "Little Blue Book Man," 335–36. Sue, his secretary, reported that an employee was worried about what the sale would do to Girard's economy. Emanuel told him not to worry, because the process was just "an advertising gimmick." Folder 12, box 3, HJC.
37. Cothran, "Little Blue Book Man," 236–37.
38. Cothran, "Little Blue Book Man," 337–38.
39. EHJ to Max and Dick (Simon and Schuster), 7 March 1929, folder 97, EHJC.
40. Cothran, "Little Blue Book Man," 339–40.
41. Cothran, "Little Blue Book Man," 341–44.
42. Cothran, "Little Blue Book Man," 528–29.
43. EHJ to "Dearest Sweetheart," 7 November 1929, folder 105, EHJC.

6. THE GREAT DEPRESSION
1. S. Haldeman-Julius, "An Intimate Look," 12.
2. S. Haldeman-Julius, "An Intimate Look," 12–13, 19.
3. EJH to MHJ, n.d., file 114, EHJ.
4. MHJ, "The Charming Humanness of Joseph McCabe," *American Freeman*, 19 July 1930.
5. *American Freeman*, 24 May 1930.

6. MHJ's thoughts on Tom Mooney, folder 108, EHJC.

7. MHJ to "Dearest Auntie," 7 June 1930, folder 110, EHJC.

8. MHJ to Jane, 21 April 1931, folder 107, EHJC.

9. MHJ to Dear Auntie, 21 April 1931, folder 107, EHJC.

10. MHJ to Jane Addams, 21 April 1931, folder 107, EHJC.

11. EHJ to Alice, 16 June 1930, folder 110, EHJC; Marcet essay, *American Freeman*, 15 March 1930.

12. MHJ to Alice 7 July 1930, folder 113, EHJC.

13. MHJ to Alice, 4 August 1931, folder 129, EHJC.

14. *American Freeman*, 4 October 1930.

15. *American Freeman*, 11 October 1930.

16. *American Freeman*, 18 October 1930.

17. *American Freeman*, 2 May 1931.

18. *American Freeman*, 9 May 1931.

19. *American Freeman*, 18 July 1931.

20. *American Freeman*, 1 August 1931.

21. *American Freeman*, 8 August 1931.

22. *American Freeman*, 14 November 1931.

23. Jane Addams to MHJ, 1 October 1931, folder 121, EHJC.

24. *American Freeman*, 31 October 1931.

25. *American Freeman*, 2 November 1931 (Chicago visit); Fry, "Generous Spirit," 135–37 (Henry and repacking).

26. Quoted in Watkins, *The Great Depression*, 338.

27. *American Freeman*, 12 December 1931.

28. *American Freeman*, 19 December 1931.

29. *American Freeman*, 2 January 1932.

30. *American Freeman*, 23 January 1932.

31. Lowe to MHJ, *American Freeman*, 8 December 1931; EHJ to MHJ, 10 December and 13 December 1931, folder 121, EHJC.

32. *American Freeman*, 28 November 1931.

33. *American Freeman*, 26 December 1931.

34. *American Freeman*, 26 December 1931.

35. *American Freeman*, 26 December 1931.

36. *American Freeman*, 5 March 1932.

37. *American Freeman*, 5 March 1932.

38. *American Freeman*, 5 March 1932.

39. *American Freeman*, 15 November 1932.

40. *New York Times*, 28 June 1931, 11 October 1932.

41. Cothran, "Little Blue Book Man," 354–55.

42. Lee, *Bizarre Careers*, 138–47.
43. Vanderbilt to EHJ, 7 April 1933, folder 128, EHJC.
44. *American Freeman*, January 1934.
45. Lou to MHJ, 14 August and 27 December 1933, folder 130, EHJC.
46. Fry, "Generous Spirit," 131.
47. MHJ to Alice, 15 March 1933, folder 127, EHJC.
48. Cochran, "Little Blue Book Man," 368–72.
49. MHJ to "Manuel Boy," 17 June 1933, folder 129, EHJC.
50. Cothran, "Little Blue Book Man," 373–75.
51. MHJ to Esther, 15 December 1933, folder 130, EHJC.
52. MHJ to Esther, 18 December 1933 and 18 January 1934, folder 133, EHJC.
53. Cothran, "Little Blue Book Man," 375.
54. Gunn to EHJ, n.d., folder 123, EHJC.
55. Cothran, "Little Blue Book Man," 379.
56. Fry, "Generous Spirit," 143.
57. Cothran, "Little Blue Book Man," 378–79.
58. Cothran, "Little Blue Book Man," 380–81.
59. Weber Linn to MHJ, 19 July 1935, folder 161, EHJC.
60. MHJ to Weber, 25 July 1935, folder 161, EHJC.
61. Cothran, "Little Blue Book Man," 381–82.
62. Cothran, "Little Blue Book Man," 392.
63. Alice to MHJ, 6 August 1936, folder 137, EHJC.
64. Alice to MHJ, 18 October 1936, folder 36, EHJC.
65. EHJ to MHJ, 2 October 1935, folder 111, EHJC.
66. Alice to Daddy, 27 February 1935, folder 35, EHJC.
67. Alice to Daddy, 2 March 1935, folder 35, EHJC.
68. Daddy to Alice, n.d., and Alice to Daddy, 17 March 1935, folder 146, EHJC.
69. Alice to Bo-Peep, n.d., folder 5, EHJC.
70. Alice to Bo-Peep, n.d., folder 5, EHJC.
71. EHJ to Goldberg, 22 June 1935, folder 5, EHJC.
72. Copeland to EHJ, 6 February 1936, folder 120, EHJC.
73. EHJ to MHJ, n.d., folder 164, EHJC.
74. EHJ to Fielding, 4 January 1938, and Fielding to EHJ, 5 January 1938, folder 181, EHJC.
75. Alice to Bo-Peep, 12 January 1938, folder 181, EHJC.
76. Henry to Bo-Peep, 29 November 1937, folder 179, EHJC.
77. Lee, *Bizarre Careers*, 103–4. For a more thorough account of this quack see Juhnke, *Quacks and Crusaders*.
78. *American Freeman*, July 1937, December 1937, January 1938, March 1938.

7. RESURRECTION

1. *American Freeman*, April 1936.

2. *American Freeman*, January, March 1937.

3. *American Freeman*, March 1938.

4. Alice to Daddy, 4 March 1938, folder 183, EHJC.

5. Bo-Peep to Hank, 4 December 1938, folder 199, EHJC.

6. Cothran, "Little Blue Book Man," 395.

7. Caspar W. Ooms to "Mr. Julius," 23 March 1939, folder 18, EHJC; *American Freeman*, May 1951.

8. Brown, "Five Cent Culture," Conclusion, p. 17, citing the *Pittsburg Morning Sun*, 3 November 1938.

9. MHJ to Child Placement Bureau, 26 April 1939, folder 187, EHJC.

10. *American Freeman*, May 1941.

11. Gunn's eulogy is in folder 170, EHJC.

12. *American Freeman*, June 1941.

13. Cothran, "Little Blue Book Man," 396–97.

14. *American Freeman*, September 1941.

15. S. Haldeman-Julius, "An Intimate Look," 13.

16. Their marriage license is reproduced in Ancestry.com, Missouri marriage records, 1805–2002.

17. S. Haldeman-Julius, "An Intimate Look," 5–7.

18. Folder 12, box 3, HJC.

19. S. Haldeman-Julius, "An Intimate Look," 16–18.

20. EHJ to Bertrand Russell, 19 August 1942, folder 192, EHJC.

21. Dorothy Fiske to Haldeman-Julius Company, 21 April 1941, and EHJ to Fiske, 23 April 1941, folder 190, EHJC.

22. Cothran, "Little Blue Book Man," 400.

23. *American Freeman*, April 1941.

24. Cothran, "Little Blue Book Man," 401.

25. *American Freeman*, June 1941.

26. *American Freeman*, October 1941.

27. Cothran, "Little Blue Book Man," 406–10.

28. *American Freeman*, October 1948.

29. Cothran, "Little Blue Book Man," 419–22.

30. Cothran, "Little Blue Book Man," 422–24.

31. *American Freeman*, November 1948; EHJ to J. Edgar Hoover, 23 July 1948, folder 201, and Hoover to EHJ, 4 February 1949, folder 204, EHJC.

32. EHJ will, folder 116, EHJC.

33. *Girard Press*, 12 April 1951.

34. *American Freeman*, March 1950.
35. Cothran, "Little Blue Book Man," 427–28.
36. IRS report of 26 April 1950, folder 210, EHJC.
37. Milton Rippey to Arthur J. Mellott, 7 May 1951, folder 213, EHJC.
38. Cothran, "Little Blue Book Man," 429–30.
39. EHJ to "Dear Friends," n.d., folder 210, EHJC.
40. *Fort Scott Tribune*, 19 April 1951, folder 12, box 3, HJC.
41. Pegler to EHJ, 10 July 1951, folder 214, EHJC.
42. EHJ to Pegler, 13 July 1951, folder 214, EHJC.
43. *American Freeman*, October 1951.
44. Cothran, "Little Blue Book Man," 434–35.
45. Folder 17, box 3, HJC.
46. Folder 12, box 3, HJC.
47. Cothran, "Little Blue Book Man," 436.
48. Folder 12, box 3, HJC.
49. *American Freeman*, June 1951.
50. *American Freeman*, August 1951.
51. Folder 19, box 3, HJC.
52. *American Freeman*, November 1951.
53. *American Freeman*, November 1951.
54. Quoted in Cothran, "Little Blue Book Man," 443–44.
55. EHJ, *My Second 25 Years*, 95–96.
56. Brown, "Five Cent Culture," Conclusion, p. 18.

EPILOGUE

1. Sharon E. Neet, "Does Story Trump History? Emanuel and Marcet Haldeman-Julius and Girard, Kansas" (paper presented at Missouri Valley History Conference, Omaha, 5 March 2015).
2. Scott, "Little Blue Books," 171.
3. Dale M. Herder, "Haldeman-Julius, the Little Blue Books, and the Theory of Popular Culture," http://www.autodidactproject.org/other/hjl.html.

BIBLIOGRAPHY

MANUSCRIPT COLLECTIONS

Axe Library, Pittsburg State University, Pittsburg, Kansas
E. Haldeman-Julius Collection
Daley Library, University of Illinois at Chicago
Haldeman-Julius Family Papers
Hale Library, Morse Department of Special Collections, Kansas State University, Manhattan, Kansas
Haldeman-Julius Collection

PUBLISHED SOURCES

Baron, Salo W. *The Russian Jew under Tsars and Soviets*. New York: Macmillan, 1976.

Barrett-Fox, Jason. "Feminism, Socialism, and Pragmatism in the Life of Marcet Haldeman-Julius, 1887–1941." Master's thesis, University of Kansas, 1908.

Brinkley, Douglas. *The Wilderness Warrior: Theodore Roosevelt and the Crusade for America*. New York: Harpers, 2009.

Brown, Melanie Ann. "Five Cent Culture at the 'University in Print': Radical Ideology and the Marketplace in E. Haldeman-Julius's Little Blue Books, 1919–1929." PhD diss., University of Minnesota, 2006.

Buhle, Paul. *Marxism in the United States*. New York: Verso, 1987.

Clark, Norman. *Deliver Us from Evil*. New York: Norton, 1976.

Cothran, Andrew Neilson. "The Little Blue Book Man and the Big American Parade: A Biography of Emanuel Haldeman-Julius." PhD diss., University of Maryland, 1966.

Fry, Paul E. "Generous Spirit: The Life of Mary Fry." Unpublished MS. Copy in Axe Library, Pittsburg State University.

Ginger, Ray. *The Bending Cross: A Biography of Eugene V. Debs*. New Brunswick NJ: Rutgers University Press, 1949.

Haldeman-Julius, Emanuel. *First Hundred Million*. Vancouver: Anglican Press, 1928.

———. *My First 25 Years: Instead of a Footnote, an Autobiography*. Big Blue Book #B-788. Girard KS: Haldeman-Julius Publications, 1949.

———. *My Second 25 Years: Instead of a Footnote, an Autobiography*. Big Blue Book #B-814. Girard KS: Haldeman-Julius Publications, 1949.

Haldeman-Julius, Marcet. *Famous and Interesting Guests at a Kansas Farm*. Girard KS: Haldeman-Julius Publications, 1936.

———. *Jane Addams as I Knew Her*. Girard KS: Haldeman-Julius Publications, 1936.

———. *Why I Believe in Companionate Marriage*. Little Blue Book #1258. Girard KS: Haldeman-Julius Publications, 1927.

Haldeman-Julius, Sue. "An Intimate Look at Haldeman-Julius." *Little Balkans Review* 2 (Winter 1981–82): 1–19.

Herder, Dale Marvin. "Education for the Masses: The Haldeman-Julius Little Blue Books as Popular Culture during the Nineteen-Twenties." PhD diss., Michigan State University, 1975.

———. "Haldeman-Julius, the Little Blue Books, and the Theory of Popular Culture." *Journal of Popular Culture* 4, no. 4 (Spring 1971): 881–91.

Israel, Gerard. *The Jews in Russia*. Trans. Sanford C. Chernoff. New York: St. Martin's Press, 1975.

Juhnke, Eric. *Quacks and Crusaders*. Lawrence: University Press of Kansas, 2002.

Lee, R. Alton. *The Bizarre Careers of John R. Brinkley*. Lexington: University Press of Kentucky, 2003.

Le Sueur, Meridel. *Crusaders: The Radical Legacy of Marian and Arthur Le Sueur*. St. Paul: Minnesota Historical Society Press, 1984.

Lord, Walter. *The Good Years*. New York: Bantam Books, 1962.

Martinek, Jason D. *Socialism and Print Culture in America, 1897–1920*. London: Pickering and Chatto, 2012.

Mattson, Kevin. *Upton Sinclair and the Other American Century*. New York: Wiley, 2006.

Miller, Frederic M., Morris J. Vogel, and Allen F. Davis. *Still Philadelphia*. Philadelphia: Temple University Press, 1983.

Mordell, Albert. *Trailing E. Haldeman-Julius in Philadelphia and Other Places*. Girard KS: Haldeman-Julius Publications, 1949.

———, comp. *The World of Haldeman-Julius*. New York: Twayne, 1960.

Murray, Robert K. *Red Scare: A Study in National Hysteria, 1919–1920*. New York: McGraw-Hill, 1984.

Niven, Penelope. *Carl Sandburg: A Biography*. New York: Scribner, 1991.

Perrett, Geoffrey. *America in the Twenties: A History*. New York: Simon and Schuster, 1982.

Potts, Rolf. "The Henry Ford of Literature." *The Believer* 6, no. 7 (September 2008): 2–38.

Rogger, Hans. *Jewish Policies and Right-Wing Politics in Imperial Russia*. New York: Macmillan, 1986.

———. *Russia in the Age of Modernisation and Revolution, 1881–1912*. New York: Longman, 1983.

Ross, Jack. *The Socialist Party of America*. Lincoln: Potomac Books, 2015.

Schiffrin, André. *The Business of Books: How International Conglomerates Took Over Publishing and Changed the Way We Read*. New York: Verso, 2000.

Scott, Mark. "The Little Blue Books in the War on Bigotry." *Kansas History: A Journal of the Central Plains* 1 (Autumn 1978): 155–76.

Shore, Elliott. *Talkin' Socialism: J. A. Wayland and the Radical Press*. Lawrence: University Press of Kansas, 1988.

Tichi, Cecelia. *Jack London*. Chapel Hill: University of North Carolina Press, 2015.

Watkins, T. H. *The Great Depression: America in the 1930s*. Boston: Little, Brown, 1993.

Weinstein, James. *The Decline of Socialism in America, 1912–1925*. New York: Monthly Review, 1967.

Woollcott, Alexander. "After June 30, the Deluge." *New Yorker*, 20 June 1925, 7–8.

INDEX

Adamic, Louis, 142, 152

Addams, Jane: avoiding influenza, 84; death of, 169; family relationships of, 69; gravesite of, 170; Marcet Haldeman-Julius, relationship with, 62, 65, 68, 70–73, 79–80, 86–87, 88–90, 100–101, 107, 149–50, 156–57, 226n27; name change suggested by, 75; at Sarah Alice Haldeman's bedside, 64

Addams, John Huy, 62, 171

Addams, Laurie, 74

Addams, Sarah Alice. *See* Haldeman, Sarah Alice Addams

Addams, Sarah Weber, 62

advertising: free, 187; after Great Depression, 147; in *Haldeman-Julius Weekly*, 109, 129; Harrison-Rippey handling, 191–92; by Julius Augustus Wayland, 58; in magazines and journals, 105, 107; methods of, 131–32, 201, 231n36; in *New Appeal*, 94, 95–96, 99–100; Post Office considering illegal, 107; selling business by, 194

African Americans, 14–15, 51, 68, 117, 135–37, 183, 201

"After June 30, the Deluge" (Woollcott), 114, 225n14

Aker's grocery store, 17

Alexander II, Czar, 2

Alexander III, Czar, 2, 3–4

Allen, F. C., 137

All Quiet on the Western Front (film), 150

All's Well, 118

America, 188

America, changes in, 60–61, 74, 93–94, 143–44, 199

American Academy of Dramatic Arts, 63

American Bankers Association, 153

American Bond and Mortgage Company, 154, 156

American Civil Liberties Union, 198. *See also* National Civil Liberties Union

American Freeman: advertising books, 100, 179, 184, 188, 189; Catholic Church and, 187–88; changes in, 141–42, 166, 169; circulation of, 161–62, 163, 169, 174, 180, 187; on Emanuel Haldeman-Julius, 195, 196; finances of, 166, 172; Marcet Haldeman-Julius as reporter for, 154; on Nazis, 164; "Questions and Answers" series in,

American Freeman (continued)
128; reporting on scandals, 155–56, 160–61, 176–77; subscriptions to, 154; World War II and, 186. See also *Haldeman-Julius Weekly*

American Magazine, 107

American Mercury, 121

American Parade, 141–42, 143. See also *Haldeman-Julius Quarterly*

amnesty for political prisoners, 94–95, 106

Anthony, Rowe, 161

anti-Semitism, 1–2, 4, 11–12, 21

Aphrodisiacs and Anti-Aphrodisiacs, 179

Appeal Army, 58, 95, 103

"The Appeal Army" (Brewer), 58

Appeal Pocket Series. *See* Little Blue Books; Pocket Series

Appeal to Reason: beginnings of, 57; book division of, 95–96, 102–3; Emanuel Haldeman-Julius involved with, 54, 76–79, 142, 191, 192; financing School of Social Economy, 98; Louis Kopelin running, 101, 123; merging with *Coming Nation*, 45; name changes of, 76, 95; as socialist publication, 58–60; subscriptions to, 58, 76; Upton Sinclair buying, 102–3; used for book sale promotion, 99–100; used to denounce socialism, 72; on World War I, 76. See also *Haldeman-Julius Weekly*; *New Appeal*

Arbuckle, Fatty, 103

Armistice, 87

"Arouse, Ye Slaves" (Debs), 59

assassin, Russian, 68

Atlantic Monthly, 100–101

auctions, 15

Austin, Minnie, 59

The Autobiography of a Madame, 179

The Autobiography of a Pimp, 174, 179

automobiles, 20, 61, 143, 180

Baer, David R., 12–13

Bailey, Liberty Hyde, 61

Baker, Newton D., 85

Baker, Norman, 176–77, 180

Baldwin, Roger, 87

The Ballad of Reading Gaol (Wilde), 94

Balta, Russia, 2–3

Baltimore Sun, 100

Bennett, Clifton, 189–90

Benson, Allan, 41, 75, 77

Berger, Victor L., 30, 41–42, 44

Berkman, Alexander, 39–40

Bernarr McFadden Publications, 142–43

Bewick, Moreing and Company, 153–54, 160–61

Bible, 13, 39, 116

Bidwell, Bertha, 170

Bielaski, Bruce, 225n6

Big American Parade (E. Haldeman-Julius), 143–44

Big Blue Books, 130–31, 188, 198

Billings, Warren, 148–50

The Black International, 186, 188

Black International, 187

blacks. *See* African Americans

Bledsoe, Milton H., 183

Bloor, Ella Reeve, 31, 35

Blue Book franchises, 112; special sales, 131

Bob, Ruthie, 90, 132–33

Bohn, Frank, 82

bombings, 2, 48, 59, 95, 148

bookskrieg, 186–87

"The Booster" (M. Haldeman-Julius), 79

Bo-Peep, 221n7. *See also*, Haldeman-Julius, Marcet

Brackett, Mr., 171

Bradbury, John W., 140

Brady, Diamond Jim, 53

The Brass Check (Sinclair), 118

brawls, 65–66

Breed, Austin A., 111

Brentano, Lowell, 101, 104

Brewer, George, 98

Brewer, Grace, 58

Brinkley, John R., 163, 177, 227n74, 230n3

British mining interests, 153, 160

Brown's preparatory school, 33

Bryan, William Jennings, 27, 116

Bryher, Winifred. *See* Euterpe (friend of Marcet Haldeman-Julius)

burglary, 190

Burkhead, L. M., 139, 140, 193

Burns, William J., 48

Burr, Walter, 136

bus incident, 137

"Business" (E. Haldeman-Julius), 41

butter churn party, 120

Butterfield, Kenyon L., 61

California: Emanuel Haldeman-Julius visits, 30–31, 50, 87, 102–3; legal proceedings in, 48, 149–50; socialism in, 30–31

candy store operator, 43–44

Capital (Marx), 37

capitalism, 58, 60

Carlyle, Thomas, 38

Carnegie, Andrew, 60

cars, 20, 61, 143, 180

Catherine the Great, 1

Catholic Chronicle, 188

Catholic Exponent, 188

Catholics, 11, 21, 74, 108–9, 186, 187–88

Catholic Universe Bulletin, 188

"Caught" (E. Haldeman-Julius and M. Haldeman-Julius), 101

Cauldwell, David Oliver, 198

Cedarville IL: Alice Haldeman-Julius on farm near, 152; Emanuel Haldeman-Julius's connection to, 190; Haldeman family in, 62, 68; Haldeman farm near, 80, 101, 122; Jane Addams's connection to, 169–70; Josephine Haldeman-Julius on farm near, 112–13, 135; Julius-Haldeman wedding in, 73–75; Marcet Haldeman-Julius's connection to, 63, 70, 84, 165–66, 171

Chamber of Horrors, 24

Chang Yen-Mao, 153–54

Chaplin, Charlie, 103

Charles H. Kerr Company, 97–98, 202

Chicago IL, 30, 45, 50, 112

Chicago Daily News, 112

Chicago World, 44

Child Placement Bureau (Kansas City), 181

Child's restaurant, 16–17

China, 153–54, 160

Chinese Engineering Company, 154

Chinz, Albert, 144

christenings, 79

Christianity and Jews, 1, 3

Churchill, Winston, 186

cigar-store Indian, 25

Clugston, W. G., 163

Cohen, John E., 31

Cohen, Joseph, 37

Collier's, 162

The Color of Life (E. Haldeman-Julius), 10–11, 41, 79

Columbus High School, 136

Coming Nation, 45

communes, 159

Communist Manifesto, 37

Communists, 157, 159, 164

companionate marriage, 74, 133–35, 138–39

Comstock, Anthony, 38–39

Conant, James B., 37

Connelly, John B., 31

"The Conquest of Prudery" (E. Haldeman-Julius), 49

conscientious objectors, 87–88

conspiracy theories, 187–88, 195–96

contraception, 134, 135

Coolidge, Calvin, 121

coolies, 160

Copeland, Lewis, 174–75

copyright issue, 186

Cosmopolitan, 60, 107

Coughlin, Charles, 186–87

Country Life Commission, 61

Cowley, Malcolm, 157–58

Cox, Kenneth, 150

Crawford, Nelson Antrim, 115, 121

Crawford County KS, 57, 82, 83, 98, 136

Creatore, Luigi, 26

Crisis, 136

Crowder, Enoch H., 84, 86

Curran, A. J., 75

Curtis, Charles, 154–55

Damrosh, Benjamin, 13

Darrow, Clarence, 48–49, 116–17, 155

Darwinism, 47

death penalty, 67–68

Debs, Eugene V.: as chancellor of School of Social Economy, 98; Emanuel Haldeman-Julius and, 31, 37, 75, 199; Emma Goldman on, 39; on Harrison Gray Otis, 48; Job Harriman and, 49; political aspirations of, 49, 102; as prisoner, 94–95, 102, 106; Robert Ingersoll and, 32; as socialist, 35, 40, 59

Debs, Theodore, 95

Debunker, 141–42, 143, 156. See also *Haldeman-Julius Monthly*

Defense Fund (Deficit Fund), 177, 180

Delaware River, 6, 7, 13

DeMille, Cecil. B., 103

Democrats, 83, 150, 162

Department of Agriculture, 121

Department of Justice, 95

Detroit Free Press, 187

The Diary of a Bell Boy (Smith), 189

Diaspora, 1

Dime Museum, 23

district attorney, socialist, 43–44

divorce, 74, 133–35

dog manure collecting as business, 21

"Don't Lower Your Standard of Living" (H. Hoover), 153

Doran and Company, 64

drafts, military, 82–87

"Dreams and Compound Interest" (E. Haldeman-Julius and M. Haldeman-Julius), 101

Drentein, Alexander, 2

Du Bois, W. E. B., 68, 201

Durant, Will, 109–10, 122, 203

Dust (E. Haldeman-Julius and M. Haldeman-Julius), 104, 148, 196–97, 228n35

Dvorkin, Mayer, 143

dynamiters, 148, 149

Eikhoff and Kraemer, 5

Einstein, Albert, 164

Eisenhower, Dwight, 12

Eisenhower, Milton, 121

elections, 21, 35, 76, 78, 98, 102, 162–63

Emerson, Ralph Waldo, 37–38

Espionage Act (1918), 89, 95–96

The Essence of Catholicism, 193

The Essence of Unitarianism (Burkhead), 193

European Museum, 24

Euterpe (friend of Marcet Haldeman-
   Julius), 71, 72, 86, 88, 90, 225n17

extortionists, 165

Facts You Should Know about Illinois
   (Smith), 189

Fagnani, Mr., 141–42

Fairbanks, Douglas, 103

false news, 43

family marriage, 134

farms: collective, 148, 159; fictional, 104;
   in Illinois, 80, 81–82, 84–85, 112–13,
   122, 165, 174–75; in Kansas, 85, 90,
   99, 104, 117, 118–19, 120, 122–23, 195

FBI (Federal Bureau of Investigation),
   98, 100, 189–90

"The FBI—The Basis of an American
   Police State" (Bennett), 189–90

fictional characters, 10–11, 101, 104, 143,
   196–97

Fielding, William J., 175

Fields, W. C., 18

Finger, Charles H., 109, 118–19, 129

Finland and Finns, 158

fires, 41, 70, 198

fireworks, 132, 198

First Hundred Million (E. Haldeman-
   Julius), 142, 176

Fishbein, Morris, 112

flea shows, 23–24

Florence (maid), 89

Flynn, Elizabeth Gurley, 148

Foodtown, 16

Fort Scott KS, 98

Fort Scott Tribune, 192

Fourth of July celebrations, 21, 198

France and the French, 163–64

franchises, 111–12

"Fred Warren issue," 59–60

Free Library, 32, 36, 37

Frick, Henry Clay, 40, 60

Fry, Homer, 81–82

Fry, Mary, 68–69, 71, 80–81, 112–13,
   157, 165, 168–69

funerals, 22, 26, 42, 182, 190

Funeral Services without Theology, 182

Gaitskill, B. S., 83, 85–86

games, street, 20

George (servant), 165

Germans, 21

Germany, 163–64

Gilbert, Clinton W., 163

Girard KS: as American socialism center,
   57; Chamber of Commerce, 107, 110;
   Emanuel Haldeman-Julius moving to,
   54–55; in Marcet Haldeman-Julius's
   eyes, 63–64; publishing business helping, 106, 110, 126, 174, 231n36; school
   football team in, 136; small town
   atmosphere of, 57, 69, 140, 174, 195

Girard Press, 131

girl falling out of window, 43

Giteau, Flora, 74, 170

"goat gland" doctor. *See* Brinkley, John R.

"God and My Neighbor" (Seal), 53

Goering, Hermann, 164

Goldberg, Isaac, 167, 174

Golden, Harry, 37

Golden Rule, 31

Goldman, Emma, 39–40, 78

Grant, Jane, 114, 121–22

The Great American Parade, 168

Great Depression, 147, 152, 168, 175

Great Fingall mine, 161

Greenwich Village NY, 53–54

Gross, Al, 155

Gunn, John, 61, 132, 167–69, 172, 182–83, 196, 230n3

Guy, Leburn, 135

Haldeman, Anna Hostetter, later Addams, 62, 69, 73, 80–81, 101, 112

Haldeman, George, 62

Haldeman, Henry, 62–63

Haldeman, Henry J. (Emanuel Haldeman-Julius's son). *See* Haldeman-Julius, Henry

Haldeman, John, 62

Haldeman, Marcet. *See* Haldeman-Julius, Marcet

Haldeman, Sarah Alice Addams, 62–63; death of, 64–65

Haldeman-Julius, Alice: christening of, 79; communicating with family, 132–33, 165–66; Emanuel Haldeman-Julius and, 84, 126, 150–51, 175–76, 190, 191, 192; Marcet Haldeman-Julius and, 68, 79–80, 88, 89–90, 113, 117, 122, 150–52, 169; marrying Carroll W. Smith, 188; as university student, 169, 171–73, 180–81; on West Coast, 148, 150–51

Haldeman-Julius, Emanuel, influences on: early childhood, 5–6; ethnic, 21–23, 26; family of origin, 6, 9–11, 32; formal education, 12–14, 33–34, 36; Jewish heritage, 1, 11–12, 17–18, 75, 189; learning about socialism, 29, 30–32, 35, 37, 39–40; music, 13, 18–19, 33; neighborhood events, 18–19, 21; neighborhood traditions, 15–17, 19–20, 25, 26; reading, 6, 31–32, 36–38, 40, 94; self-education, 36–37; "street

education," 13, 14–15, 18, 23–24, 27–28; zoo, 26–27

Haldeman-Julius, Emanuel, personal characteristics of: alcoholism, 168, 194; atheism, 11, 32, 49, 96; compared to well-known persons, 111–12, 131, 199, 202; dishonest actions, 18, 29–30, 231n36; education important to, 96–97; fund-raising abilities, 99, 105–6, 114, 177, 192; Marcet Haldeman-Julius on, 73; publicity seeking, 107, 138–39, 162, 187; public speaking, 107–8; racial tolerance, 11–12

Haldeman-Julius, Emanuel, personal life: acquaintance with Marcet Haldeman-Julius, 51, 62, 69–72; in Boston, 28–30; in California, 30–31; in car accident, 181; causes undertaken by, 136–37, 199–200, 201; daily routine of, 125–26, 184–85; death of, 195; doing farm work, 7, 9; family of origin and, 80; during Great Depression, 147–48; interests of, 126, 128–29, 151, 185–86; John Gunn and, 61, 196; legal difficulties of, 176, 191–94; marital agreement of, 73–74, 113, 164–65; marital separation of, 165–67; marriage of, to Marcet Haldeman-Julius, 74–75, 76, 115, 123–25, 140, 152, 160, 200–201; marriage of, to Sue Haney, 184; military draft and, 82–88, 227n61; money matters and, 76, 111, 114–15, 122–23, 144–45, 164–65, 172, 175–77, 191–92; name change of, 75–76; as outsider in small towns, 57, 61–62, 69; overview, ix–x; as parent, 138–39, 140, 169, 171–73, 191, 192, 200–201; politics and, 138, 155–56, 162–63, 200; on religion,

108–9, 121, 144, 187–88, 189; self-reflection by, 44–45, 123, 194, 197; short excursions, 24–25, 25–26; Sinclair Lewis and, 150; swimming pool incident, 195; will and funeral plans, 190; women and, 50, 124, 184, 200

Haldeman-Julius, Emanuel, pre-publishing life of: in California, 49–50; celebrities living nearby, 53–54; on Clarence Darrow, 48–49; as employee, 29, 33–34, 36, 37, 40–45, 51, 54–55; Jack London and, 46–47; in New York, 49–54; as subject of joke during, 44

Haldeman-Julius, Emanuel, publishing career of: advertising and sales techniques, 95–96, 99–101, 105, 129, 131–32, 179–80, 184, 189; in California, 103; changing titles, 127–28, 141–42; Charles Coughlin and, 186–87; expanding business, 45, 106, 110–11; exposing Herbert Hoover, 152–53; goals, 128; helping Eugene Debs, 94–95; John Gunn and, 167–68; Lawrence Tibbett and, 119–20; legal difficulties, 103–4, 186; Louis Adamic and, 152; low pricing of books, 96, 103–4, 105, 113, 129, 131–32; M. Lincoln Schuster and, 121–22; overview, 199–200, 201–3; selling newspaper business, 102–3; types of publications, 98–99, 141–42

Haldeman-Julius, Emanuel, writings of: Big American Parade, 143–44; "Caught," 101; The Color of Life, 10–11, 41, 79; "The Conquest of Prudery," 49; Dust, 104, 148, 196–97, 228n35; Marcet Haldeman-Julius collaborating in, 100; "Mark Twain: Radical," 40; on Nazis and Germany,

163–64; The Outline of Bunk, 144; pen name in, 41; on presidential campaign, 75; "Questions and Answers," 128; sales of books written by, 128; Violence, 143, 148; "What the Editor Is Thinking About," 109

Haldeman-Julius, Henry, 90, 122, 126, 132, 150, 152, 165, 166, 171, 175–76, 180–81, 197–98

Haldeman-Julius, Josephine: as adopted child, 90, 140; divorce and remarriage of, 141; on farms, 112–13, 120; as good student, 89; Marcet Haldeman-Julius and, 157, 183; wedding ceremony of, 139, 193; as young adult, 132–33, 135, 137–39, 140–41

Haldeman-Julius, Marcet: acquaintance with Emanuel Haldeman-Julius, 51, 62, 69–72; alcoholism of, 168–69; as banker, 63, 65, 68–69, 71–72, 76, 78–79, 85, 86–87, 123; Ben B. Lindsey and, 133; birth and youth of, 62, 63–64; "Caught," 101; causes undertaken by, 65–68, 71–72, 134–35, 136–37, 181–82, 183, 201; cigarette habit of, 63, 65, 73; death and funeral services of, 182–84; draft status of Emanuel Haldeman-Julius and, 83–84; Dust, 104, 148, 196–97, 228n35; on Emanuel Haldeman-Julius, 6–7, 9, 10–11, 107, 113, 119–20; Emanuel Haldeman-Julius's draft status and, 84–87; family of origin and, 80–82; farms and, 85, 90, 175; health problems of, 84, 113, 122, 133, 169, 182; as hostess, 117–18; insecurities of, 67, 115; John Gunn and, 168, 169; Julius family and, 90–91, 221n7; lacking birth certificate, 157; "Marcet's

Haldeman-Julius, Marcet *(continued)*
Fairyland," 64; marital agreement of,
73–74, 76, 164–65; marital separation
of, 165–68; marriage of, 74–75, 113,
115, 123–25, 140, 152, 201; Mary Fry
and, 71, 80–81, 112–13, 157; money
matters of, 76, 85, 113, 122–23,
164–66, 169–72; names of, 68, 75–76,
221n7; in New York, 121; as parent,
88, 132, 138–39, 140, 152, 181; political leanings of, 66–67, 72–73, 78–79,
200, 226n27; pregnancies of, 76,
88–89; as reporter, 116–18, 149–50; in
Ridley PA, 67; in Russia, 148, 156–60;
Sinclair Lewis and, 150; *Story of a
Southern Lynching*, 127; *Violence*, 143,
148; *Why I Believe in Companionate
Marriage*, 133; wills of, 69, 164–65; as
writer, 64, 79, 100–101, 115
Haldeman-Julius Company, 123, 130,
148, 162, 167, 169, 181, 190, 197–98
Haldeman-Julius Monthly, 141. See also
Debunker
Haldeman-Julius Quarterly, 115, 141. See
also *American Parade*
Haldeman-Julius Weekly, 108–9, 111, 116,
123, 129, 141. See also *American Free-
man*; *Appeal to Reason*; *New Appeal*
Hamilton, Alice, 68
Haney, Sue, 147, 184–85, 190, 194, 195–96
"Hanlon's Superba," 23
Hansen, Harry, 112
Harding, Warren, 102, 106
Hardy, Thomas, 186
Harnell, John, 162
Harper & Brothers, 186
Harriman, Job, 49–50
Harrison, Benjamin, 2–3
hats, 19, 29, 46–47

Hays State Teachers College dean, 136
Haywood, William "Big Bill," 40, 59, 148–49
heating methods, 19–20
Hecht, Ben, 112
Herron, George D., 82
Hitler, Adolph, 163–64, 186, 187
Hoffman, C. B., 98
Hollywood CA, 30, 46
Hoover, Herbert, 152–54, 160–61, 162
Hoover, J. Edgar, 189–90
horses, 15–16, 19–20, 23, 126
Hostetter, Anna. *See* Haldeman, Anna
Hostetter, later Addams
Howat, Alexander, 82
Howe, E. W., 49
"How To" books, 105
Hudson, Douglas, 191, 192
Hull House, 68
Hungarians, 22

immigrants, 1, 5, 7, 10, 30, 57
incubator for chicks, 185–86
Indiana, 59, 108
Industrial Workers of the World (IWW),
148–49
influenza pandemic (1918-19), 84
Ingersoll, Robert, 32, 36, 53
Internal Revenue Service (IRS), 191–92
International Socialist Review, 40
Irving, Washington, 38
Israel, 189
Italians, 21
IWW (Industrial Workers of the World),
148–49

Jardine, William, 121
Jenkins, Mel, 89–90
Jewish cooking, 17–18
Jewish theater, 24

Jews, 1–5, 7, 21, 24, 164, 189
Jo (inmate), 67
John Moffet Elementary School, 12–13
Johnson, James Weldon, 201
Jones, Mother, 148
Jordan, David Starr, 154
Jouralovitch, Mr., 41
journalists, 60, 108
Journal of the American Medical Association, 112
Julius, David, 10, 32–33, 36, 80, 200; name change, 4–5
Julius, Elizabeth Zamustin, 4–6, 10, 20, 25
Julius, Emanuel. *See* Haldeman-Julius, Emanuel
Julius, Esther, 4, 9, 12, 32
Julius, Josephine, 6
Julius, Lillian, 6
Julius, Nathan, 4, 12, 32, 80
Julius, Rosalie, 6, 40
The Jungle (Sinclair), 95

Kansas, ix, 57, 78, 98, 161
Kansas Authors Club, 121
Kansas City MO, 57, 99, 121, 124, 130, 139, 140, 150
Kansas City Advertising Club, 128
Kansas City Star, 107, 139
Kansas City Times, 83–84, 107
Kansas State Agricultural College, 108, 121, 136
Keith's theater, 36
Kelly, Florence, 68
Kensington PA, 6, 7
Kensington theater, 36
Kerr (Charles H. Kerr Company), 97–98, 202
KFKB, 230n3
The Kid (film), 103

kidnapping of labor leaders, 59
Kiev, Ukraine, 2
kilhozes, 159
King, Nelson, 150
Kinnerly, Mitchell, 103
Kirkpatrick, George R., 31, 35, 37, 41
Knight, John, 187
Knights of Labor, 148
Knowlton, Mrs., 170
Kopelin, Louis: death of, 196; as editor, 41, 60, 77; Emanuel Haldeman-Julius and, 40, 54, 61, 123, 196; as *New Appeal* owner, 78, 94, 99, 101, 102–3, 106; war and, 77, 82–83, 86
kosher cooking, 17–18
Krishna Menon, V. K., 97
Krueger, Karl, 172
Ku Klux Klan, 108–9, 200

labor issues, 48, 59, 148, 149, 160
Landon, Alf, 163
Larsen, Vic, 149
Lathrop, Julia, 68
law and laws: federal, 82, 101; Jewish, 4; state, 78, 87–88, 115–16, 134, 135, 161
lawyers: Clarence Darrow, 48–49, 116–17; defending Hoover, 162; defending Jews, 3; Emanuel Haldeman-Julius and, 167, 169, 170, 191, 192; Marcet Haldeman-Julius and, 116–17, 164–65, 167, 170; socialist, 120
Leavenworth Federal Prison, 87
Lee, Joseph, 190
Lee, Raymond, 190
"A Legal But Bad Ruling" (*St. Louis Post-Dispatch*), 107
Leroy (servant), 165
Leslie's Illustrated Weekly, 99

LeSorge, Dorothy, 181
Le Sueur, Arthur, 98
Le Sueur, Marion, 98
Lewis, Sinclair, 64, 150
Lewis Copeland Company, 174
libel suits, 155–56, 176
Liberty Encyclopedia, 167–68
librarian at School for Girls, 37–38, 40, 44
Life's Little Ironies (Hardy), 186
Lightfoot, E. G., 195
Lindeman, Edouard, 113
Lindley, E. H., 135–36
Lindsay, Ben, 74
Lindsey, Ben B., 133–34, 139–40, 201
Literary Digest, 105
Little Blue Books, ix; affordability of, 131; beginnings of, 94; Ben B. Lindsey writing for, 133; criticism of, 144, 187–88; cultural role of, 93–94, 96–97, 136, 201–2; Emanuel Haldeman-Julius's plans for, 114, 122, 131, 174, 189, 194; financial worth of, 101, 142, 170; format of, 77; as franchise business, 111–12; Marcet Haldeman-Julius and, 184; name of, 99; Nelson Antrim Crawford recruited for, 121; physical production of, 130; sales of, 128, 174, 181; second series of, 102; stopping publication, 198; subjects dealt with, 49, 100, 188–89, 193. *See also* Pocket Series
Little Blue Book Shoppes, 110–11
Little Rock AR, 137
London, Jack, 30, 46–47, 60–61
Long, Fred, 31, 37
Los Angeles CA, 45–46, 50
Los Angeles Citizen, 45
Los Angeles Times, 48
Loving, Pierre, 129–30
Lowe, Caroline, 98, 120–21, 159

Loyal Socialist Mission, 77
Lyttleton, Alfred, 160

machinery, printing, 106, 130–31
mail order, 108, 109, 185
Manley (reporter), 42–44
A Man of Learning (Crawford), 121
"The Man without a Country," 66
Marcet, Jean. *See* Haldeman-Julius, Marcet
"Marcet's Fairyland" (M. Haldeman-Julius), 64
"Mark Twain: Radical" (E. Haldeman-Julius), 40
marriage, 74, 133–35, 138–39
Marxism, 30. *See* also socialism and socialists
Mary (friend of Marcet Haldeman-Julius), 67
Mason, Miss, 37–38
Maxwell family, 152
Maybrie, Hamilton Wright, 38
Mayflower hotel, 154–55
McAuliffe, Clarence, 188
McCabe, Joseph, 114, 115, 187, 188
McClure's, 60
McGill, George, 162–63
McKinley, William, 19, 35
McNamara, James, 48, 49
McNamara, John, 48, 49
McParland, James, 59
Meghan, Thomas, 103
Mellot, Arthur, 191–92
Mencken, Henry L., 40, 103–4, 121
Merchants, Manufacturers, and Employers Association, 148
Mercure France, 144
"Merrie England" (Seal), 53
Michaelson, Grace, 74
Michaelson, Peter, 74

migrations, 1, 3–5
Mills, Walter, 98
Milwaukee WI, 30, 50
Milwaukee Journal, 42–43
Milwaukee Leader, 41–43
miners, 21, 65–66, 67, 90
mining industry, 57, 152–54, 160–61
Mining Manual, 153–54
Mining Year Book, 153–54
"Miss History," 13–14
Miss Mason's School for Girls, 37–38
Missouri, 57, 136
The Modern Sex Book, 179
"Mom and Pop" stores, 16
Monroe, Elizabeth, 18
Monroe, Hugh F., 13
Montessori method, 89–90
Mooney, Rita, 148
Mooney, Tom, 148–50, 199
Moore, "Ed," 37, 53
Moore, Harold, 155–56
Moore, William J., 154–56
Moreing Company. *See* Bewick, Moreing
    and Company
Morrison, Alfred H., 74
Moscow, Russia, 3
Moscow News, 121
Mother Earth, 40
Mother Jones, 148
Moyer, Charles, 59
muckrakers, 60
Murphy, Mrs., 27–28

The Naked Truth, 176
Nathan, George Jean, 40
The Nation, 107
National Association for the Advance-
    ment of Colored People, 117–18
National Association of Publishers, 113

National Civil Liberties Union, 87. *See
    also* American Civil Liberties Union
National Conference of Christians and
    Jews, 189
Nazis and Nazism, 47, 163–64
Negroes. *See* African Americans
New Appeal: advertising books, 95–96,
    99, 101, 105–6; amnesty focus of,
    94–95; dissolution of, 166; financial
    worth of, 164; possible sale of, 99,
    105; replacing *Appeal to Reason*, 76,
    78; as socialist publication, 83, 101–
    2; subscriptions to, 93, 105; World
    War I and, 83, 84, 86, 227n61. See
    also *Appeal to Reason*; *Haldeman-
    Julius Weekly*
New Appeal company, 85, 167
New Deal, 30
The New Republic, 107
news, false, 43
New York (state), 38, 101–2
New York Call, 38, 40–41, 49, 52, 54–55
New York City NY, 24–25, 30, 50
New Yorker, 52, 114, 121, 225n14
"New York Letter" (Nortizen), 109
New York School of Social Research, 113
New York Times, 126, 139
New York World, 144
Norris, J. Frank, 143
North, Dorothy, 74
Nortizen, Julius, 109

Ochremenko, Peter, 148
October Revolution celebration, 158
Odessa, Ukraine, 3
O. D. Jennings Company, 181
O'Hare, Frank, 89
O'Hare, Kate Richards, 89
Oklahoma, 57, 136

Olson, Cuthbert, 150

Orchard, Harry, 59

Organized Farmer, 161

osoaviachim, 158

Otis, Harrison Gray, 48, 59

The Outline of Bunk (E. Haldeman-
Julius), 144

Outlook, 107, 152

Owensby, O. M., 88–89, 227n74

Paine, Tom, 36

Pale of Settlement, 1, 3

Palestinian Settlement, 189

Palmer, A. Mitchell, 95, 101

paperbacks, 97, 180

Pasteur, The Man and His Work (Fishbein), 112

Paulen, Ben, 162–63

Peace Jubilee, 18–19

Pegler, Westbrook, 193

Penguin Books, 97

Penn, William, 7

Perrett, Geoffrey, 93

Pettibone, George, 59

Philadelphia PA, 5–6, 7, 12–14

Philadelphia Enquirer, 187–88

Philadelphia Press and Record, 34, 37

Pittsburg Daily Sun, 84, 104, 105

Pittsburg Headlight, 136

Pocket Book of Baby and Child Care
(Spock), 202

Pocket Library of Socialism, 202

Pocket Series, 93, 96, 99, 101. *See also*
Little Blue Books

pogroms, 2–3

Poland, 1, 3

police, 18, 21, 28, 40, 137

pond on farm, 118

pornography, 38–39

Post Office, 103, 107, 126, 156, 161, 162,
174, 176

Preparedness Day Parade, 148

"Prince of Peace" sermon (Bryan), 27

Prison Memoirs of an Anarchist (Berkman), 40

Prohibition, 61

prostitution, 24, 27–28

Protestants, 108

Provisional Rules (1882), 3

Publisher's Weekly, 110, 111

publishing business, ix, 97–98, 105, 108,
112, 179–80

"Questions and Answers" (E. Haldeman-
Julius), 128

rabbis, 4, 11

racial discrimination, 47, 135–37, 210

radio, 128, 163, 176, 186, 230n3

Ralston, John T., 116

Rand School of Social Science, 39

Ray, Roberta, 111–12

Red Bank, 18

Red Scare, 78, 87, 101, 105, 108

Reeve, Ella. *See* Bloor, Ella Reeve

Reich Crystal Night, 164

Reitman, Ben L., 39

Republicans, 35, 57–58, 66–67, 72, 83,
102, 138, 162–63, 200

Review of Reviews, 107

Rider, Tony, 66

Ridley KS, 67

right of courtesy, 164–65

Rippey, Milton, 191–92

Roaring Twenties, 49, 63, 93–94, 115,
134, 144

Rockefeller, John D., 60

Roman Empire, 1

Roosevelt, Franklin, 30, 162, 188

Roosevelt, Theodore, 59, 61

Rosell, Aubrey, 132–33, 135, 137–39, 141, 157

Rosell, Josephine. *See* Haldeman-Julius, Josephine

Ross, Harold, 114, 121–22

"roughnecks," 23–24

royalties, 148, 174

The Rubaiyat of Omar Khayyam, 94

Russell, Bertrand, 186

Russell, Charles Edward, 82

Russia, 1–4, 119, 148, 158–60. *See also* Soviet Union

Sachs, Sophia, 5–6

saloons, 22, 23, 61

Salvation Army, 28–29

Sandburg, Carl, 42

San Francisco Argonaut, 127

San Francisco Call Bulletin, 149

Sartor Resartus (Carlyle), 38

Saturday Evening Post, 107

scandals, 154–55, 160–61, 176–77

School for Girls, 37–38

School of Social Economy, 98

Schuster, M. Lincoln, 121–22

Schuylkill River, 6, 7

Scopes, John, 115–17

Scopes trial, 113, 115–17

Seal, Charlie, 53

Sears, Amelia, 171

segregation, 136–37

Seiler, Albert, 87

serfs, 1–2

The Sermon on the Mount, 193

sex: attitudes toward, 133; as book topic, 94, 97, 102, 179, 186, 201–2; in companionate marriage, 73–74, 134, 201;

Emanuel Haldeman-Julius on, 49; premarital, 134–35

Shackles of the Supernatural (Fielding), 175

Shaeffer, Oscar, 78, 85, 86–87, 123

Shakespeare's works, 106–7

Shaver, Muriel, 121

Sheppard, Jake, 84, 85, 86, 98

Simon and Schuster, 121–22, 143

Simons, A. M., 77, 82

Sinclair, Harry, 155

Sinclair, Upton, 30, 47–48, 77, 95, 102–3, 105, 106, 109, 118–19

"slave trading," 160–61

sleighs, horse-drawn, 19–20

Smart Set, 40

Smith, Carrie, 74

Smith, Carroll W., 188–89

Smith, Lloyd E., 114

Social Democrat, 45, 49

Social Democratic League, 30, 77

socialism and socialists: in America, 30–31, 35–36, 41, 45, 57–58; definition of, 31, 223n53; education, involved in, 98; Emanuel Haldeman-Julius learning about, 29, 30–32, 35, 37, 39–40; in Europe, 52, 164; running for office, 75, 94–95, 101–2, 162; World War I and, 50–51, 60, 76–77, 82–83; written works of, 36, 97

Socialist Literary Syndicate, 41

Socialist Party, 35, 41, 120

sombrero incident, 46–47

Soupy Island, 18

South Africa, 160

Soviet Union, 120–21, 157–60. *See also* Russia

Spalding's Commercial College, 132

Spargo, John, 41, 77, 82

Spock, Benjamin, 202

"spookology," 47–48
State Bank of Girard, 85
steamship voyages, 4–5
Stearns, Harold, 54
Stephenson County IL, 82, 93
Steunenberg, Frank, 59
Stevens, William, 148–49
St. Louis Post-Dispatch, 107
stock market crash (1929), 144–45
stock shares, 50, 84, 85, 97–98, 103, 114, 145, 153–54, 166, 194
Story of a Southern Lynching (M. Haldeman-Julius), 127
The Story of Philosophy (Durant), 109–10, 122
The Strange Career of Mr. Hoover under Two Flags (Harnell), 162
Strong, Anna Louis, 120–21
suicides, 13, 59–60
supermarkets, 16
Sweet, Henry, 117
Sweet, Ossian H., 117

Taylor, William, 59
Teapot Dome Scandal, 155
Tennessee, 115–16
theaters, 23–24
Third Partition of Poland, 1
Tibbett, Lawrence, 119–20
TNT enterprises, 176
tobacco and candy store, 6, 25
Tom (friend of Marcet Haldeman-Julius), 71, 72, 73
Tom Sawyer (Twain), 66
toy factory, 33
Train, Arthur, 162
Triangle Shirtwaist Company fire, 41, 60
Truscan Steel Company, 110
Twain, Mark, 38, 40

Ukraine, 159
Unitarian Church, 193
United Mine Workers of America, 82
United States Attorney, 103
"The University in Print," 105
University of Kansas, 135–37, 169
University of Missouri, 112

Vanderbilt, Cornelius, 163–64
Vedder, Henry C., 129
Violence (E. Haldeman-Julius and M. Haldeman-Julius), 143, 148
Vlag, Piet, 39
Voroshilov, Kliment, 158

Wagner, Rob, 103
Wagner, Robert, 60
Wagner Act (1935), 60
Wallace, Henry, 61
Walleck, Walter, 136
Walling, William English, 77
Wall Street crash, 144, 152
Wall Street Journal, 126
Wanhope, John, 41
Wanhope, Joshua, 52
Warren, Fred, 58, 59–60, 95, 98
Wayland, Jon, 60, 78
Wayland, Julius Augustus, 57–58, 59–60, 225n6
Wayland, Walter, 60, 78
Wayland, Warren, Mrs., 62
Wayland, William, 94, 176
Weber, Sarah. See Addams, Sarah Weber
Western Comrade, 45, 49, 50
Western Federation of Miners, 59
Western Union boy, 27–28
Wettstein, Josephine. See Haldeman-Julius, Josephine
Wettstein, Maggie, 133

Wettstein, Mr., 133
"What the Editor Is Thinking About"
    (E. Haldeman-Julius), 109
White, Stewart Edward, 103
White, Walter, 117–18
White, William Allen, 135–36, 138
Whitman, Walt, booklet, 103–4
Who's Who in America, 203
Why I Believe in Companionate Marriage
    (M. Haldeman-Julius), 133
Wilde, Oscar, 94
"Wild Women in History" (series), 179
wills, 63, 69, 122–23, 164–65, 190, 225n14
Wilson, Stanley B., 45
Wilson, Woodrow, 77, 82, 148–49
Wisconsin News, 43
Wood, Clement, 115
Woollcott, Alexander, 52–53, 225n14
Work, John M., 41
"Workers' English" (M. Le Sueur), 98

World War I, 30, 50–51, 52, 60, 76–78,
    82–84, 98
World War II, 186
Wright, Chester M., 42, 43, 44–45, 49,
    51–52, 76, 201
Writer's Guild, 112
W. T. Raleigh Company, 93

Yaros family, 157

Zamustin, Boris, 4
Zamustin, Elizabeth. *See* Julius, Eliza-
    beth Zamustin
Zolajefski, David. *See* Julius, David
Zolajefski, Elizabeth. *See* Julius, Eliza-
    beth Zamustin
Zolajefski, Esther. *See* Julius, Esther
Zolajefski, Nathan. *See* Julius, Nathan
Zolajefski, Rose, 4
zoos, 26–27